Master Your Mac

Simple Ways to Tweak, Customize, and Secure OS X

MATT CONE

First printing

16 15 14 13 12   1 2 3 4 5 6 7 8 9

ISBN-10: 1-59327-406-8
ISBN-13: 978-1-59327-406-1

Publisher: William Pollock
Production Editor: Serena Yang
Cover Design: Serena Yang
Cover Photo: Kazuya Minami
Interior Design: Octopod Studios
Developmental Editor: Tyler Ortman
Technical Reviewer: Wayne Linder
Copyeditor: Paula L. Fleming
Compositor: Serena Yang
Proofreader: Ward Webber
Indexer: Nancy Guenther

For information on book distributors or translations, please contact No Starch Press, Inc. directly:

No Starch Press, Inc.
38 Ringold Street, San Francisco, CA 94103
phone: 415.863.9900; fax: 415.863.9950; info@nostarch.com; http://www.nostarch.com/

Library of Congress Cataloging-in-Publication Data
A catalog record of this book is available from the Library of Congress.

Dedication

This book is dedicated to Emily and Finn. I couldn't have done it without their love and support.

Acknowledgments

I want to thank the following people who helped make this book possible.

First, the people who inspired me. My parents, Steve Cone and Kathie Lathan, taught me how to learn and fostered my interest in technology. Wayne Linder, Ric Getter, Rick Myers, and Jeremy Bechtold proved to be an endless supply of great OS X tips and tricks. Robin Williams, John Tollett, and Juan Torrez all provided excellent mentorship and guidance.

Last but certainly not least, the people at No Starch Press who worked long hours to make this book a reality: Bill Pollock, the founder of No Starch Press; Serena Yang, Production Manager; Tyler Ortman, my editor; and the rest of the No Starch Press staff.

Brief Contents

Contents in Detail

Part 6: Serious Security

Introduction

If you're like most Mac users, you already know the ins and outs of OS X. You're familiar with the Finder, and you know how to use the most popular apps. But there are lesser known ways to make your Mac even better—ways to customize it and make it yours. That's what this book is all about: mastering your Mac.

The first time you used a Mac, your first thought was probably, "Wow, cool!" And then after you used it for a while, you probably wondered: "What can I use this for?" Slowly you discovered the apps. You surfed the Web with Safari, created movies with iMovies, and cued up playlists with iTunes. But that left you wanting more. Now you're thinking, "How do I change this computer and customize it for my needs?"

You've come to the right place!

What This Book Is About

This is a book about unlocking your Mac's full potential. Instead of rehashing the basics and covering popular apps like iMovie, it looks beyond the obvious applications and documented uses of OS X. It's a workbook full of advanced projects that push the limits of OS X. You'll get started with scripting and automation, configure new shortcuts, secure your Mac against invisible threats, and learn how to repair your hard drive.

The goal of the projects is twofold. Each project helps you implement an immediate solution to a real problem, and then it provides guidance on going above and beyond the project. When you learn AppleScript in Chapter 12, for example, you'll create your very own script, but you'll also learn how to incorporate other data structures and interface elements to build a much more advanced script.

While most of the projects are written so an intermediate user could follow them, this is not a book for the faint of heart. Follow the instructions carefully and pay special attention to the warnings and notes.

What's in This Book

The wide variety of projects touch on just about every part of OS X. Start with whichever project catches your eye. Since most projects don't build on others, you can skip around the book and follow your interests.

This book is divided into seven parts, each covering a different aspect of OS X:

▶ **Part 1: Back to Basics** eases you into the book with some introductory projects that tackle some common OS X annoyances and pitfalls.

▶ **Part 2: Boosting Productivity** provides tricks and tips for optimizing your setup and squeezing even more out of your Mac.

▶ **Part 3: Automation** presents several methods for automating common tasks that you perform regularly.

▶ **Part 4: Managing Your Life** breathes new life into boring areas of OS X like music and email.

▶ **Part 5: Internet and Networks** explores how you can share data and devices wirelessly, and how you can access them when you're away from home.

▶ **Part 6: Serious Security** looks at some of the threats you can encounter while using your Mac and how you can protect your data and accounts.

▶ **Part 7: Monitoring, Troubleshooting, and Maintenance** help you keep your Mac in tip-top shape, before or after you experience a problem.

Excited yet? Go ahead, skip to a project and get started!

PART 1

Back to Basics

1 The Best Shortcuts (and How to Make Your Own)

You can always find more than one way to do something with your Mac. The question is, which method is the fastest, easiest, and most efficient? When it comes to opening applications, executing menu commands, and launching AppleScripts or shell scripts, there's a clear winner: keyboard shortcuts.

Instead of using the mouse to select Print from the File menu, you could just press the ⌘ and P keys to print a document. There are hundreds of preset keyboard shortcuts built into OS X, and you can also map custom keyboard shortcuts to actions you perform regularly.

Of course, using keyboard shortcuts is totally unnecessary. If productivity is not a concern of yours, by all means feel free to continue using the mouse or trackpad. But you'll be missing out on a huge time-saving feature. Like people who take typing classes for the first time and stop hunting and pecking for letters on the keyboard, first-time users of keyboard shortcuts may feel like they've discovered a whole new world!

Project goal: Learn to use keyboard shortcuts to run software, use commands, and launch scripts.

What You'll Be Using

To use the power of keyboard shortcuts with your Mac, you'll use the following:

 System Preferences

 Shortcuts (*http://nulana.com/shortcuts/*, $)

Using Keyboard Shortcuts Built into OS X

Even if you're a complete beginner when it comes to keyboard shortcuts, you probably already know some basic shortcuts. You might press ⌘-P to print or ⌘-O to open a document in a word processing application. Apple has thoughtfully placed keyboard shortcuts like these throughout OS X to make your life easier.

There are two types of keyboard shortcuts: system level and application level. System-level shortcuts work no matter what application you're using. Application-level shortcuts work only in the active application. For example, pressing SHIFT-⌘-Q logs you out of OS X whether you're using Preview or iPhoto, but pressing ⌘-Q quits only the active application.

Learning Keyboard Shortcuts

With all of the keyboard shortcuts available in OS X and the applications pre-installed on your Mac, learning shortcuts can seem daunting. The first thing to remember is that you won't need to memorize every shortcut. Like shortcuts you use in the real world—the route from your house to the grocery store, for example—you'll only learn the ones you need to use regularly.

There are two ways to learn keyboard shortcuts: Check the menus or use a reference guide. Most keyboard shortcuts for menu commands are displayed in the menu next to the command, as shown in Figure 1-1. The next time you select a command with the mouse for the umpteenth time, try to memorize the corresponding keyboard shortcut. With a little time and effort, you'll be able to commit at least a couple of commands to memory.

FIGURE 1-1: *Keyboard shortcuts are usually displayed next to the menu commands.*

Did you notice the symbols in the shortcuts? Those are the *modifiers*—the special keys that change the way keystrokes are interpreted by the operating system. The modifiers in keyboard shortcuts—keys like ⌘, CONTROL, and SHIFT—are represented by hieroglyphics that are not at all intuitive. Use Table 1-1 as a reference to decipher these cryptic symbols.

Table 1-1: Common Modifiers

Symbol	Key
⌘	COMMAND
⇧	SHIFT
⌥	OPTION (called ALT on non-Mac keyboards)
⌃	CONTROL
⌫	DELETE
⏏	EJECT

Some keyboard shortcuts are more common than others. Use Table 1-2 to familiarize yourself with some of the shortcuts you'll be using most often.

Table 1-2: The Best OS X Shortcuts

Key combination	What it does
CONTROL-⌘	Puts the active application in Full Screen mode
⌘-SHIFT-3	Takes a screenshot
⌘-OPTION-H	Hides all applications except the active application
⌘-H	Hides the active application
⌘-CONTROL-D	Defines a highlighted word
⌘-OPTION-D	Shows or hides the Dock
⌘-D	Duplicates the selected file
⌘-M	Minimizes the active window to the Dock
⌘-W	Closes the active window

(continued)

Table 1-2: The Best OS X Shortcuts (*continued*)

Key combination	What it does
⌘-[	Goes back in a folder or web browser
⌘-]	Goes forward in a folder or web browser
⌘-SHIFT-?	Opens Mac help
SHIFT-⌘-DELETE	Empties the Trash
OPTION-SHIFT-⌘-ESC (hold for three seconds)	Force-quits the active application
SHIFT-⌘-Q	Logs out
OPTION-⌘-⏏	Puts the computer to sleep

For those obscure keyboard shortcuts that are difficult to find in a menu, you can use a reference guide. Apple maintains an excellent reference guide to most keyboard shortcuts on its website (*http://support.apple.com/kb/ht1343*). Also, a couple of third-party application reference guides, available in the Mac App Store, publish all of the keyboard shortcuts available on your computer.

Changing System-Level Keyboard Shortcuts

Now that you've started memorizing and using keyboard shortcuts, you're ready to change system-level keyboard shortcuts to match your personal preferences. This is a basic first step toward customizing your Mac. In later sections, you'll take the concept a step further by changing application-level keyboard shortcuts and even creating your own custom shortcuts.

＊ **NOTE:** Apple doesn't allow you to change every system-level keyboard shortcut. To edit system-level keyboard shortcuts that aren't available in System Preferences, try using the Shortcuts application discussed later in this chapter.

Here's how to change system-level keyboard shortcuts:

1. From the **Apple** menu, select **System Preferences**.
2. Click **Keyboard**.
3. Click **Keyboard Shortcuts**. The window shown in Figure 1-2 appears.
4. From the left pane, select a category. The keyboard shortcuts in that category appear in the right pane.
5. Select a checkbox to enable a keyboard shortcut; deselect a checkbox to disable a shortcut.
6. Double-click a shortcut and then to edit the shortcut's key combination, press the keys you want to use for that shortcut.

Click this button to modify some of the the keyboard shortcuts built into OS X.

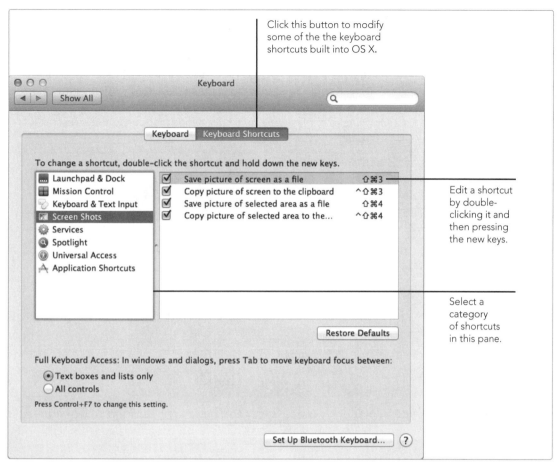

Edit a shortcut by double-clicking it and then pressing the new keys.

Select a category of shortcuts in this pane.

FIGURE 1-2: *Use System Preferences to modify system-level keyboard shortcuts.*

✳ **NOTE:** **If you're a former Windows user who just can't stop using** CONTROL **for your shortcut commands, you can retrain your Mac—just change the modifier keys for shortcuts in System Preferences. To do this, click** *Keyboard Settings* **and then** *Modifier Keys,* **and then assign Control (^) to Command (⌘) and vice versa, as shown in Figure 1-3.**

FIGURE 1-3: *Change modifier keys in System Preferences to ease the transition to OS X.*

Changing and Adding Application-Level Keyboard Shortcuts

Many of the menu commands available in applications have keyboard shortcuts, but there are always some commands that don't have any keyboard shortcut assigned, like the one shown in Figure 1-4. These commands were "left behind" by the developers, who decided that the commands were not important enough to assign keyboard shortcuts. Fortunately, you can use System Preferences to add keyboard shortcuts to application menu commands that don't have any shortcuts assigned by default.

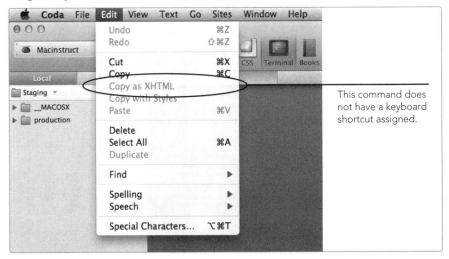

FIGURE 1-4: *Not every menu command has a keyboard shortcut assigned.*

You can also change existing keyboard shortcuts for application menu commands. For example, if you wanted to change the default keyboard shortcut for copying text from ⌘-C to ⌘-SHIFT-C in your word processing program, you could do that in System Preferences.

Here's how to change application keyboard shortcuts:

1. From the **Apple** menu, select **System Preferences**.
2. Click **Keyboard**.
3. Click **Keyboard Shortcuts**.
4. Select **Application Shortcuts** from the left pane. The window shown in Figure 1-5 appears.
5. Click the **+** button to add a new application shortcut. The window shown in Figure 1-6 appears.
6. Select an application from the **Application** menu.
7. Enter the menu command you want to modify in the **Menu Title** field, exactly as it appears in the application's menu.
8. Click the **Keyboard Shortcut** field and then press keys to set the keyboard shortcut for the menu command.

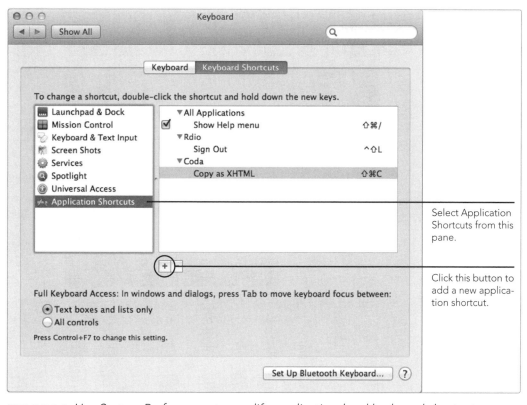

FIGURE 1-5: Use System Preferences to modify application-level keyboard shortcuts.

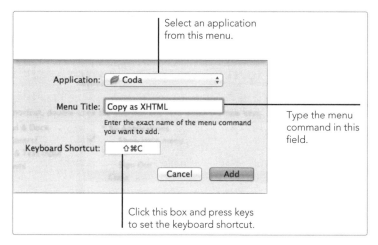

FIGURE 1-6: Set an application-level keyboard shortcut by selecting the application, typing the name of the menu command, and then pressing the keys to record the keyboard shortcut.

9. Click **Add**. The keyboard shortcut is now displayed in the application, next to the menu command, as shown in Figure 1-7.

Now that you've set the keyboard shortcut, you can quickly access the menu command.

FIGURE 1-7: *The command now has a keyboard shortcut assigned— just press the keys when you're in the application to execute the command.*

Remember, the custom keyboard shortcuts you create in System Preferences are available only within the application you specify. This is an advantage if you want use the custom commands only with a specific application (you want to "sandbox" them in that application). But if you wanted to change a keyboard shortcut that is universally available within all applications, like ⌘-C for copying text, you would need to change the command in every application.

Creating Your Own Shortcut Commands

Changing system- and application-level shortcuts has prepared you for the holy grail of keyboard shortcuts—the ones you create yourself, entirely from scratch. OS X doesn't provide support for this itself, but a third-party application called Shortcuts (*http://nulana.com/shortcuts/*, $) allows you to create brand-new keyboard shortcuts to launch applications; open files, folders, and websites; and run AppleScripts and shell scripts.

These custom shortcuts are system level, so you can use them no matter which application is currently active. You can also use the Shortcuts application to change existing system-level keyboard shortcuts that are not modifiable in System Preferences.

Here's how to create your own keyboard shortcuts:

1. Start the Shortcuts application.
2. From the left pane, select any category except All Categories or System. (You can't add new keyboard shortcuts in those categories.) The window shown in Figure 1-8 appears.

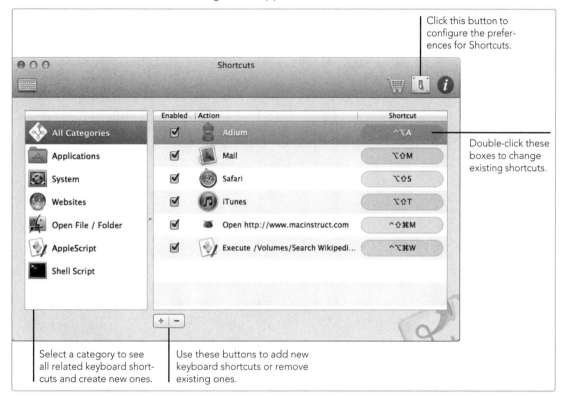

Click this button to configure the preferences for Shortcuts.

Double-click these boxes to change existing shortcuts.

Select a category to see all related keyboard shortcuts and create new ones.

Use these buttons to add new keyboard shortcuts or remove existing ones.

FIGURE 1-8: Create custom keyboard shortcuts with the Shortcuts application.

3. Click the **+** button to create a new keyboard shortcut in the selected category.
4. Depending on the category, you'll need to select an application, file, folder, AppleScript, or shell script. If you're creating a shortcut in the Websites category, you'll need to enter the URL of the website. The new keyboard shortcut appears in the Shortcuts application window.
5. Double-click the gray Shortcut box next to the new shortcut and then press the keys you want to use for that shortcut.

You can add as many of these keyboard shortcuts as you want. Go ahead—go wild!

For these custom keyboard shortcuts to work, the Shortcuts application needs to be running in the background. You can change the application's preferences to add it as a login item and hide the Dock and/or menu bar icon (see Chapter 2).

Additional Ideas for Controlling Your Mac with Keyboard Shortcuts

Other applications provide some of the same features as the Shortcuts application. Apptivate (*http://www.apptivateapp.com/*, $), for example, allows you to launch any application with a system-level keyboard shortcut that you specify. You'll learn about another application in Chapter 7 called LaunchBar (*http://www.obdev.at/products/launchbar/*, $$$), which provides a lot of the same features as the Shortcuts application. And in Chapter 11 you'll learn about Keyboard Maestro (*http://www.keyboardmaestro.com/*, $$$), a useful application for assigning keyboard shortcuts to *macros*, which automate sequences of time-consuming keystrokes and mouse actions.

2

Starting Applications Automatically at Login

Do you know that your Mac can automatically launch applications and restore your work environment when you log in? Two features in OS X, *login items* and *resume*, do exactly that.

By specifying login items, you tell your Mac to open applications, scripts, or documents when you log in to your computer. With the resume feature enabled, your Mac takes a snapshot of open applications and documents before you shut down and then automatically restores everything again when you log in. It's like waking your Mac up from sleep mode. You can use login items and the resume feature separately or with each other.

Project goal: Configure login items and set applications and windows to resume automatically when you log in.

What You'll Be Using

To pick up where you left off, even after logging off, you'll use the following:

 System Preferences

 Exhaust (*http://mrgeckosmedia.com/applications/info/exhaust/*, free)

Adding Login Items

Users can add just about anything as a login item—everything from applications and documents to custom AppleScripts and Automator actions. You can even automatically mount network drives by adding them as login items. Plus, every user on your Mac can specify his or her unique login items.

Here's how to add login items for an individual user:

1. From the **Apple** menu, select **System Preferences**.
2. Select **Users & Groups**. The window shown in Figure 2-1 appears.

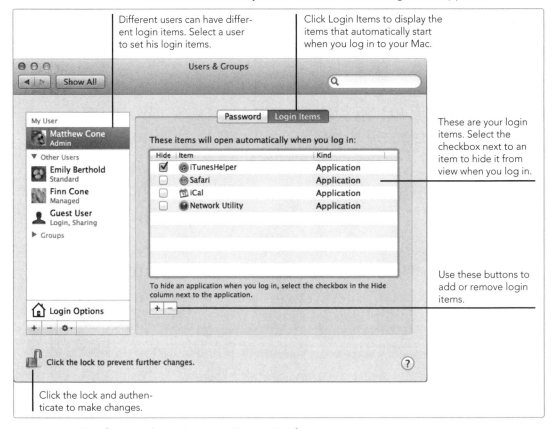

FIGURE 2-1: *Configuring login items in System Preferences*

3. From the sidebar, select a user.
4. Click the **Login Items** button.
5. Click the **+** button to add a login item. You can select applications, documents, AppleScripts, network drives, and Automator actions.

To hide a login item so it doesn't appear on the screen when it starts, select the **Hide** checkbox next to the item. To remove a login item, select the item, and then click the **–** button.

＊ **NOTE:** Some applications, like iTunes, automatically install *helper applications* as login items. Do not remove these items—doing so may prevent the applications from functioning correctly!

Adding Global Login Items

In situations where every user on your computer needs to have the same login items, like an enterprise environment or a home where all family members share a Mac, you can set *global login items* for all users on a particular Mac.

To add global login items, open the Terminal application and type the following command as an administrator:

```
sudo defaults write /Library/Preferences/loginwindow AutoLaunchedApplicationDictionary -array-add
'{ "Path" = "/path/to/item"; "Hide" = "0"; }'
```

Replace */path/to/item* with the path to the login item. To hide the login item, change the hide value to 1. Execute the command again to add another global login item.

To remove all global login items, open the Terminal application and type the following command:

```
sudo defaults delete /Library/Preferences/loginwindow AutoLaunchedApplicationDictionary.
```

Performing Actions on Sleep or Wake

Login items are perfect for opening files and running scripts when you log in to your computer, but what about actions that need to be performed every time you put your Mac to sleep or wake it up? For example, you might want to mute the volume when you put the computer to sleep and then reconnect to a network drive or virtual private network (VPN) when you wake it up.

SleepWatcher (*http://www.bernhard-baehr.de/*, free) is an open source command-line tool that can automatically execute Unix commands on sleep or wake. Knowledge of the command line is required to use this tool—you'll need to create bash scripts to really tap SleepWatcher's full potential.

Resuming Applications and Reopening Windows at Login

Do you want to save your work environment configuration when you restart or shut down and then restore it when you log back in? You can do so by turning on the resume feature.

Here's how to resume applications and reopen windows at login:

1. From the **Apple** menu, select **System Preferences**.
2. Select **General**. The window shown in Figure 2-2 appears.

When this checkbox is not selected, changes are automatically saved when a document is closed.

Select this checkbox to prevent windows from being restored when you reopen applications.

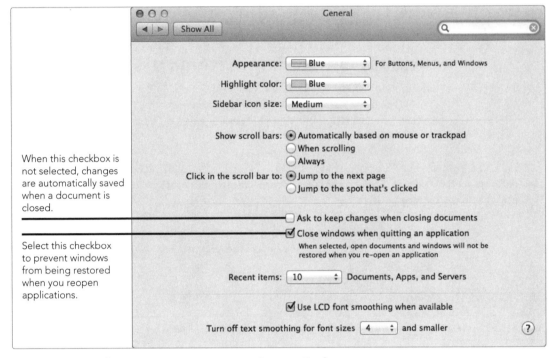

FIGURE 2-2: *Configuring resume settings in System Preferences*

3. To automatically save changes to documents when you close them, deselect the **Ask to keep changes when closing documents** checkbox.
4. To automatically reopen the active windows when you quit and reopen an application, deselect the **Close windows when quitting an application** checkbox.
5. From the **Apple** menu, select **Restart** or **Shut Down**. A dialog like the one shown in Figure 2-3 appears.

Select this checkbox to automatically resume open applications when you log back in.

FIGURE 2-3: *Use the Restart or Shut Down prompt to control the resume feature.*

6. Select the **Reopen windows when logging back in** checkbox.
7. Click the **Restart** or **Shut Down** button.

The next time your Mac starts up, all of the applications and windows you had open when you restarted or shut down will automatically open. If you ever want to turn off the resume feature, just deselect the checkboxes.

Configuring Advanced Login Item Settings with Exhaust

You can use System Preferences to add, hide, and remove login items—and that's it. If you need the ability to configure advanced settings for your login items, take a look at Exhaust (*http://mrgeckosmedia.com/applications/info/exhaust/*, free). This open source application lets you rearrange the order in which items load, modify the commands that call the items, and set timing options to control when items launch. For example, you could set a 30-second delay to automatically start iTunes *after* your Mac has connected to the network drive that your music is stored on. Or you could move your email client to the end of the list so it starts only after your Mac has connected to a VPN.

Use the Exhaust interface to interact with your login items, as shown in Figure 2-4. The items shown at the top of the sidebar load first when you log in—you can rearrange the launch order by dragging and dropping items in the list.

By default, commands for login items are set to the application paths, but you can change the commands to anything you want. If a login item takes arguments, you can add one or more in the Arguments box. And the timing options are useful for managing multiple AppleScripts or Automator actions.

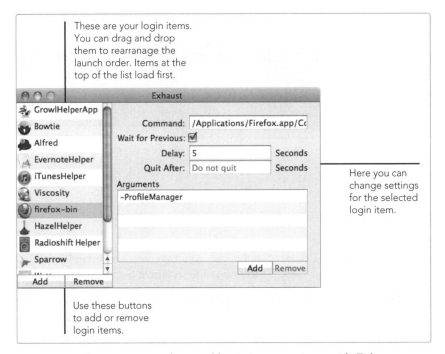

These are your login items. You can drag and drop them to rearrange the launch order. Items at the top of the list load first.

Here you can change settings for the selected login item.

Use these buttons to add or remove login items.

FIGURE 2-4: *Customizing advanced login item settings with Exhaust*

Additional Ideas for Starting Applications Automatically at Login

Most login items can be removed by opening System Preferences or the Exhaust application, selecting the item, and then clicking the **–** or **Remove** button. But in rare instances, login items may not appear in System Preferences at all. To track down these rogue applications and scripts, check the following locations:

▶ **Items that launch at startup:** */Library/StartupItems*, */Library/ LaunchDaemons*, and */System/Library/LaunchDaemons*

▶ **Items that launch at login:** */Library/LaunchAgents* and */System/Library/ LaunchAgents*

Delete the item you want to remove and then restart your computer. The item should not launch at startup or login.

3

Finding Files and Folders Fast

The typical Mac has hundreds of thousands of files stored on the hard disk. If you misplace a critical file or folder, how do you find it? It's a little like looking for a needle in a haystack—if you don't have the right tools for the job, you're going to walk away frustrated and empty-handed.

Unfortunately, the search capabilities built into OS X are only moderately effective. The Finder's Find feature isn't very accurate. Spotlight searches many different file types quickly and accurately—as long as it has indexed all of the files and folders on your Mac, which isn't always the case.

For these reasons and others, many Mac users choose to customize Spotlight and use third-party tools to locate files and folders. You may not need these tips right now, but when disaster eventually strikes and you lose a file or folder, you'll know what to do!

Project goal: Customize Spotlight and use third-party tools to find missing files and folders.

What You'll Be Using

To find the file you need efficiently, you'll use the following:

 Spotlight

 Find Any File (*http://apps.tempel.org/FindAnyFile/*, $)

Mastering Spotlight Searches

Spotlight is the revolutionary search technology built into OS X. You access it by clicking the magnifying-glass icon in the menu bar or by pressing the ⌘ key and spacebar. When the familiar Spotlight box appears, start typing, and search results will appear in real time, as shown in Figure 3-1.

FIGURE 3-1: *Performing a search with Spotlight*

Spotlight works fairly well out of the box, but you'll get even more out of this tried-and-true search feature with these tricks and tips.

Improving Spotlight's Search Results

Spotlight creates an *index* of practically everything on your hard drive—including email messages, contacts, and even Calendar events—and it uses this index to search your hard drive. That's fine if you don't have any inkling what you're searching for, but if you're looking for a specific file or folder, the last thing you want to do is wade through email messages in the search results. Fortunately, you can improve Spotlight by prioritizing search results and turning off some document categories when you perform a search.

Why would you disable document categories? To free up space in Spotlight's menu—which shows only a couple of results in every category—and concentrate searches in the categories where the document mostly likely lives. After you make the changes, the most useful results appear in the Spotlight menu, and everything else is hidden. This can make Spotlight a lot more useful, especially if it hasn't worked very well for you in the past.

✳ *NOTE:* Turning off document categories does not change Spotlight's index. Only displayed results are modified—Spotlight's index is not.

Here's how to deactivate Spotlight document categories:

1. From the **Apple** menu, select **System Preferences**.
2. Select **Spotlight**. The window shown in Figure 3-2 appears.
3. Deselect categories to prevent these types of files from appearing in the search results.
4. Drag categories up and down the list to prioritize the search results. Categories at the top of the list appear first in the results.

Hiding Dictionary and Calculator Results

You can't disable the dictionary and calculator search results in System Preferences, but don't worry—you can manually hide those results if you don't want to see them. Just open the Terminal application and type the following:

```
defaults write com.apple.spotlight DictionaryLookupEnabled NO
```

Press RETURN and then type the following:

```
defaults write com.apple.spotlight CalculationEnabled NO
```

Press RETURN again and then restart your computer. From now on, all of the dictionary and calculator search results will be hidden when you perform a search with Spotlight.

To start showing the dictionary and calculator search results again, type the same commands but replace the NO at the end of the commands with YES.

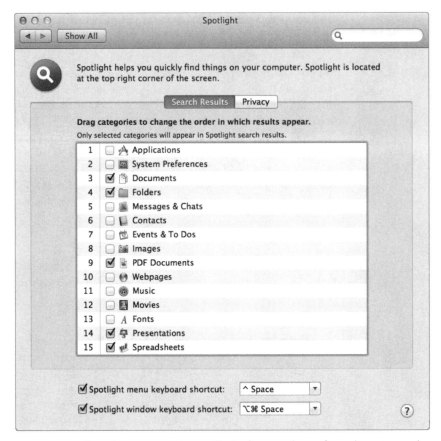

FIGURE 3-2: *Deselect categories to limit the number of results returned by Spotlight and drag categories to prioritize the search results.*

The next time you perform a search with Spotlight, you'll have to sort through fewer search results. Just remember that you'll need to reselect categories in System Preferences if you ever want to search for files in different categories.

Using Operators to Focus Searches

Limiting search categories and prioritizing results effectively focuses Spotlight searches, but it's a lot of work to open System Preferences every time you want to limit Spotlight's categories for one search. A better idea is to use *search operators*. These prefixes tell Spotlight to use a single search category or metadata variable for your current search.

Table 3-1 lists some examples of search operators you can use in Spotlight.

Table 3-1: Spotlight Search Operators

To search for documents...	Use...
In a specific category	kind:audio, kind:email, kind:folder, kind:word, etc.
Created by a specific author	author:*name*
Created or modified on or within specific dates	date:today, created:12/14/11-12/25/11, modified:<01/01/12
With Boolean operators	"master your mac" OR "my new mac", Matt AND Emily, apple NOT Microsoft

To use a search operator, enter it with a keyword in the Spotlight box to perform the search, as shown in Figure 3-3.

FIGURE 3-3: *Use search operators to eliminate irrelevant results.*

Search operators work for only one search—future Spotlight searches will return the usual results.

Adding Metadata to Find Files Quickly with Spotlight

Here's something that can prevent future headaches: Enter Spotlight metadata in the Get Info window so you can quickly locate a file or folder in the future. When you perform a Spotlight search for a keyword or phrase stored in metadata, Spotlight returns the file or folder at the top of the search results.

Of course, you'll need to enter the metadata *before* you lose the file or folder. You'll also have to remember the keywords you entered in the metadata to find the documents, so choose the keywords or the phrase carefully.

Here's how to add metadata in the Get Info window of a file or folder:

1. Select a file or folder.
2. Select **File ▸ Get Info**. The window shown in Figure 3-4 appears.
3. Click the triangle next to **Spotlight Comments** to reveal the field.
4. Enter keywords or a phrase in the **Spotlight Comments** field.
5. Close the Get Info window.

Now when you perform a Spotlight search for the keyword or phrase, the file or folder appears at the top of the search results, as shown in Figure 3-5.

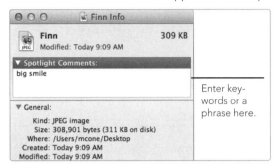

Enter keywords or a phrase here.

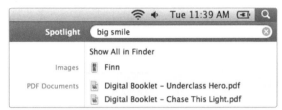

FIGURE 3-4: *Enter metadata to find a file or folder quickly in a Spotlight search.*

FIGURE 3-5: *Search for the keyword, and the file or folder appears at the top of the search results.*

Rebuilding Spotlight's Index

Spotlight performs searches by parsing through an index of all the files and folders on local hard drives connected to your computer. OS X is supposed to update this index in real time when you create or modify files or folders, but problems occasionally crop up. Spotlight won't work correctly if this index is incomplete or corrupted. When search results don't appear as expected, it's probably time to manually rebuild Spotlight's index.

Here's how to rebuild Spotlight's index:

1. From the **Apple** menu, select **System Preferences**.
2. Select **Spotlight**.
3. Click **Privacy**. The window shown in Figure 3-6 appears.
4. Click the **+** button.
5. Select a hard disk or volume.
6. Click the **−** button. Spotlight rebuilds the index of the selected hard disk or volume—a process that can take between 30 minutes and a couple of hours, depending on how many files you have.
7. Select the **Spotlight** menu to verify that the index is being rebuilt, as shown in Figure 3-7.

Your searches should be more accurate after Spotlight rebuilds the index.

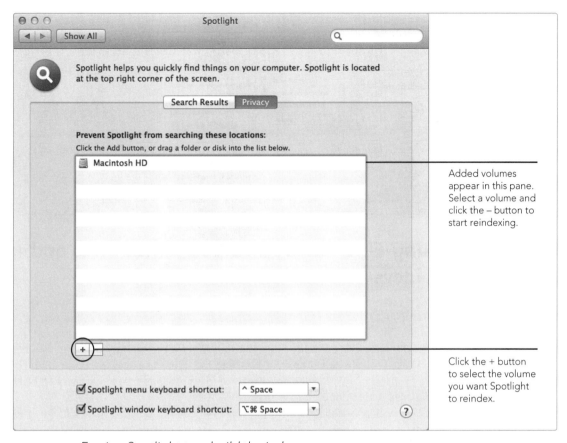

Added volumes appear in this pane. Select a volume and click the – button to start reindexing.

Click the + button to select the volume you want Spotlight to reindex.

FIGURE 3-6: *Forcing Spotlight to rebuild the index*

FIGURE 3-7: *Verifying that Spotlight is rebuilding the index of your hard disk*

Using Find Any File to Search for Files and Folders

If you're not a big fan of Spotlight or don't enjoy remembering all those search operators like NOT, kind:, or date:, you have another option. Find Any File (*http://apps.tempel.org/FindAnyFile/*, $) is a shareware application that quickly locates files and folders on your Mac with amazing accuracy. You start by entering search criteria like filename, creation date, size, and file type code, and then click Find to search your hard disk. Results are displayed in a simple interface that makes it easy to find files and folders.

There is one big limitation: Find Any File searches only the names of files and folders—it cannot search inside files. If that doesn't matter to you, this tool might fit the bill for finding files and folders on your Mac.

Here's how to search for files and folders with Find Any File:

1. Open the Find Any File application.
2. Select a volume or category of volumes from the menu at the top of the window.
3. When you open Find Any File, one criterion is displayed. Click **More Choices** to add additional criteria, as shown in Figure 3-8.
4. Edit a criterion by selecting a category from the menu in the first column.
5. Specify limits for the criterion by selecting a variable from the menu in the second column.
6. If available, enter a value for the criterion in the field in the third column.
7. Repeat the process as necessary to add additional search criteria. When you've specified the search criteria, click **Find** to search for the file or folder. The search results window appears, as shown in Figure 3-9.
8. Select a file or folder to reveal its location in the lower pane.

You can customize the results window. For example, select the **Show** dropdown menu from the **Invisibles** menu to see invisible files.

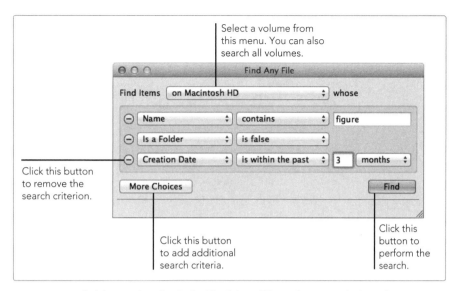

Select a volume from this menu. You can also search all volumes.

Click this button to remove the search criterion.

Click this button to add additional search criteria.

Click this button to perform the search.

FIGURE 3-8: *Add search criteria in Find Any File to locate missing documents.*

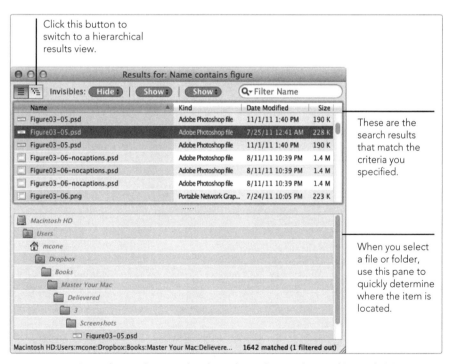

Click this button to switch to a hierarchical results view.

These are the search results that match the criteria you specified.

When you select a file or folder, use this pane to quickly determine where the item is located.

FIGURE 3-9: *Search results are displayed in a list. Select a file or folder to see where it's located on your computer.*

If you plan on using Find Any File regularly, you might want to set a global hotkey in the preferences to launch Find Any File quickly when you're using the Finder or a certain application.

Additional Ideas for Finding Files and Folders

Plenty of other applications can also help you find files and folders on your Mac. EasyFind (*http://www.devontechnologies.com/products/freeware.html*, free) is another powerful application that some find preferable to Find Any File. It can't search inside of documents, but it can find hard-to-find files like system-level objects, packaged objects, and hidden objects.

One geeky command-line tool conspicuously absent from this chapter is grep. This powerful UNIX-based application comes preinstalled on every Mac. It can search inside of files, look for a particular file or folder in a specific location, and use regular expressions, among other things. The downside is that grep has a serious learning curve.

For a Mac-friendly introduction to grep, see Kirk McElhearn's article on *Macworld*'s website (*http://www.macworld.com/article/41504/2004/12/jangeekfactor .html*). Once you have the basics down, take a look at the *Grep Pocket Reference* by John Bambenek or *Mastering Regular Expressions* by Jeffery Friedl, both of which are available from O'Reilly (*http://oreilly.com/*).

4

Organizing Windows

Many people find themselves fighting OS X when switching between applications and windows, losing precious time to the mundane tasks of resizing windows and clicking frantically to find the correct application.

It doesn't have to be this way. With application switchers and window managers, you can manage applications and windows in a whole new way.

Project goal: Quickly switch between applications and windows, and maximize screen space for multiple applications and windows.

What You'll Be Using

To move easily from application to application and see what you're doing, you'll use the following:

 Mission Control

 Divvy (*http://mizage.com/divvy/*, $$)

 Moom (*http://manytricks.com/moom/*, $)

 Cinch (*http://irradiatedsoftware.com/cinch/*, $)

Switching Between Applications

The application switcher built into OS X allows you to flip quickly between applications without taking your hands off the keyboard.

Here's how to switch to a different application:

1. Press the ⌘ and TAB keys on the keyboard. The application switcher window shown in Figure 4-1 appears.

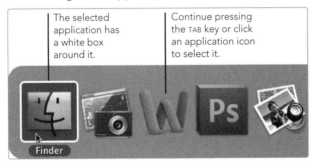

The selected application has a white box around it.

Continue pressing the TAB key or click an application icon to select it.

FIGURE 4-1: *Press the ⌘ and TAB keys to use the application switcher.*

2. While holding down the ⌘ key, press the TAB key repeatedly until the application's icon is selected. (By default, the application selection box moves from left to right when you press the TAB key. Hold down the SHIFT key while pressing TAB to reverse that.) Or you can use the mouse or trackpad to click the application's icon.
3. When the application is selected, let go of the ⌘ and TAB keys. The application you selected appears on the screen.

The order of the icons in the application switcher is not arbitrary. The active application is displayed first, and the other applications are displayed in the order in which you last used them, from left to right.

This shortcut really shines when you're switching between two applications, like Safari and Microsoft Word. If you're using Safari, and Word was previously active, just press ⌘-TAB to switch to Word. To jump back to Safari, press the ⌘ and TAB keys once again. For continuous switching back and forth between two applications, using this shortcut is much faster than anything else.

If you're switching among three or four applications, you may be better off using Mission Control (see "Mission Control: The Ultimate Application and Window Switcher" below).

Opening Files with the Application Switcher

Here's a bonus tip: You can use the application switcher to open a file with an application that's already open. Just select a file in the Finder by clicking it and holding the mouse button, press ⌘-TAB to show the application switcher, and then drag and drop the file onto the application you want it to open in.

Cycling Through Windows

Fans of the application switcher will be happy to know about a similar shortcut for cycling through all of the open windows in a single application. Just press the ⌘ and ` (the grave accent, above TAB) keys repeatedly to flip through all of the windows in an application, such as multiple documents in Microsoft Word or all your open Safari windows.

Mission Control: The Ultimate Application and Window Switcher

Mission Control is a feature in OS X that combines Exposé, Dashboard, and Spaces—three tools available in older versions of OS X—in a single, powerful interface. Its power lies in its simplicity. When you enter Mission Control, it displays all open applications and windows—all you have to do is select an application or window, and it becomes active.

As with any productivity application, it takes time and practice to effectively integrate Mission Control into your lifestyle. But once you get used to the bird's-eye view of all the applications, windows, and spaces open on your Mac, you'll be switching applications like a pro!

Configuring Mission Control's Settings

Before you start using Mission Control in earnest, you'll want to customize the settings. By default, you can open Mission Control by using a trackpad gesture (a four-finger swipe up) or a keyboard shortcut (pressing CONTROL and the up arrow). These default settings can be changed in System Preferences. You'll need to experiment to find settings that feel natural.

Here's how to configure Mission Control's settings:

1. From the **Apple** menu, select **System Preferences**.
2. Click **Mission Control**. The window shown in Figure 4-2 appears.

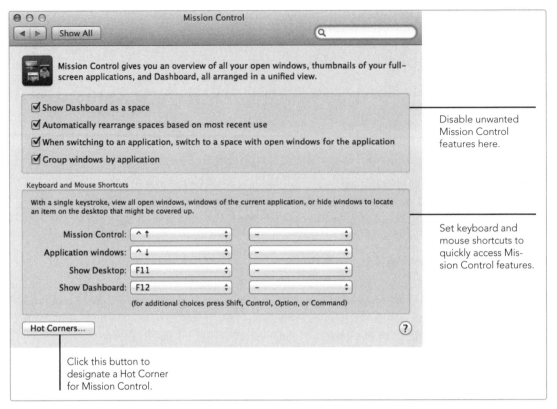

Disable unwanted Mission Control features here.

Set keyboard and mouse shortcuts to quickly access Mission Control features.

Click this button to designate a Hot Corner for Mission Control.

FIGURE 4-2: *Configuring Mission Control settings*

3. (Optional) Dashboard is shown as a space by default. Deselect the **Show Dashboard as a space** checkbox to prevent Dashboard from appearing as a space.

4. (Optional) By default, spaces are automatically rearranged based on most recent use. This means that the space most recently used is displayed first, just as applications appear in the application switcher. If you want spaces to always appear in the order in which you created them, deselect the **Automatically rearrange spaces based on most recent use** checkbox.

5. (Optional) By default, when you select an application, you are automatically switched to the space the application is open in. To prevent this behavior and force the application to be displayed in the current space, deselect the **When switching to an application, switch to a space with open windows for the application** checkbox.

6. (Optional) By default, all of an application's windows are grouped together in Mission Control. To prevent this behavior and display each window individually in Mission Control, deselect the **Group windows by application** checkbox. You don't want to deselect this checkbox if you frequently have many windows open.

7. (Optional) Change the keyboard and mouse shortcuts by selecting options from the menus. You can hold down the SHIFT, CONTROL, OPTION, or ⌘ keys to modify the options in the menus.

You can also change other Mission Control keyboard shortcuts in the Keyboard section of System Preferences.

Here's how to change keyboard shortcuts associated with Mission Control:

1. From the **Apple** menu, select **System Preferences**.
2. Click **Keyboard**.
3. Click **Keyboard Shortcuts**. The window shown in Figure 4-3 appears.

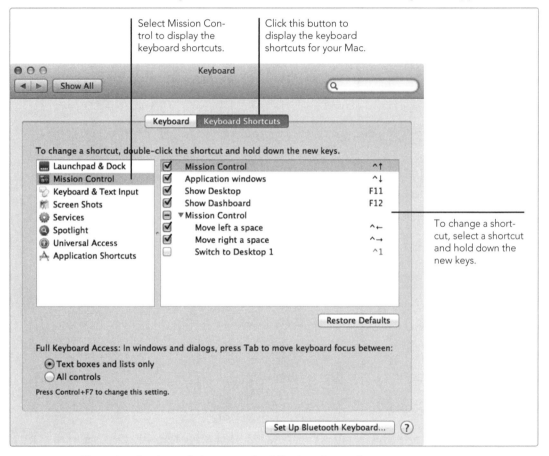

FIGURE 4-3: *Changing keyboard shortcuts for Mission Control*

4. Select checkboxes to enable the keyboard shortcuts; deselect checkboxes to disable shortcuts.
5. To change a shortcut, double-click it and hold down the new keys you want to activate the command.

You should practice using the keyboard shortcuts for Mission Control whether you have changed them or not. If a keyboard shortcut doesn't feel natural, keep changing it until you find something that feels right. The goal is to find a keyboard shortcut that you'll actually *use*.

Switching Between Applications and Windows with Mission Control

Now comes the fun part—actually using Mission Control. It's a regular Mac application, so you can open it by double-clicking its icon in the Applications folder. If keyboard shortcuts and trackpad gestures are your thing, press F3 or CONTROL and the up arrow, or swipe up with four fingers. (Of course, if you changed the keyboard shortcut in the section above, you'll need to use the new shortcut.) The screen shown in Figure 4-4 appears.

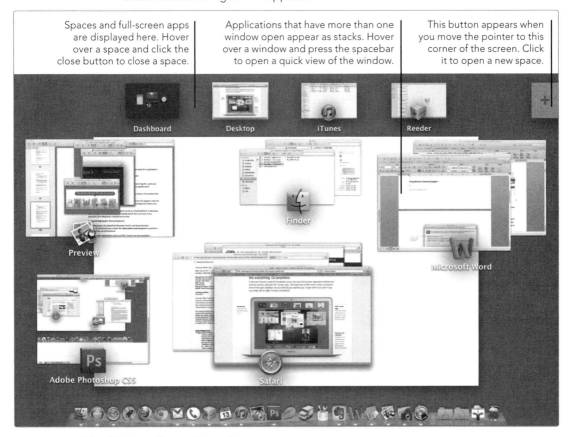

Spaces and full-screen apps are displayed here. Hover over a space and click the close button to close a space.

Applications that have more than one window open appear as stacks. Hover over a window and press the spacebar to open a quick view of the window.

This button appears when you move the pointer to this corner of the screen. Click it to open a new space.

FIGURE 4-4: *The Mission Control interface*

Spaces and applications in full-screen mode are displayed at the top of the screen. The most recently opened applications are displayed in the rest of the screen. Just click an application or window to switch to it.

If you have multiple windows open in an application, you'll notice that the windows are stacked in a pile. You can move the pointer over a window and press the spacebar to display a preview of the window without leaving Mission Control. To close the preview, press ESC or click the mouse button.

When you open Mission Control, it displays the open applications in the current space. To move between spaces while in Mission Control, press CONTROL and the right or left arrow key, or swipe with four fingers to the left or right.

Creating Virtual Desktops with Spaces

OS X's virtual desktop feature, called Spaces, can help you organize applications and windows. For example, you can research and write in one space while iTunes plays music in a second. Spaces can be especially handy for managing applications with lots of little windows and dialogs—just put your most complicated applications in a stand-alone space.

Try creating a second space by using Mission Control. In Mission Control, move the pointer to the upper-right corner and click the **+** button to create a new space, or use full-screen mode to put an application in a new space by itself. (To put an application in full-screen mode, click the two arrows in the top-right corner of a window.) You can switch between spaces with Mission Control, keyboard shortcuts, or even gestures. The default gesture is a four-finger swipe left or right; the default keyboard shortcut is pressing the CONTROL key and the left or right arrow key.

Spaces aren't quite as effective as using two monitors, but they're a viable alternative for portable Mac users who are looking to seriously boost productivity. If you're writing a book, for example, you could create a space for taking screenshots of applications and another space for typing the book in a word processor. You'll avoid confusion and reduce application switching by performing different tasks in separate spaces. Experiment to find the best configuration for you!

Maximizing Your Screen Space

What if you need to display two or more windows on the screen at once? The usual procedure is to manually resize the windows to fit them next to each other—a cumbersome process that can quickly frustrate and discourage even the most determined user.

A better solution is to use a window management application to quickly and precisely resize the windows in a layout of your choosing. There are many great window management applications for Mac users. In this section, you'll learn about three of the best options: Divvy, Moom, and Cinch. All of these applications have free trials, and it's likely you'll need to use only one of the three, so test them out before forking over any money.

Using Divvy

If you need an easy and accurate method to resize windows on your screen, try a little application called Divvy (*http://mizage.com/divvy/*, $$). It's flexible enough to be used by both novices and advanced users. Beginners can click the menu bar icon to manually resize windows, and advanced users can set global keyboard shortcuts to resize windows without opening Divvy's interface.

Here's how to use Divvy to resize a window:

1. Click the **Divvy** menu bar icon. The window shown in Figure 4-5 appears.

FIGURE 4-5: *Select the boxes in the Divvy window to resize the active application.*

2. Drag the pointer to select the boxes in the Divvy window. As you select boxes, the corresponding portion of the screen is highlighted to show you how the application window will be resized when you release the mouse button.

3. Release the mouse button. The window is resized accordingly.

The features for advanced users are hidden in Divvy's preferences—just right-click the menu bar icon or click the gear icon in Divvy's window. There you can set a global keyboard shortcut to show Divvy's interface so you don't have to click the menu bar icon every time you want to resize a window. And if you want to avoid using the Divvy interface entirely, you can specify *shortcuts* to instantly resize a window according to the setting you specify in the shortcut.

Using Moom

One of OS X's biggest weaknesses is the infamous green "zoom" button in the corner of every window. Clicking that button never really resizes a window the way you expect it to—unless you use an application called Moom (*http://manytricks .com/moom/*, $). Install this app and you'll be able to resize a window by moving the pointer over the green button and then selecting one of five resizing presets from the pop-up menu.

If you need more control over window size, you can turn on the *move and zoom grid* to display an interface like Divvy's—and as with Divvy, you can create global keyboard shortcuts to instantly resize windows without using Moom's interface.

Here's how to use Moom to resize a window:

1. Move the pointer over the green "zoom" button. The Moom pop-up menu appears, as shown in Figure 4-6.

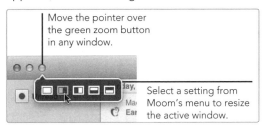

FIGURE 4-6: *Move the pointer over the green button to display Moom's menu.*

2. Select a setting. The window is resized according to the option you've chosen.

Moom's features are very similar to the ones provided by Divvy. Deciding to use one application over the other is a matter of personal preference. Try them both and purchase the one you like!

Using Cinch

Maybe you've heard of the new feature in Microsoft Windows 7 called Areo Snap that allows users to automatically resize windows by dragging them to the right, left, or top of the screen. This feature can be added to OS X with the help of Cinch (*http://irradiatedsoftware.com/cinch/*, $). Dragging a window to the left or right side of the screen resizes the window to exactly half of the screen; dragging a window to the top of the screen maximizes it to the entire screen.

✱ **NOTE:** Cinch isn't for everyone. Some Windows 7 users complain that Areo Snap resizes windows when they least expect it, and your experience with Cinch might be similar.

Here's how to use Cinch to resize a window:

1. Drag a window to the left, right, or top of the screen. The dotted line shown in Figure 4-7 appears.
2. Release the mouse button to resize the window.

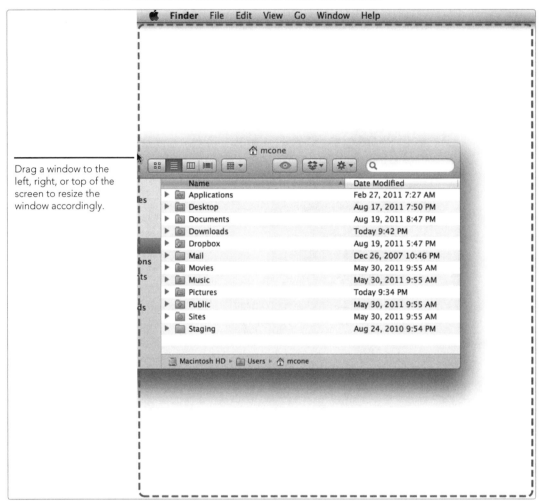

Drag a window to the left, right, or top of the screen to resize the window accordingly.

FIGURE 4-7: *Start Cinch and then drag a window to the left, right, or top of the screen to resize it.*

One thing you'll quickly discover is that Mission Control can interfere with Cinch. By default, dragging a window to the left or right side of the screen in OS X moves it to a different space after approximately 0.75 seconds. Invoking Cinch before Mission Control is all about timing. If you're still having problems after practicing, visit Irradiated Software's website (*http://irradiatedsoftware.com/cinch/*) to find some workarounds to this problem.

Additional Ideas for Managing Applications and Windows

If you'd like more features from the application switcher (⌘-TAB), try an application called Witch (*http://manytricks.com/witch/*, $$). It replaces the default application switcher with a window that displays applications and open windows—functionality that power users may find much better than that provided by the classic and clunky application switcher.

And if for some reason Divvy, Moom, and Cinch don't fit your bill, you can find plenty of other applications to help you maximize your screen space. Another excellent option is an application called MercuryMover (*http://www.heliumfoot .com/mercurymover/*, $$). This is the best choice for the keyboard-shortcut lovers out there—all you have to do is press a couple of keys, and the active window is resized.

5 Cleaning House

If you've been following along so far, it's likely that you've installed a few new applications on your Mac, some of which you may never want to use again. Downloading and installing applications on your Mac is a relatively trivial matter—removing them is another story. You would think you could just drag an application to the Trash to remove it, but it's not always that simple.

When you install an application, you also install *related files* on your Mac's hard disk. Most related files don't do anything other than support the application, so it's a good idea to delete them when you remove the application. Related files can be quite large, and they just take up unnecessary space after you remove the application. The problem is that you'll never be able to find all of the related files by yourself. The files are scattered all over the hard disk, so you'll need to use a couple of tools to find and delete them.

In this chapter, you'll learn how to use Launchpad and AppCleaner to permanently remove applications and their related files. You'll also learn how to use System Preferences to delete unwanted preference panes, a special kind of program.

Project goal: Permanently remove applications and preference panes from your Mac.

What You'll Be Using

To get rid of unwanted applications and preference panes, you'll use the following:

 Launchpad

 AppCleaner (*http://freemacsoft.net/*, free)

 System Preferences

Removing Applications with Launchpad

The Mac App Store makes it easy to find and install applications, and Launchpad makes it easy to get rid of those applications when you're ready to delete them permanently from your Mac. The process of removing apps with Launchpad is similar to removing apps in iOS—you're already familiar with this process if you own an iPad, iPhone, or iPod Touch. The only caveat is that this only works to remove applications downloaded from the Mac App Store.

Here's how to use Launchpad to remove applications downloaded from the App Store:

1. Open the Launchpad application.
2. Click an application icon until all of the icons start wriggling. Applications that can be deleted in Launchpad have an X button displayed on their icon.
3. Click the **X** on the application icon you want to remove. The dialog shown in Figure 5-1 appears.
4. Click **Delete**. The application and all of its related files are permanently deleted from your computer.

Did you delete an application by accident? No problem. Apple keeps track of the applications you download, so it's easy to reinstall any application that you've purchased or downloaded for free from the App Store.

Just open the App Store and hold down the OPTION key when you click the **Purchased** button, and an **Install** button will appear next to any application you have deleted from your Mac. Click **Install** to download and install the application on your Mac again.

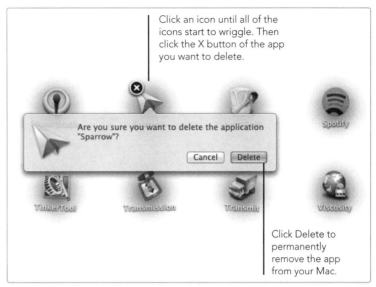

Click an icon until all of the icons start to wriggle. Then click the X button of the app you want to delete.

Are you sure you want to delete the application "Sparrow"?

Cancel   Delete

Spotify

TinkerTool   Transmission   Transmit   Viscosity

Click Delete to permanently remove the app from your Mac.

FIGURE 5-1: *Use Launchpad to remove applications downloaded from the Mac App Store.*

Removing Applications with AppCleaner

Launchpad removes only applications downloaded from the App Store. To remove the other applications installed on your Mac—the ones you downloaded directly from developer websites—you can use an application called AppCleaner (*http:// freemacsoft.net/*, free).

When you open AppCleaner and select an application to remove, it locates all of the files associated with the application and marks them for deletion. Click **Delete**, and the application and all of its support files are permanently removed from your computer.

Here's how to remove applications with AppCleaner:

1. Open the AppCleaner application.
2. Drag an application's icon to the AppCleaner window. Or click the **Applications** button, select an application, and then click **Search**. The window shown in Figure 5-2 appears.
3. All files related to the application are selected by default. To keep some files, deselect the checkboxes next to the ones you want to keep.
4. Click **Delete**. The application and all selected files are moved to the Trash.

You may have noticed two other buttons in the AppCleaner window: Widgets and Others. Use those buttons to remove unwanted Dashboard widgets, browser plug-ins, preference panes, and more.

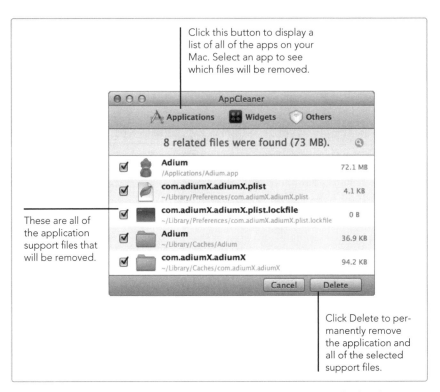

Click this button to display a list of all of the apps on your Mac. Select an app to see which files will be removed.

These are all of the application support files that will be removed.

Click Delete to permanently remove the application and all of the selected support files.

FIGURE 5-2: *Use AppCleaner to remove applications installed independently of the App Store.*

But wait, there's more! AppCleaner allows you to automate the process of deleting related files when you remove an application. When the *SmartDelete* feature is enabled and you drag an application to the Trash, AppCleaner automatically notifies you of any related files that should also be deleted. It's a great way to automate the process of removing applications—just drag an application to the Trash, and AppCleaner takes care of the rest.

Here's how to turn on and use SmartDelete:

1. Open the AppCleaner application.
2. Select **File ▸ Preferences**.
3. Click **SmartDelete**. The window shown in Figure 5-3 appears.
4. Slide the switch to the **On** position. The SmartDelete feature is now enabled.
5. To test SmartDelete, drag an application to the Trash. The dialog shown in Figure 5-4 should appear.
6. Click **Delete** to move the selected files to the Trash. Click **Cancel** to keep all of the files.

FIGURE 5-3: *Turn on App-Cleaner's SmartDelete feature to automatically find and delete an application's related files when you drag it to the Trash.*

FIGURE 5-4: *AppCleaner's SmartDelete finds the related files of an application that's been dragged to the Trash.*

✳ **NOTE:** In Chapter 14 you'll learn about Hazel, a third-party preference pane that is also capable of monitoring the Trash and notifying you when related files need to be deleted.

Removing Preference Panes

Sometimes after installing a new application, you'll see a new icon in your System Preferences for that application. These *preference panes* can be used to interact with applications, configure settings, and add functionality to your Mac. In addition, some applications (sometimes called *plug-ins*) can be uninstalled *only* by removing their preference panes. Some common examples of preference panes include Adobe Flash Player and Flip4Mac. If you no longer need the functionality provided by a preference pane, you'll want to permanently remove it.

Here's how to remove a preference pane:

1. From the **Apple** menu, select **System Preferences**.
2. In the Other section of the window, right-click the preference pane you want to remove. The menu shown in Figure 5-5 appears.
3. Select **Remove Preference Pane**. You may have to enter your administrator password. The preference pane is permanently removed from your Mac.

Don't forget that you can also use AppCleaner to remove preference panes.

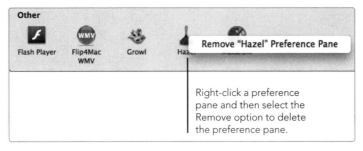

FIGURE 5-5: Use System Preferences to remove preference panes.

Additional Ideas for Removing Applications

By now you probably appreciate the need to properly remove applications. You can't just drag an application to the Trash to remove it—doing so removes the application but leaves behind all of the related files. Using one of the methods described in this chapter ensures that all of the files related to the application are also deleted.

You can use a couple of other methods to remove applications. The original application remover is AppZapper (*http://appzapper.com/*, $$), which has a loyal customer base but is expensive and rarely updated. In some cases, you can use an application's installer to uninstall the application. If all else fails, check the developer's website for uninstall instructions.

6

Adjusting Energy and Display Settings

We know how it goes. Someone says "energy and display settings," and your eyes glaze over. But as boring as this subject might seem, tailoring your Mac to your physical environment can save energy, boost productivity, and even protect your health.

It starts with modifying the default energy and display preferences built into OS X—the baseline operating settings you have to live with day in and day out. Then you'll use a couple of third-party applications to further adjust these settings. For example, you'll use an application called Caffeine to temporarily suspend the settings when you're using your Mac to deliver a business presentation or watch a movie. And you'll use another application called F.lux to change the color of your display at night to a softer, warmer color that is easier on the eyes.

Project goal: Adjust energy and display settings, temporarily disable energy settings, and configure display brightness for nighttime use.

What You'll Be Using

To save energy and optimize your Mac's display for the way you're using it at any given moment, you'll use the following:

 System Preferences

 Caffeine (*http://lightheadsw.com/caffeine/*, free)

 F.lux (*http://stereopsis.com/flux/*, free)

Understanding Energy and Display Settings

First things first. Let's start by customizing the energy and display settings that control when your display, hard drive, and computer go to sleep.

Why bother? Because putting your computer and display to sleep when you're not using them can help you conserve energy. If you're running on battery power, the settings can help you use your Mac longer before reconnecting the power adapter. Be careful, though. If you're too conservative with the settings, your computer can go to sleep too soon. That's annoying, and it could actually *increase* your Mac's energy usage.

The settings can also help your Mac automatically adjust the brightness of the display depending on your environment and use custom settings depending on whether you're using battery power or the power adapter.

Here's how to configure your Mac's energy and display settings:

1. From the **Apple** menu, select **System Preferences**.
2. Click **Energy Saver**. The window shown in Figure 6-1 appears.
3. Move the sliders to change when your Mac and display go to sleep—shorter times put your computer to sleep faster.
4. Select the checkboxes to put your hard disk to sleep when possible and reduce the display's brightness when it's running on battery power.
5. Click **Show All**.
6. Click **Displays**. The window shown in Figure 6-2 appears.
7. Select the **Automatically adjust brightness** checkbox to enable your Mac's ambient light sensors, if available.

That should do it. You've created some baseline energy and display settings that control how your Mac operates under normal conditions. In the following sections, you'll learn how to adjust those settings on the fly in special circumstances.

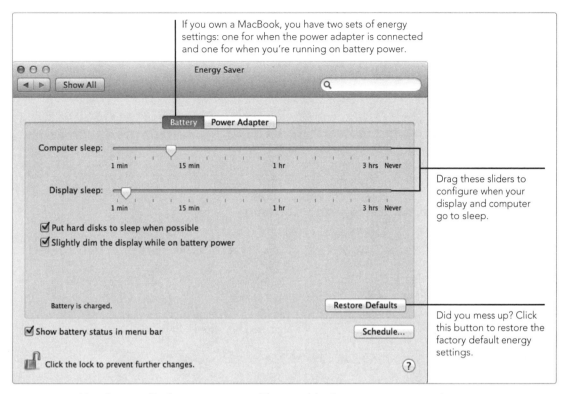

FIGURE 6-1: *Use System Preferences to modify your Mac's energy saver settings.*

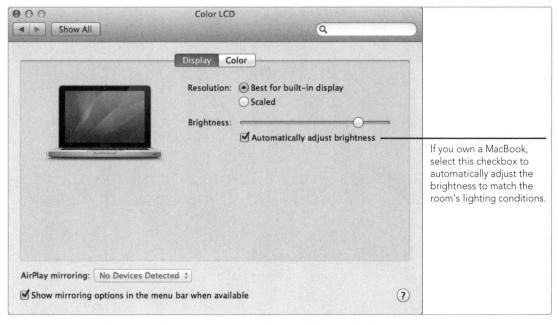

FIGURE 6-2: *Use System Preferences to modify your display's brightness settings.*

Temporarily Disabling Energy Settings

Now that you've customized your Mac's energy settings, you're faced with a new problem: What to do on the rare occasions when you need to temporarily disable the energy settings altogether? You don't want the display going to sleep during a business presentation or when you're watching a movie.

Enter Caffeine (*http://lightheadsw.com/caffeine/*, free), an application that provides an alternative to manually modifying the energy settings every time you need to make a temporary change. It's easy to use. Just click Caffeine's menu bar icon to prevent your Mac from going to sleep, dimming the display, or starting screensavers. Click the menu bar icon again to turn Caffeine off.

Getting Started with Caffeine

When you open Caffeine for the first time, it places an icon (a coffee cup) in the menu bar and asks you to configure the application's preferences, as shown in Figure 6-3.

You can set Caffeine to automatically start when you log in and even to disable the energy settings when it starts. You'll also need to set the default duration—the amount of time for which Caffeine disables your energy settings. You can change the duration when you activate Caffeine from the menu bar.

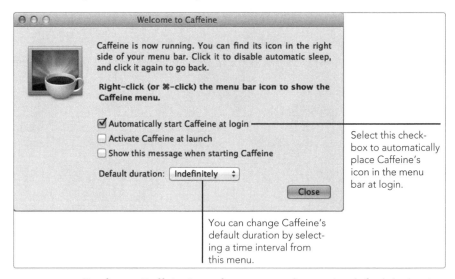

Select this check-box to automatically place Caffeine's icon in the menu bar at login.

You can change Caffeine's default duration by selecting a time interval from this menu.

FIGURE 6-3: *Configure Caffeine's preferences to change its default behavior.*

Turning Caffeine On and Off

To turn Caffeine on with the default duration, just click the menu bar icon. You can tell at a glance when Caffeine is turned off—the icon is dimmed and the cup is empty. When Caffeine is enabled, the icon is black and the cup is full and steaming, as shown in Figure 6-4.

FIGURE 6-4: *Click Caffeine's menu bar icon to turn it on and off.*

Caffeine automatically turns off after the default duration times out. (If the default duration is set to Indefinitely, Caffeine stays turned on until you manually turn it off.) To turn Caffeine on for a duration other than the default, right-click the menu bar icon and select a setting from the **Activate for** menu, as shown in Figure 6-5.

To stop Caffeine manually before the duration you've specified has ended, just click the menu bar icon.

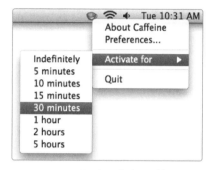

FIGURE 6-5: *Right-click Caffeine's menu bar icon to activate Caffeine for a specific time interval.*

Adjusting Your Display's Color at Night

Apple says its displays provide a "brilliant viewing experience," which means your Mac's display is very bright. That's great during the day, when you probably need the display to be as bright as possible, but what about at night? Recent research suggests that staring at computer screens after sunset can disrupt your sleep cycles.[1]

The F.lux application (*http://stereopsis.com/flux/*, free) customizes your display's lighting by changing the color of your screen, so you're not as wired when you try to go to sleep. At night, F.lux changes the brilliant "blue light" brightness that mimics sunlight to one that closely resembles the warm "red light" brightness of an incandescent light bulb or candle.

When you open F.lux for the first time, it determines your geographic location by using data from your Mac's Internet connection. It uses this information to determine the time of sunset and the moment at which F.lux will start transitioning your display from day to night settings. Once F.lux has pinpointed your location, a map appears on the screen, as shown in Figure 6-6. Click **Confirm** if the location is correct.

---

1. See, for example, Laura Beil, "In Eyes, a Clock Calibrated by Wavelengths of Light," *New York Times*, *http://www.nytimes.com/2011/07/05/health/05light.html.*

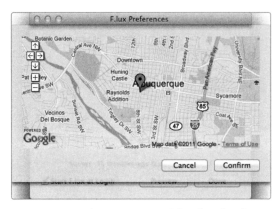

FIGURE 6-6: *When you start F.lux for the first time, it automatically pinpoints your location.*

Now you can configure F.lux's preferences, as shown in Figure 6-7. Move the sliders to adjust the lighting settings for day and night—dragging the slider left adds red light to create a warmer light; dragging the slider right adds blue light to create brighter light. You can test the settings by clicking **Preview**. It's best to preview the night settings in the dark, of course.

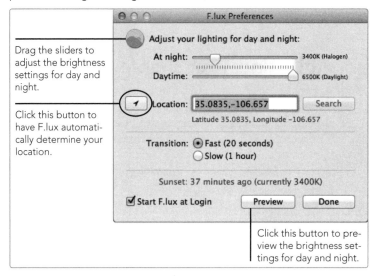

FIGURE 6-7: *Configure F.lux's preferences to customize your computer's brightness settings for day and night.*

Another setting you might want to play with is Transition. When F.lux determines that the sun has set, it starts transitioning your display to the night setting. You can set F.lux to perform the transition in 20 seconds, which can be quite jarring, or over a 1-hour period, which is much easier on the eyes.

Use the F.lux menu to change the nighttime settings on the fly or disable the default setting for an hour, as shown in Figure 6-8.

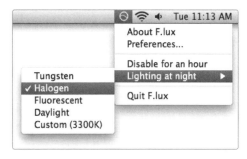

FIGURE 6-8: *Use the F.lux menu to change the nighttime settings.*

Additional Ideas for Adjusting Energy and Display Settings

If you're using Caffeine to keep your Mac awake when you're away from home, you should know about two other options that might be more effective. The Wake for network access setting in the Energy Saver preferences turns your Mac on when it detects traffic attempting to access your Mac. This setting is perfect when you will need to remotely connect to your Mac but don't want to keep it awake all day. It's available only when your Mac is connected to a power adapter.

Another option is Aurora (*http://www.metakine.com/products/aurora/*, $$), an application that can wake your Mac or put it to sleep at a specific time of day.

F.lux can be customized for lots of situations—use your imagination. For example, individuals who work night shifts might reverse the brightness settings for night and day to fake their brains into thinking it's day when it's really night.

Finally, remember that most of the settings discussed in this chapter are a matter of personal preference. You'll need to play around with the settings to find a configuration that works for you.

PART 2

Boosting Productivity

7

Launching Applications Fast

Ready to open an application on your computer? You know the drill. Click the application's icon on the Dock or—if it's not there—open the Applications folder, find the application, and then double-click the icon. Ditto for documents, songs, preference panes, system services, and just about anything else you can open on your Mac.

But what if there were a shortcut? With a type of tool called an *application launcher*, there is. Just as keyboard shortcuts help you perform actions nearly instantaneously and window management utilities take the work out of switching between applications and windows, application launchers make opening applications and files a piece of cake. Using only the keyboard, you'll be able to find and open applications, documents, and system settings. Plus, you can use the more advanced application launchers to perform actions within applications by just typing a couple of commands into a window.

You'll cut your teeth on Spotlight, Apple's built-in search tool that can moonlight as an application launcher. Once you're familiar with the concept, you'll transition to an intermediate application launcher, Alfred, which lets you open applications and interact with them. Then you'll take the final step with LaunchBar, an advanced application launcher that lets you do practically everything with your keyboard.

Project goal: Launch applications and open files fast, without touching the mouse or trackpad.

What You'll Be Using

To open applications and files on your Mac quickly, you'll use the following:

 Spotlight

 Alfred (*http://www.alfredapp.com/*, free)

 LaunchBar (*http://www.obdev.at/products/launchbar/*, $$$)

Getting Your Feet Wet with Spotlight

When you think of Spotlight, you probably think of searching your computer for files and folders. But Spotlight can also function as a basic application launcher. Press ⌘-spacebar and start typing the name of the application you want to open, and Spotlight locates the matching applications or preference panes and displays them in the results list, as shown in Figure 7-1. (You could click the Spotlight menu with the mouse or trackpad, but the goal of application launchers is for you to use the keyboard only.)

With any luck, the application you want to open will be displayed as the *Top Hit* in Spotlight's results list and you won't have to enter its full name. For example, you should be able to enter **itu** for iTunes to appear as the Top Hit. Once you see the application at the top of the list, press RETURN to open it—there's no need to use the mouse or trackpad.

Start typing, and the Top Hit is automatically highlighted—just press RETURN to open the application.

FIGURE 7-1: When you open Spotlight and start typing an application's name, it appears as the Top Hit in the search results.

Configuring Spotlight as an Application Launcher

Since Spotlight is configured as a search utility by default, you'll probably want to disable most of the categories if you plan on using it primarily as an application launcher. This ensures that you see results in only the Applications and System Preferences categories. Of course, disabling these categories means that you won't see documents, email messages, or results from any of the other categories (one reason why you might not want to use Spotlight as your primary application launcher).

Here's how to disable Spotlight categories to configure it as an application launcher:

1. From the **Apple** menu, select **System Preferences**.
2. Click **Spotlight**.
3. Click **Search Results**. The window shown in Figure 7-2 appears.
4. Deselect all of the checkboxes except **Applications** and **System Preferences**.
5. Close System Preferences.

FIGURE 7-2: Turn off all categories except Applications and System Preferences to maximize Spotlight's effectiveness as an application launcher.

Now you can try out your "new" Spotlight application launcher. Press ⌘-spacebar to open the Spotlight window and then start typing an application's name. When it's displayed as the Top Hit, press RETURN to open the application.

Hiding Developer Files in Spotlight

In Chapter 3, you learned how to hide dictionary and calculator entries in Spotlight's search results. Now that you're using Spotlight as an application launcher, you're probably seeing Developer files—another category of results that you can't disable in System Preferences unless you have installed Xcode, Apple's integrated developer environment. (Of course, you don't necessarily want to disable these results if you're a developer.)

However, there's a way to hide the developer results in Spotlight searches without installing Xcode. Just enter the following command into the Terminal application:

```
defaults write com.apple.spotlight orderedItems -array-add
"<dict><key>enabled</key><false/><key>name</key><string>
SOURCE</string></dict>"
```

Then log out and back in—the developer results won't appear when you perform a new search.

Using Alfred

Spotlight works as an application launcher, but it's a bit rudimentary. Alfred (*http://alfredapp.com/*, free), an intermediate-level application launcher, allows you to open applications *and* interact with your computer.

If you know how to use Spotlight, you'll feel right at home using Alfred. The general concept is the same. Press a keyboard shortcut to open Alfred's heads-up display, start typing, and then select a result that appears in the list, as shown in Figure 7-3.

In addition to launching applications, Alfred can do math, look up definitions, search websites, and even control your computer. If those features don't pack enough of a punch, install the Alfred Powerpack (*http://www.alfredapp.com/powerpack/*, $$) to unlock a slew of powerful functionality.

Setting Up Alfred

You'll need to take care of some preliminary setup tasks before using Alfred. The first order of business is adding Alfred as a login item, setting its *hotkey* so you can quickly open the heads-up display with your keyboard, and entering your geographic location so it knows which websites to open. Next, you'll change the appearance settings to suit your personal preferences.

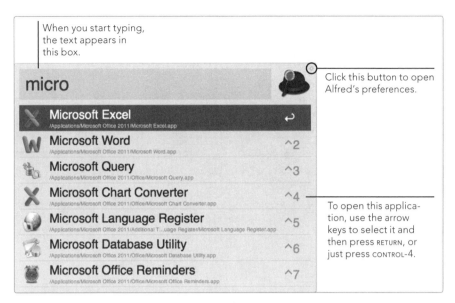

When you start typing, the text appears in this box.

Click this button to open Alfred's preferences.

To open this application, use the arrow keys to select it and then press RETURN, or just press CONTROL-4.

FIGURE 7-3: Alfred's user-friendly interface is accessible even to new Mac users.

Here's how to set up Alfred:

1. Open Alfred. (It's in your Applications folder.) The window shown in Figure 7-4 appears.
2. Select the **Launch Alfred at login** checkbox to add the Alfred application as a login item.
3. Click the **Alfred hotkey** box and then press the key combination you want to use to open Alfred. (⌘-spacebar is the keyboard shortcut assigned to Spotlight by default. To use that shortcut as Alfred's hotkey, you need to first change Spotlight's keyboard shortcut by opening System Preferences, clicking **Spotlight**, clicking **Search Results**, and then selecting a new shortcut from the **Spotlight menu keyboard shortcut** menu.)
4. Select your country from the **Where are you** menu. This customizes Alfred's web search feature—something you'll learn about later in this chapter—for your geographic location.
5. Click **Appearance**. The window shown in Figure 7-5 appears.
6. Select the **Hide menu bar icon** checkbox to remove Alfred's icon from the menu bar. Don't worry—you won't be missing much. All of the important options available from the menu bar icon are also available in the heads-up display.
7. You can change the number of results shown in the heads-up display by selecting a different value from the **I want to see** menu.
8. If you'd like to change the color of the heads-up display, click **Theme**. You'll be able to select from a few color combinations.
9. Close the Alfred Preferences window.

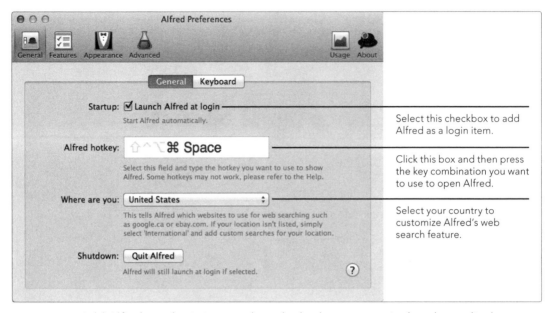

Select this checkbox to add Alfred as a login item.

Click this box and then press the key combination you want to use to open Alfred.

Select your country to customize Alfred's web search feature.

FIGURE 7-4: *Add Alfred as a login item and set the hotkey to open its heads-up display.*

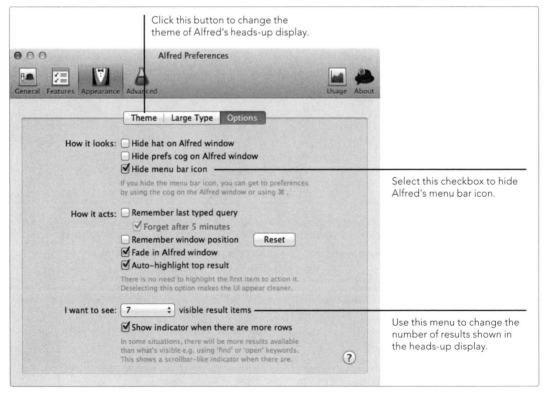

Click this button to change the theme of Alfred's heads-up display.

Select this checkbox to hide Alfred's menu bar icon.

Use this menu to change the number of results shown in the heads-up display.

FIGURE 7-5: *Customize Alfred's appearance to fit your personal preferences.*

Now you can press the hotkey combination to open the heads-up display. Try opening a couple of applications and documents to get a feel for Alfred's interface.

Doing Math

The next time you need to perform a calculation, enter the expression into Alfred's heads-up display. It displays the answer in the results list, as shown in Figure 7-6. Select the answer and press RETURN to copy it to the clipboard.

FIGURE 7-6: *Enter an expression to turn Alfred into a calculator.*

The advanced calculator is disabled by default, but you can enable it in Alfred's Preferences. (Click **Features**, select **Calculator** from the sidebar, and then select the **Advanced** checkbox.) With the advanced calculator enabled, you'll be able to enter common trigonometric expressions like sin, cos, and tan.

Defining and Spelling Words

You can use Alfred to interact with the Dictionary application. To see a word's definition, open the heads-up display, type **define**, and then enter the word. Alfred shows the first part of the definition, as shown in Figure 7-7. Select the word and press RETURN to see the word's full definition in the Dictionary application.

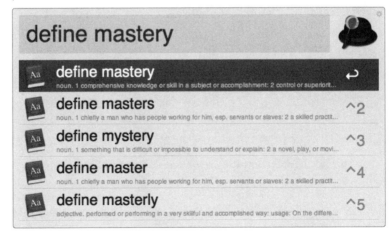

FIGURE 7-7: *Use Alfred to interact with the Dictionary application.*

If you don't know exactly how to spell a word, you can use Alfred as a spell-checker. Enter **spell** and then start typing the word—Alfred displays suggestions as you type. Select a word and press RETURN to copy it to the clipboard.

Searching the Internet

This is one of Alfred's best features. To search for a website, open the heads-up display, enter a predefined keyword for a website, enter your search query, and press RETURN. Alfred opens your web browser and searches the website for the query. For example, to search Amazon.com for the movie *Iron Man*, enter **amazon iron man dvd** and press RETURN.

To see which websites you can search with Alfred, open **Preferences**, click **Features**, and then select **Web Searches** from the sidebar. The window shown in Figure 7-8 appears.

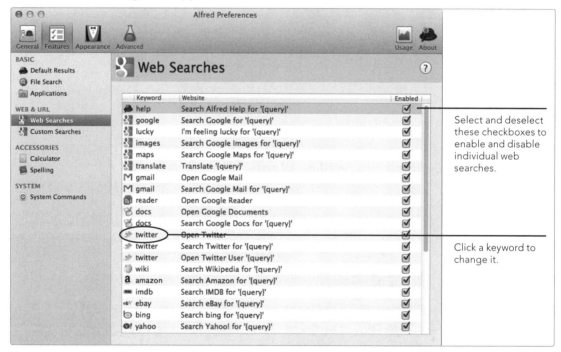

FIGURE 7-8: *Search websites by using predefined keywords.*

* *NOTE:* You can modify a website's keyword by clicking the keyword and entering a new one.

You can create custom searches for websites that are not already defined in Alfred. To do so, open Alfred's **Preferences**, click **Features**, select **Custom Searches** from the sidebar, and click the **+** button. Enter the website's search URL (usually the first part of the URL that displays search results with {query} where the search keyword would normally be, like `http://store.apple.com/us/search?find={query}`), title, and keyword. Test the search to make sure it's working by clicking **Test**.

If you'd just like to visit a website, type a URL into the heads-up display, like `apple.com`. Alfred opens a web browser and displays the website.

Finding Files

In Chapter 3, you learned how to search your Mac like a pro. Alfred also has a couple of search tricks up its sleeve.

To open a file with Alfred, enter **open** and start typing the name of the file. To reveal a file in the Finder, enter **find** and start typing the name of the file—select the file to see it in the Finder. You can also search inside documents by prefacing a search query with `in`.

Like Spotlight, Alfred allows you to exclude certain categories of files from search results. To modify the excluded categories and search scope, open **Preferences**, click **Features**, select **File Search** from the sidebar, and click **Exclusions & Scope**. The window shown in Figure 7-9 appears.

Change the search scope to **Everything** to improve Alfred's search results. Use the **Result limit** menu to change how many search results are shown in the heads-up display.

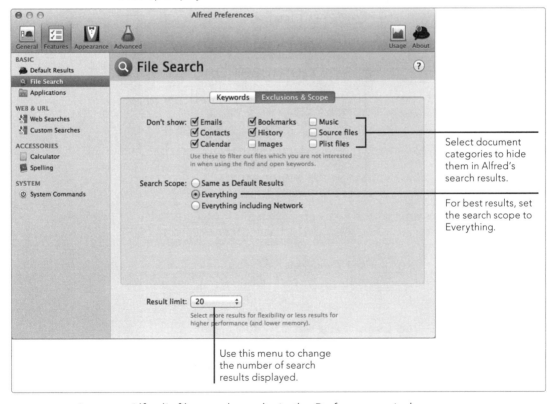

FIGURE 7-9: Improve Alfred's file search results in the Preferences window.

Controlling Your Computer

Shutting down your computer at the end of the day can be much easier when you use Alfred to execute common system commands by entering keywords into its heads-up display. For example, enter **sleep** to put your computer into sleep mode or **lock** to secure the screen before you walk away from the computer. The full list of commands is shown in Figure 7-10. You can change the keywords for the commands by opening Alfred's **Preferences**, clicking **Features**, and selecting **System Commands** from the sidebar.

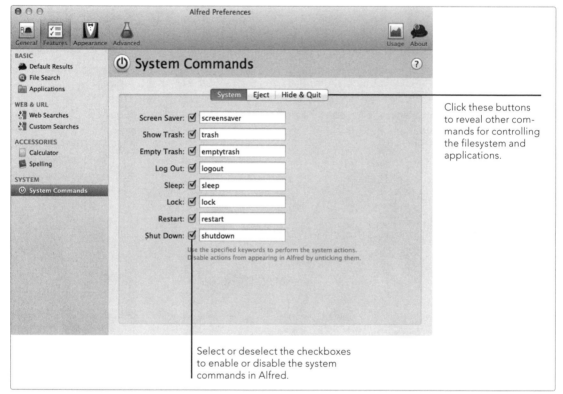

Click these buttons to reveal other commands for controlling the filesystem and applications.

Select or deselect the checkboxes to enable or disable the system commands in Alfred.

FIGURE 7-10: *Many system commands can be executed from Alfred's heads-up display.*

A few more commands are hiding in the Eject and Hide & Quit sections. For example, enter **eject** to pop out an inserted CD or DVD and type **hide** to hide any open application.

Doing Even More with Alfred

So far, everything you've learned can be performed using the free version of Alfred. If the basic features leave you hungry for more, consider purchasing the Alfred Powerpack (*http://www.alfredapp.com/powerpack/*, $$). This upgrade is especially beneficial for advanced users who want more power from their keyboard and Alfred's interface.

The Powerpack unlocks advanced features like the ability to execute shell scripts and AppleScripts, navigate the filesystem, access your contacts in the Address Book application, interact with iTunes, and email attachments—all without using the mouse or trackpad. As you'll learn in the next section, many of these features are also available in the LaunchBar application.

Using LaunchBar

Alfred has a good balance of power and usability for casual users. You can use it to launch applications with its cool-looking heads-up display and even dabble in some advanced features, like executing system commands from the heads-up display. But Alfred won't be enough for the Mac power user.

Enter LaunchBar (*http://www.obdev.at/products/launchbar/*, $$$), arguably the best, and most advanced, application launcher available. Like Alfred, LaunchBar sports a heads-up display, as shown in Figure 7-11, and it can also find documents and perform system commands. But that's where the resemblance ends.

FIGURE 7-11: *Beneath the simple interface, LaunchBar is very powerful.*

LaunchBar has literally hundreds of features, including filesystem operators, iTunes playback control, and AppleScript and macro support. It also has a steep learning curve. But with LaunchBar, any time and energy you invest will be handsomely rewarded with improved productivity. Longtime users think of LaunchBar as an appendage—an indispensible application that helps them perform work quickly and efficiently.

Setting Up LaunchBar

Like Alfred, LaunchBar has some settings that need to be configured before you start using it. You'll set a keyboard shortcut to activate the heads-up display and change the retype delay interval—a setting you'll learn more about in the next section.

Here's how to set up LaunchBar:

1. Open LaunchBar. (It's in the Applications folder.)
2. From the **LaunchBar** menu, select **Preferences**.

3. Click **General**. The window shown in Figure 7-12 appears.

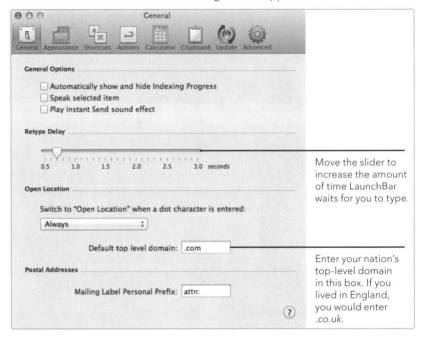

FIGURE 7-12: *Configure LaunchBar's general options to make it easier to live with.*

4. Move the **Retype Delay** slider to change the amount of time LaunchBar waits for you to type characters on the keyboard.
5. If you live in a location that has a default top-level domain other than *.com*, enter that in the **Default top level domain** field.
6. Click **Shortcuts**. The window shown in Figure 7-13 appears.
7. Set keyboard shortcuts for LaunchBar and Spotlight by clicking the **Search in LaunchBar** and **Search in Spotlight** boxes and pressing the keys. (By default, LaunchBar's keyboard shortcut is set as ⌘-spacebar—the same shortcut that Spotlight uses. Be sure to change Spotlight's shortcut in System Preferences if you want to continue using ⌘-spacebar for LaunchBar.)
8. For super-fast access to the LaunchBar heads-up display, select a modifier key from the **Search in LaunchBar** menu.
9. Click **Advanced**. The window in Figure 7-14 appears.
10. Click **Hide Dock Icon** to hide LaunchBar's Dock icon. This has some drawbacks—read the warnings in the window that appears after you click the button.
11. Close the LaunchBar preferences window.

    Now you're ready for the next part—actually using LaunchBar!

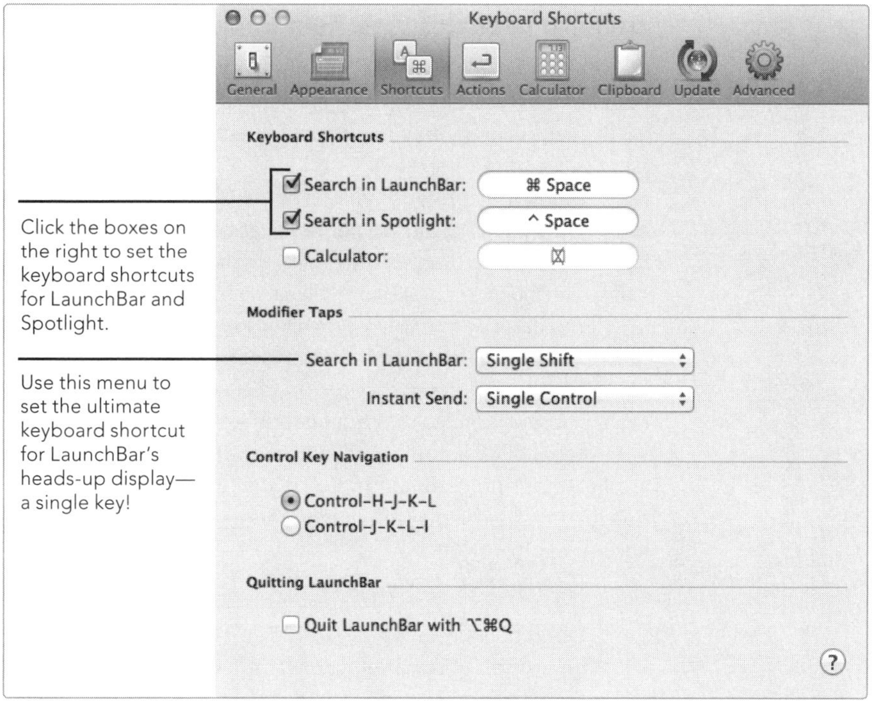

Click the boxes on the right to set the keyboard shortcuts for LaunchBar and Spotlight.

Use this menu to set the ultimate keyboard shortcut for LaunchBar's heads-up display— a single key!

FIGURE 7-13: *Set shortcuts to display LaunchBar's heads-up display quickly.*

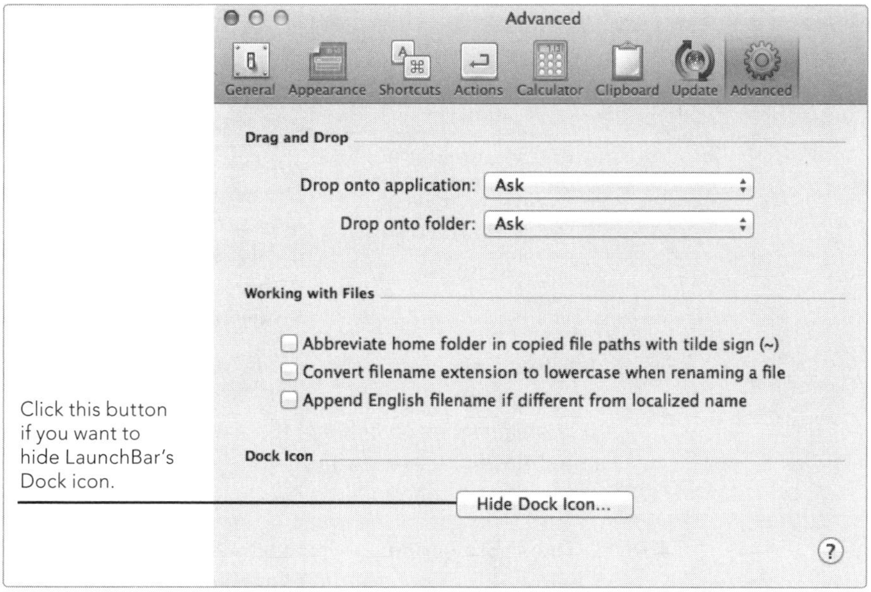

Click this button if you want to hide LaunchBar's Dock icon.

FIGURE 7-14: *LaunchBar's Advanced window allows you to hide the Dock icon.*

Training LaunchBar to Remember Abbreviations

LaunchBar can seem a little unwieldy to users who have used Spotlight or Alfred. For example, you can leisurely type an application's name in Alfred and know that it will eventually appear in the search results. Since LaunchBar is all about speed, it functions a little differently.

LaunchBar's *retype* delay is set to 0.7 seconds by default, so it's a fool's errand to try typing the full names of applications. Unless you type extraordinarily fast, LaunchBar will probably think you started typing something new when you're halfway through the application's name and reset everything you've typed!

You can change the retype delay in LaunchBar's general preferences. Alternatively, you can use *abbreviations* for applications and commands. For example, if you open the Calendar application frequently, you'll want to create a short, memorable abbreviation for that application—something like *ca* or *cal*.

LaunchBar automatically remembers the abbreviations you use to launch applications and commands. Once you use an abbreviation to open an application, LaunchBar displays that application at the top of the list the next time you enter that abbreviation.

Here's how to train LaunchBar to remember abbreviations:

1. Open LaunchBar's heads-up display.
2. Enter the abbreviation you want to use for the application. The text you type appears in the heads-up display, as shown in Figure 7-15.

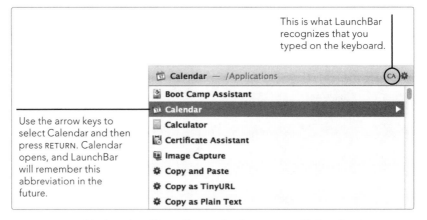

FIGURE 7-15: Notice that Boot Camp Assistant, not Calendar, is currently at the top of the results list for the ca abbreviation. Just open Calendar once to change that—it'll appear at the top of the list the next time you enter ca.

✳ **NOTE:** The abbreviation you choose needs to be fairly close to the application's name—close enough that LaunchBar will display the application in the results list. Otherwise you won't be able to select the application.

3. Use the arrow keys to select the application. Then press RETURN to open the application and train LaunchBar to remember the abbreviation for the application you selected.

4. Verify that you trained LaunchBar by opening the heads-up display again and entering the abbreviation—the desired application should now appear at the top of the list. If it doesn't, repeat this process until it does.

The key to creating a good abbreviation is to make it short enough to remember and type quickly, but long enough to differentiate it from the other applications on your computer. Use the shortest abbreviations for the applications you use the most. If you use Calculator more than Calendar, for example, you would want to use *c* as the abbreviation for Calculator, not Calendar.

Launching Items Fast

If you need another reason to use abbreviations, LaunchBar's *instant open* feature provides a pretty good one. It allows you to open the selected item without pressing RETURN. Just type the abbreviation into LaunchBar's heads-up display and continue holding down the last key of the abbreviation when the item's name is highlighted in red, as shown in Figure 7-16.

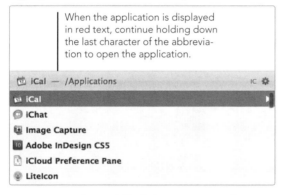

FIGURE 7-16: LaunchBar's instant open feature lets you open an application by holding down the last letter of the abbreviation—in this case, the A key to open the Calendar application.

If you know your abbreviations, this is a great way to open items fast. No more pressing RETURN!

Accessing Websites

Accessing websites with LaunchBar is a breeze. Just open the heads-up display and type a period, and LaunchBar displays an empty URL with the top-level domain you entered in the preferences, as shown in Figure 7-17. Type the middle part of the URL, like **CNN**, and press RETURN to open CNN's website in your default web browser.

FIGURE 7-17: *Type a period to enter the middle part of the URL.*

It's also easy to open bookmarks and other websites that you visit frequently. LaunchBar indexes bookmarks and the web browser's history so you can access them from the heads-up display. Type the name of a website to pull it up in Launch-Bar's search results. You can use abbreviations to quickly access bookmarks or the previously visited websites in your history.

Composing Email Messages

LaunchBar excels at performing small actions that are otherwise time consuming. For example, you can use LaunchBar to compose a short email message to a friend, family member, or coworker—something that's usually done by opening the Mail application, creating a new message, entering the recipient's name, typing the message, and clicking Send. With LaunchBar, you do the same thing by pressing a couple of keys on the keyboard.

Here's how to use LaunchBar to compose an email message:

1. Open LaunchBar's heads-up display.
2. Enter **email**. The window shown in Figure 7-18 appears.

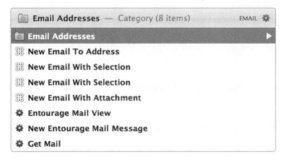

FIGURE 7-18: *LaunchBar provides a variety of services for composing email messages.*

3. For the purposes of this example, select the **Email Addresses** category, as shown in Figure 7-18. (If necessary, use the arrow keys.) This category provides access to all of the email addresses stored in the Contacts application. Select one of the other services, such as **New Email To Address**, to email an individual not stored in the Contacts application.
4. Press the spacebar. The window shown in Figure 7-19 appears.

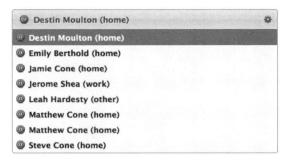

FIGURE 7-19: *Select a contact stored in the Contacts application.*

5. Select the contact you want to email and then press the spacebar. The window shown in Figure 7-20 appears.

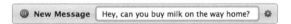

FIGURE 7-20: *Compose your email message directly in LaunchBar.*

6. Type a message to the recipient and then press RETURN. LaunchBar opens a new email message in your default email client—all you have to do is send it.

    You can also use LaunchBar to email attachments to your contacts.

Scheduling Calendar Events

Need to create a reminder or schedule an event in Calendar? Use LaunchBar's heads-up display. You can add reminders with alarms, schedule events with start and end times, and set priorities for reminders.

Here's how to create Calendar events and reminders with LaunchBar:

1. Open LaunchBar's heads-up display.
2. Enter your abbreviation for the Calendar application or type **cal**. The search results appear in the heads-up display.
3. Select **Calendar** and then press the spacebar. A list of calendars appears.
4. Select a calendar and press the spacebar. The window shown in Figure 7-21 appears. Enter a description of the event.

FIGURE 7-21: *Start by entering a description of the event.*

5.   (Optional) Press TAB. An @ character appears, as shown in Figure 7-22. Enter a location for the event.

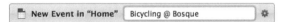

FIGURE 7-22: *Set a location for the event (optional).*

6.   Press TAB to add another @ character, as shown in Figure 7-23. Enter the date and time for the event. (See Table 7-1 for formatting options.)

FIGURE 7-23: *The event as it will be saved to the Calendar application—with name, location, and date*

7.   Press RETURN to save the event to the Calendar application.

LaunchBar's Calendar syntax is powerful, but it takes some getting used to. Use Table 7-1 to familiarize yourself with some of the most common notations.

Table 7-1: LaunchBar's Calendar Syntax

Command	What it does
Oil Change @ Feb 1	Creates an all-day event
Editorial Meeting @ Mar 3 1-3pm	Creates an event with a start and end time
Return Library Books !!	Creates a reminder with a medium priority
Vacation @ Durango @ Today	Creates an all-day event for today
Send Mom's Birthday Card > next mon !2d	Creates a reminder with a due date and an alarm two days before due
Call Jamie @ tomorrow 2w	Creates an event two weeks from tomorrow

If you'd rather not learn LaunchBar's syntax for Calendar, you can configure LaunchBar to schedule events by opening a helper application, like Fantastical (*http://flexibits.com/fantastical/*, $$) or QuickCal (*http://quickcalapp.com/*, $). To set a calendar helper application, open LaunchBar's preferences, click **Actions**, select **Options**, and then select an application from the **Create Calendar events with** menu.

Playing Songs with iTunes

iTunes plays your music, but it doesn't have to be the application you use to start playing music. LaunchBar can act as an iTunes controller, too. (You'll learn about other ways to interact with your iTunes library in Chapter 19.) This is handy when you don't want to switch to iTunes just to change playlists or start playing another song.

Here's how to use LaunchBar to play songs with iTunes:

1. Open the LaunchBar heads-up display.
2. Enter your abbreviation for the iTunes application or type **itunes**. LaunchBar displays the search results.
3. Select **iTunes Library** and then press the spacebar. LaunchBar displays all of the songs, artists, and playlists in your library. (You can also select other services, such as Next Song or Previous Song.)
4. Start typing the name of a song, artist, or playlist. Select the desired item when it appears and then press the spacebar. If a song is selected, the Launch-Bar iTunes controller appears, as shown in Figure 7-24. If you selected an artist, album, or playlist, continue selecting items and pressing the spacebar until a song starts playing.

FIGURE 7-24: Use LaunchBar's controller for iTunes.

You can use the controller to pause the track, skip ahead or move back in the song, or open the Spotify application (if it's installed on your computer). It's pretty slick!

Doing Even More with LaunchBar

Believe it or not, you've barely scratched the surface of LaunchBar's capabilities. There's plenty more you can do with this application, from navigating your computer's filesystem to instantly calling your friends with Skype. In fact, LaunchBar is almost *too* big for its own good. It's an epic application that you'll probably discover in bits and pieces.

One resource that can really help is the documentation. It's available from LaunchBar's help menu and the developer's website (*http://www.obdev.at/resources/ launchbar/help/*).

Additional Ideas for Using Application Launchers

You have a couple of other options when it comes to application launchers. Quicksilver (*http://qsapp.com/*, free) is a free, open source application that was extremely popular several years ago. After being abandoned by the original developer, it has recently seen a flurry of new development activity. Its unique interface continues to inspire and attract many Mac users.

Another advanced application launcher, Butler (*http://manytricks.com/ butler/*, $$$), is also popular among Mac users. Since it has many of the same features provided by Alfred and LaunchBar, its main differentiating feature is the interface—it's up to you to decide which one you like best.

8

Customizing Trackpad and Mouse Gestures

Multi-touch gestures are an integral part of OS X. You can use the trackpad or a compatible mouse to perform a variety of actions with your fingers—all without clicking a button. Once you start using gestures to perform actions, you'll wonder how you ever managed to use a computer the "old-fashioned" way. If you count yourself among the late-adopter crowd, you'll need to learn how to use the standard gestures built into OS X first. Once you're familiar with the concept, you can start customizing the existing gestures and add new gestures with third-party applications. You'll be a multi-touch expert before you know it!

Project goal: Start using gestures if you haven't already, customize the gestures available in OS X, and enable new gestures with third-party applications.

What You'll Be Using

To use and customize trackpad and mouse gestures, you'll use the following:

 System Preferences

MagicPrefs (*http://magicprefs.com/*, free)

jitouch (*http://jitouch.com/*, $)

BetterTouchTool (*http://www.boastr.de/*, free)

Using Gestures in OS X

To use gestures in OS X, you'll need one of three compatible devices—a Magic Trackpad, Magic Mouse, or the trackpad built into every MacBook. All of the gestures built into OS X are automatically enabled when one of these devices is found. Some of the default gestures available are shown in Figure 8-1.

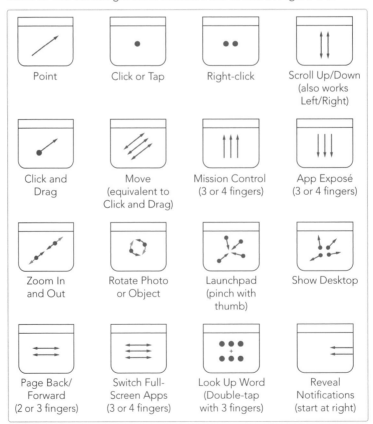

FIGURE 8-1: *Multi-touch gestures for the MacBook and Magic Trackpad*

The default functionality of the Magic Mouse is quite limited compared to that of the MacBook and Magic Trackpad, but you'll learn how to add a ton of gestures for a Magic Mouse later in this chapter.

Learning to Use Gestures

Any new technology can be difficult to learn, and gestures are no exception. If you need help visualizing gestures, open System Preferences. In the Trackpad or Mouse preferences (select the option that corresponds to your multi-touch device), you'll find short videos for every gesture available, as shown in Figure 8-2.

Gestures are categorized under three tabs. Select the different tabs to see all of the gestures.

Move the pointer over a gesture.

A video demonstrating the gesture appears here.

FIGURE 8-2: Open System Preferences to access videos illustrating multi-touch gestures.

Here's a trick that can help you rapidly learn gestures. Pick one gesture per day and use it every hour or so, whether you're at home or work. Try *really* using it, not just playing around with it. Think of ways you could incorporate the gesture into your daily work or play. Repeat this process until you've used and acquired every gesture available.

Customizing and Disabling Gestures

If you don't like a gesture in OS X, you might be able to change it in System Preferences. Not all gestures can be customized, and the gestures that are modifiable have limited alternative options available. But if you want to customize a gesture, System Preferences should be your first stop. Also, if you really don't like a gesture (or find yourself accidentally using it), you can disable it entirely.

Here's how to customize and disable gestures in System Preferences:

1. From the **Apple** menu, select **System Preferences**.
2. Click **Trackpad** or **Mouse**, depending on which one you primarily use.
3. Click **More Gestures**. The window shown in Figure 8-3 appears.

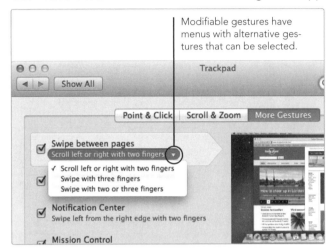

FIGURE 8-3: *Use System Preferences to customize the multi-touch gestures built into OS X.*

4. Actions that can be customized have arrows next to their gestures—these are menus that can be clicked. Select a gesture from a menu to associate it with the action.
5. (Optional) Uncheck any gestures you'd like to disable.
6. Close System Preferences. Test your new gesture to verify that it works.

Don't give up if the gesture you want to customize isn't modifiable in System Preferences. Chances are good that you can change it with one of the third-party applications presented next.

Customizing Gestures with Third-Party Applications

The multi-touch gestures built into OS X are like a gateway drug: They satisfy your productivity craving for a time, but they'll leave you wanting more and more. Indulge yourself by using *one* of the following third-party applications to add new multi-touch gestures and modify existing ones. MagicPrefs is good for people starting out, jitouch is a paid option with more polish, and BetterTouchTool is a powerful and potentially overwhelming application with lots of options. Let's go take a look.

Using MagicPrefs

MagicPrefs (*http://magicprefs.com/*, free) was created to extend the functionality of the Magic Mouse, but it has since been updated to support all of Apple's multi-touch devices. This preference pane is useful for mapping gestures to actions that aren't available with the default gestures—things like opening Spotlight, displaying the application switcher, and locking your session.

Here's how to use MagicPrefs to add and modify gestures:

1. If you haven't already installed MagicPrefs, do that now.
2. From the **Apple** menu, select **System Preferences**.
3. Click **MagicPrefs**. The window shown in Figure 8-4 appears. (Gestures for the connected multi-touch device automatically appear. If you have more than one device available, select a device at the top of the window.)

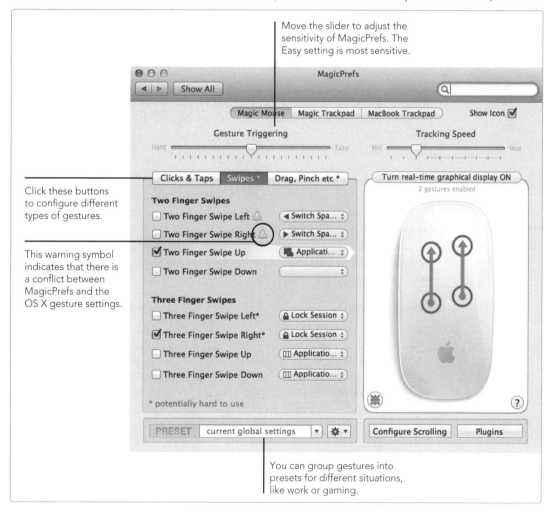

FIGURE 8-4: *The MagicPrefs interface*

4. Select a gesture's checkbox to turn it on. Click the **Clicks & Taps**, **Swipes**, and **Drag, Pinch etc** buttons to see all of the gestures available.

✳ **NOTE:** Gestures that are currently enabled in the Mouse or Trackpad area of System Preferences are not available for selection in MagicPrefs. Use the instructions in the previous section to disable any gestures you want to modify before using MagicPrefs.

5. From the menu next to the gesture, select an action to perform when the gesture is used.
6. Close System Preferences. The gesture is now turned on.

You can change the sensitivity of the multi-touch device by adjusting the **Gesture Triggering** slider. This handy feature can prevent accidental triggering. If you find that gesture actions are performed when you least expect them, move the slider toward **Hard**. Experimentation is necessary—you don't want to make gestures *too* hard to trigger.

The best way to create custom gestures with MagicPrefs is to explore. In other words, check out all of the options available and then try enabling a couple of gestures. Start with something easy, like the five-finger click or the two-finger clockwise rotate. You might use either one of those gestures to lock your screen, show the desktop, or display the application switcher.

For advanced users, MagicPrefs provides a way to group all custom gestures into *presets* for different situations, like work or gaming. (BetterTouchTool also has this feature.) For example, while using the work preset, you could set a three-finger click to activate Spotlight. Then at night, after you activate the gaming preset, you could use the same three-finger click to hide all applications and show the desktop. Of course, many people will find that assigning two or more actions to the same gesture and toggling between those actions with presets is too complicated to be worthwhile. But presets are a great option for many users who have very specific needs at different times of the day.

Using jitouch

jitouch (*http://jitouch.com/*, $), another preference pane for adding gestures, sports a clean interface. It also has some niceties like character recognition—a feature that allows you to draw characters on your multi-touch device. And it allows left-handed users to reverse all of the gestures, something that MagicPrefs and Better-TouchTool can't do.

Here's how to use jitouch to add and modify gestures:

1. If you haven't already installed jitouch, do that now.
2. From the **Apple** menu, select **System Preferences**.
3. Click **Jitouch**.
4. Click **Trackpad** or **Magic Mouse**, depending on the multi-touch device connected to your computer. The window shown in Figure 8-5 appears.
5. Double-click a gesture to edit it or click the **+** button to create a new gesture. The window shown in Figure 8-6 appears.

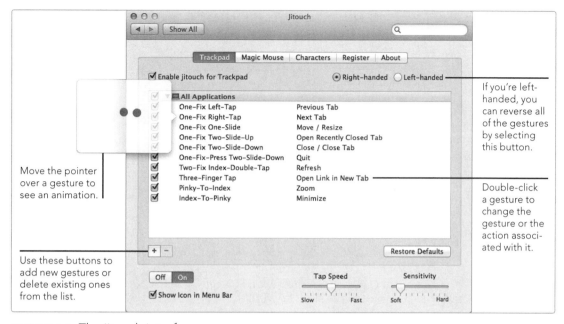

Move the pointer over a gesture to see an animation.

Use these buttons to add new gestures or delete existing ones from the list.

If you're left-handed, you can reverse all of the gestures by selecting this button.

Double-click a gesture to change the gesture or the action associated with it.

FIGURE 8-5: *The jitouch interface*

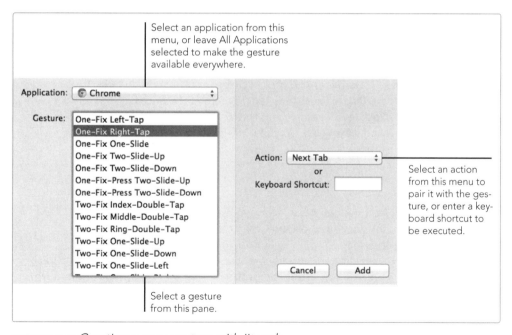

Select an application from this menu, or leave All Applications selected to make the gesture available everywhere.

Select an action from this menu to pair it with the gesture, or enter a keyboard shortcut to be executed.

Select a gesture from this pane.

FIGURE 8-6: *Creating a new gesture with jitouch*

6. From the **Application** menu, either select an application to limit the gesture to one application or leave **All Applications** selected to make the gesture available everywhere.
7. Select a gesture from the Gesture pane.
8. From the **Action** menu, select an action or enter a keyboard shortcut to pair it with the gesture.
9. Click **Add**. The gesture is now available.

You'll notice that there are more options in jitouch than in MagicPrefs. If you own a Magic Trackpad, you could use the left-side scroll and the right-side scroll gestures to trigger keyboard shortcuts. For example, you could use the left-side scroll gesture to add a bookmark in Safari and the right-side scroll to clear your browser history.

The ability to add application-specific gestures can significantly increase the usefulness of a gesture. For example, you could set a two-finger double-tap to open a new tab in the Safari application and use the same gesture to open a new document in Microsoft Word. However, to keep things simple and prevent confusion, try keeping the actions for a gesture as similar as possible across applications.

Using BetterTouchTool

BetterTouchTool (*http://www.boastr.de/*, free) is the most powerful and flexible multi-touch gesture application available. It can also be the most confusing, but once you learn how to use the interface, you'll gain access to gestures that simply aren't available in the other multi-touch applications.

Here's how to use BetterTouchTool to add and modify gestures:

1. Open the BetterTouchTool application.
2. From the **BetterTouchTool** menu, select **Preferences**.
3. Click **Gestures**. The window shown in Figure 8-7 appears.
4. Click **Magic Mouse** or **Trackpads & Tablets**, depending on the multi-touch device connected to your computer.
5. To create an application-specific gesture, select or add an application in the Select Application pane. To make a gesture available everywhere, select **Global**.
6. Click **Add new gesture**.
7. From the **Touchpad Gesture** menu, select a gesture.

✳ *NOTE:* Gestures that are already associated with an action are labeled with an *In Use* icon—do not use these gestures unless you plan to use them with a modifier key.

8. Select an action from the **Predefined Action** menu or enter a keyboard shortcut in the **Custom Keyboard Shortcut** field. The gesture is now available.

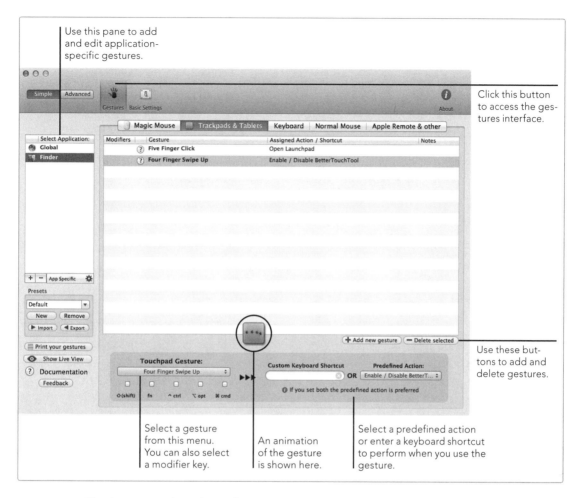

Use this pane to add and edit application-specific gestures.

Click this button to access the gestures interface.

Use these buttons to add and delete gestures.

Select a gesture from this menu. You can also select a modifier key.

An animation of the gesture is shown here.

Select a predefined action or enter a keyboard shortcut to perform when you use the gesture.

FIGURE 8-7: *The BetterTouchTool interface*

The sky's the limit! To get started, try doing something a little different—use a five-finger click to log out of your computer, for example, or a four-finger click to put your computer to sleep. The key is to find actions that you perform frequently (like logging out) and link them to gestures that feel comfortable to you and that you'll easily remember.

Of course, the list of gestures available in BetterTouchTool can be overwhelming (see the "11 Finger Tap," for example). Don't get too fancy—not at first, anyway. Complicated gestures are difficult to remember and use, so stick with simpler ones until you've gotten comfortable.

Additional Ideas for Customizing Trackpad and Mouse Gestures

A word of warning: Avoid burnout by using gestures in moderation. You don't need to map every action to a gesture. Instead, use gestures for the actions you use the most and forget about mapping the rest. If you find yourself becoming overwhelmed, scale back the number of gestures to something manageable.

9

Connecting Multiple Displays to Your Mac

Quick, what's the holy grail of Mac productivity? Many would say that it's using multiple monitors with one Mac. If you're ready to take the plunge, you'll be rewarded with more desktop space for windows, easier access to applications, and the ability to see pretty much everything at once.

But there are also plenty of pitfalls associated with using multiple displays with your Mac. The first headache is actually connecting the darn things—you might need a special adapter for your Mac's port and your display connectors. Next you'll need to tell OS X how you've positioned the displays on your desk, change the resolution, and specify a color profile. Finally, you need to learn how to display the menu bar on two screens and keep a MacBook awake with the lid closed so you can use it with the secondary display only.

Even with the challenging initial setup, the productivity payoff associated with using multiple monitors is huge. Many people swear by it. Once you get used to using two displays, you'll never want to use anything else!

Project goal: Connect multiple displays to your Mac and make using them feel natural.

What You'll Be Using

To boost your productivity with multiple displays, you'll use the following:

 System Preferences

 Stay (*http://cordlessdog.com/stay/*, $$)

 SecondBar (*http://blog.boastr.net/*, free)

 SmartSleep (*http://www.jinx.de/SmartSleep.html*, $)

Connecting the Displays to Your Mac

Connecting all of the displays to your Mac is the first step. Unfortunately, different displays have different types of connectors, and different Macs have different types of ports. Figuring out whether or not you need an adaptor—and if so, what type of adaptor—is a prerequisite to connecting the displays.

Determining the Type of Port on Your Mac

To find the right adapter, you need to know what type of port your computer has. If you've purchased a Mac in 2011 or later, it probably has a Thunderbolt port (also known as a Mini DisplayPort). Older Macs have either a Mini-DVI or Mini-VGA port, as shown in Figure 9-1. In a pinch, you can also find a display adapter that connects to a USB port, which should be available on virtually every Mac.

FIGURE 9-1: *From left to right, the Thunderbolt port, the Mini-DVI port, and the Mini-VGA port*

The type of port you have shouldn't play a big part in the display you purchase. Adapters are available for virtually every port and connector combination possible.

Finding the Right Adapter

Now you'll need to find an adapter for your particular port and connector combination. (If you don't know what type of connector your display has, check the packaging material.) Generally speaking, the display will have one of three types of connectors: DVI, VGA, or HDMI. You can find adapters at the Apple Store (*http://store.apple.com/*) or Other World Computing (*http://eshop.macsales.com/shop/video/cables_and_accessories/*).

Adjusting Display Settings in OS X

After you connect one or more displays to your computer, you'll need to configure some display settings in OS X. Your Mac needs to know how the displays are positioned on your desk, and you might need to adjust the display settings for each monitor to get its color and resolution just right.

Positioning the Monitors

First you'll need to tell OS X how the displays are positioned on your desk. That way, it'll feel natural to drag windows from one display to another. For example, if you connect a display to your MacBook and position it on the left side of your desk, you'll want to change settings in System Preferences so that windows moved to the left side of your MacBook's display appear on the other display.

You can position displays horizontally or vertically. Most people place their displays side by side on their desk, but you might personally prefer a vertical setup.

Here's how to adjust the display settings for multiple monitors:

1. Connect all of the monitors to your Mac.
2. From the **Apple** menu, select **System Preferences**.
3. Click **Displays**.
4. Click **Arrangement**. The window shown in Figure 9-2 appears.
5. All of the displays should be shown in the window—they're represented by the blue boxes. If some displays are not appearing, click **Detect Displays**.
6. Click and drag the displays to rearrange them. The graphic representation should match the way the displays are positioned on your desk so that dragging windows from one display to another feels natural.
7. (Optional) The menu bar is shown on only one display. Drag and drop the menu bar to place it on your default screen. (Later in this project, you'll learn how to use SecondBar to place menu bars on every display.)
8. (Optional) By default, different displays have separate desktops. If you want to *mirror* displays to show the same desktop on all of them, select the **Mirror Displays** checkbox.

Now your Mac's display settings correspond to your displays' physical configuration. Things are starting to feel a bit more natural!

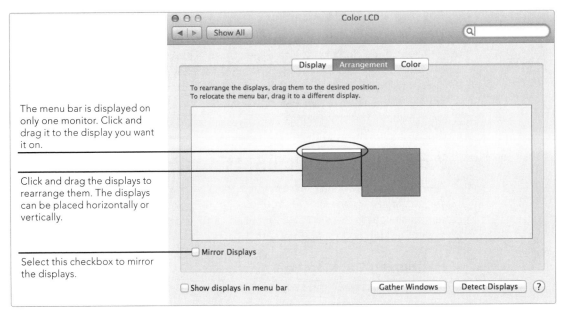

The menu bar is displayed on only one monitor. Click and drag it to the display you want it on.

Click and drag the displays to rearrange them. The displays can be placed horizontally or vertically.

Select this checkbox to mirror the displays.

FIGURE 9-2: *Use System Preferences to tell OS X how you've positioned displays on your desk.*

Adjusting Display Settings

OS X automatically sets the color and resolution settings for any displays you connect to your Mac, but sometimes they need to be adjusted. For example, if you wear glasses, you might find the resolution on a new display to be set too high. And if you're a graphic designer, you might need to calibrate the color.

Here's how to adjust display settings:

1. Connect all of the monitors to your Mac.
2. From the **Apple** menu, select **System Preferences**.
3. Click **Displays**. The System Preferences window appears on every display connected to your computer.
4. In the window on the display you want to modify, click **Display**. The window shown in Figure 9-3 appears.
5. (Optional) Select a resolution to change the virtual screen size of the display. You can also adjust the **Brightness** slider to change the brightness of the display.

* **NOTE:** **When you change the resolution of a display, a dialog appears asking you to confirm that everything looks okay. This is a failsafe—if you don't click anything, the display will return to its previous resolution after 30 seconds.**

6. Click **Color**. The window shown in Figure 9-4 appears.

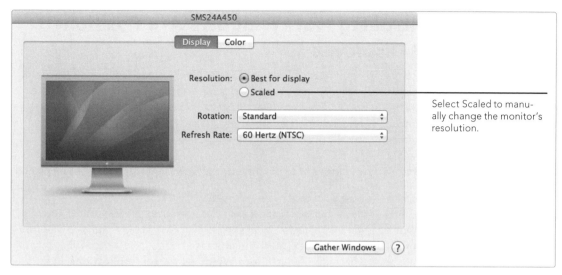

FIGURE 9-3: *Changing the resolution of a connected display*

Select Scaled to manually change the monitor's resolution.

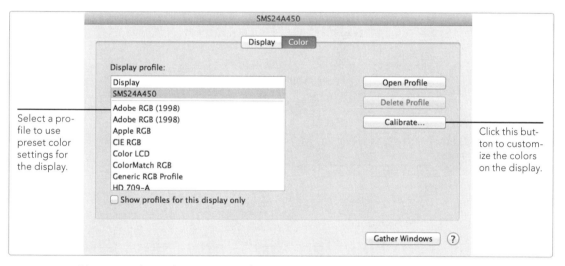

Select a profile to use preset color settings for the display.

Click this button to customize the colors on the display.

FIGURE 9-4: *Changing the color settings of a connected display*

7.   (Optional) Apple develops display profiles for many different types of displays. You can also select a different profile from the **Display profile** box, if one is available.

8.   Close the System Preferences window.

Now you've got a fully functional multiple-monitor setup—you can start using it in your day-to-day routine. But if you read the rest of this project, you can make the setup even better!

Controlling How Windows Are Positioned and Displayed

If you own a laptop, it won't take long to learn about one common annoyance: Every time you connect or disconnect a display, your windows move all over the place. A third-party application called Stay (*http://cordlessdog.com/stay/*, $$) solves this problem by remembering where your windows are positioned on the screen and then automatically moving them there when you connect or disconnect a display.

Here's how to use Stay to control how windows are positioned and displayed:

1.   Open the Stay application.
2.   Connect the secondary display(s) to your computer.
3.   Open all of the applications that you normally use and arrange the windows on the displays the way you like them.
4.   From the **Stay** menu, select **Store Windows for All Applications**. Stay saves the positions of all the open windows.
5.   (Optional) Repeat the process for your primary display. You should disconnect all of the secondary monitors from your computer before storing the windows for the primary display.
6.   From the **Stay** menu, select **Preferences**. The window shown in Figure 9-5 appears.

Select this checkbox to automatically restore the windows when a display is connected or disconnected.

FIGURE 9-5: *Configuring Stay to automatically restore windows upon display connection or disconnection or application launch*

7.   Select the **Restore Windows as displays are connected and disconnected** checkbox. This feature automatically repositions windows when you connect or disconnect a display.
8.   Select the **Restore Windows as applications are launched** checkbox. Not all of the applications or windows saved in your display profile will be open when you connect a display. This feature allows Stay to automatically position windows after you open an application.
9.   Close the Stay preferences.

From now on, Stay will handle window positioning automatically. You'll soon wonder how you ever lived without this feature.

Making the Menu Bar Available Everywhere

As mentioned earlier in this chapter, OS X displays the menu bar on only one display. That can get annoying fast, especially if you want to dedicate a secondary display to a single application, like Adobe Photoshop. Moving the pointer from one display to another just to access the menu bar is a major drag on productivity.

That problem is solved by a third-party application called SecondBar (*http://blog.boastr.net/*, free). It's easy to install and use: When you open SecondBar, it displays another menu bar for the active application on a second display. (Unfortunately, SecondBar can't display a menu bar on more than two displays.)

Once SecondBar is running, you can configure its settings to make it easier to use. Here's how:

1. Open the SecondBar application.
2. From the **SecondBar** arrow menu next to the clock, select **Preferences**. The window shown in Figure 9-6 appears.

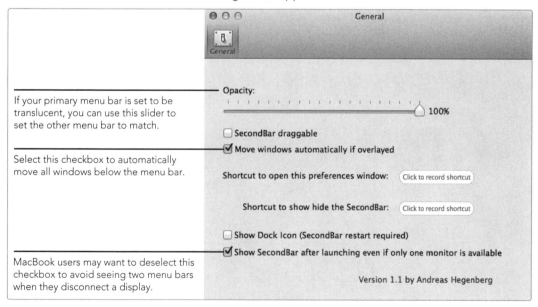

FIGURE 9-6: *Configuring SecondBar's preferences*

3. (Optional) If you're using the translucent setting for your primary menu bar, you can adjust the Opacity slider to match your other menu bar.
4. Select the **Move windows automatically if overlayed** checkbox. This automatically repositions windows below the menu bar on the secondary display.

That's it! Now both of your displays will have menu bars, resolving one of the major pitfalls of using multiple displays with OS X.

Keeping a MacBook Awake with the Lid Closed

If you're a MacBook owner with another display, you face a tough question: Do you use the MacBook's display *and* the other display or just the display without the MacBook? The MacBook's display could be quite small by comparison, and you might find that all you need is the secondary display. The problem is how to shut your MacBook's lid without putting your computer to sleep.

A third-party application called SmartSleep (*http://www.jinx.de/SmartSleep .html*, $) solves this problem. Install it, click a couple of buttons, and then close the lid. Boom—you're using the laptop with the secondary monitor, and there's no pesky notebook display staring at you.

Here's how to keep your MacBook awake with the lid closed:

1. Download and install the SmartSleepInsomnia plug-in (*http://www.jinx.de/ SmartSleep.html*, $).
2. Open the SmartSleep application. The window shown in Figure 9-7 appears.
3. Select the **Show Status in MenuBar** checkbox. The SmartSleep menu appears in the menu bar.

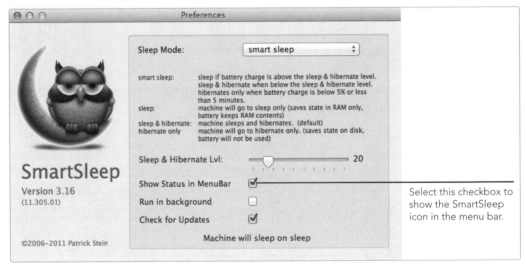

FIGURE 9-7: *Configuring SmartSleep's preferences*

4. From the **SmartSleep** menu, select **Start Insomnia (using plugin)**.
5. From the **SmartSleep** menu, select **Insomnia length** and then select a time interval. Your Mac will stay awake with the lid closed for the amount of time you selected.

Now you can close your MacBook's lid—it will stay awake! You can use your computer with the secondary display.

Additional Ideas for Connecting Multiple Displays to Your Mac

Ergonomics is one thing this chapter didn't discuss at all, but you should make it a priority in your computing environment—whether at home or work. Essentially, you need to ensure that your displays are positioned at eye level. You don't want to be slouching down to look at a display.

This is a serious issue for those who own laptops. If you plan on using your MacBook's display with a secondary monitor, consider purchasing a stand to lift your laptop to eye level. The Griffin Elevator stand (*http://store.griffintechnology .com/elevator/*) and the Belkin Zero Stand (*http://store.apple.com/us/product/ H3860ZM/A/*) are two popular options.

10 Talking to Your Mac

You don't need a degree in computer science to know that talking to your computer is one of the ultimate geek dreams. Popular culture reinforces this dream with famous talking computers like HAL and the computer that made Earl Grey tea for Captain Picard.

With OS X, the future is here today. You too can have a little piece of nerd nirvana by enabling the built-in speech recognition feature and controlling your Mac with voice commands. If you need to write a letter, you can tell your Mac exactly what to type by using the dictation feature. And if having full-blown conversations with a computer is your thing, you can give your Mac a voice so it can respond to your commands, tell you jokes, and read alerts displayed on your screen.

Project goal: Tell your Mac what to do and give your Mac a voice with the built-in speech recognition and text-to-speech features.

What You'll Be Using

To talk with your Mac, you'll use the following:

 System Preferences

 AppleScript Editor

Setting Up Speech Recognition

Speech recognition in OS X converts spoken words into commands that can be understood by your computer. When you enable your Mac's speech recognition features, you can speak dozens of recognized voice commands to do things like switch applications, create email messages, or log out of your computer.

Here's how to turn on speech recognition:

1. From the **Apple** menu, select **System Preferences**.
2. Click **Accessibility**.
3. From the sidebar, select **Speakable Items**. The window shown in Figure 10-1 appears.

FIGURE 10-1: *Enable the speech recognition settings.*

4. Select **On** to activate **Speakable Items**.
5. Click **Listening Key**. The window shown in Figure 10-2 appears.

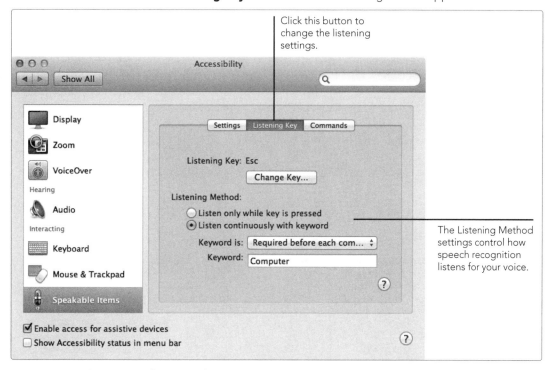

FIGURE 10-2: *Customize the speech recognition settings to match your personal preferences.*

6. Select a listening method. You can configure your Mac to listen continuously for a keyword or listen only when a key is pressed.
7. (Optional) Click **Change Key** to change the listening key. ESC is the default listening key. You'll press this key when you want the Mac to start listening to you.
8. (Optional) If you selected the **Listen continuously with keyword** option, you can change the keyword settings. *Computer* is the default keyword—it's required before every command when set to the default **Required before each command** setting. So you'll need to preface commands with "computer" like this: "Computer, tell me a joke."

Speech recognition isn't perfect—sometimes your Mac doesn't understand what you're telling it to do. That's why you'll want to pay special attention to the "command acknowledgment" settings, which you can use to tell your Mac to play a sound or speak when it recognizes a command (see Figure 10-1).

If you're having trouble getting your Mac to recognize your voice commands, click the **Calibrate** button (Figure 10-1). You'll be asked to read through a series of sentences so the microphone sensitivity level can automatically adjust to your voice.

Talking to Your Computer

When your Mac is listening for voice commands, the speech feedback window appears, as shown in Figure 10-3. You can use the window to see the current volume level being received by your Mac's microphone. If the level is too high—in the red—then you know that you're speaking too loudly or positioned too close to the microphone.

The speech feedback window floats above all other windows, but you can minimize it to the Dock by double-clicking it.

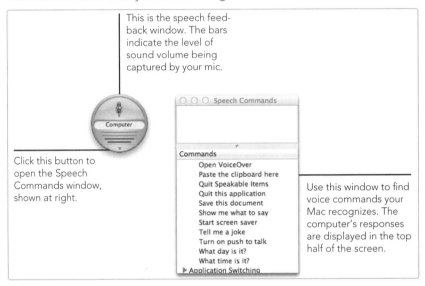

This is the speech feedback window. The bars indicate the level of sound volume being captured by your mic.

Click this button to open the Speech Commands window, shown at right.

Use this window to find voice commands your Mac recognizes. The computer's responses are displayed in the top half of the screen.

FIGURE 10-3: *Use the speech feedback and Speech Commands windows to talk to your Mac.*

It's time to talk to your computer. What should you say? You can speak any of the commands listed in the Speech Command window (see Figure 10-3).

Try it out by saying, "Tell me a joke." (Remember, if you set your Mac to listen continuously, you'll need to preface the command with a keyword, like "computer." Otherwise, you'll need to press the listening key.) The computer acknowledges the command by playing a sound or speaking a command acknowledgment. If you're lucky, the computer will tell you a knock-knock joke. It says, "Knock, knock." And then you're supposed to say, "Who's there?" You get the idea. You're having a conversation with your computer!

Many commands are straightforward and easily guessable. For example, you can say, "Switch to Safari," and your Mac should make Safari the active application. "Get my mail" retrieves your new email messages with the Mail application, and "Log me out" logs you out of your computer.

Telling Your Computer What to Type

If you'd rather tell your computer what to write in a word processing document than type it yourself, enable the dictation feature. Just open a new text file, push a button to activate dictation, and start talking. Once you're finished, your Mac will send the audio recording to Apple's servers to transcribe what you said. It all happens in the blink of an eye.

Here's how to enable and activate dictation:

1. From the **Apple** menu, select **System Preferences**.
2. Click **Dictation & Speech**. The window shown in Figure 10-4 appears.

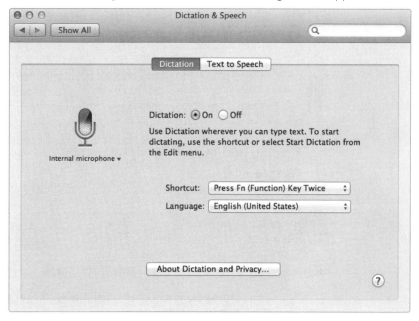

FIGURE 10-4: *Enabling Dictation*

3. Select **On** to enable Dictation.
4. From the **Shortcut** menu, set a key to activate dictation. You can press the function (FN) key twice by default.
5. Open a text document and press the shortcut key twice. The dictation icon appears, as shown in Figure 10-5.
6. Start talking. When you're finished, click **Done**. Apple's servers will transcribe what you said and then paste the text in the document.

FIGURE 10-5: *Start talking when you see this microphone on your screen.*

Here's a trick that will prevent a headache or two: Punctuation needs to be enunciated. For example, if you wanted Dictation to type the following:

Here I am, at home, alone.

---

you would say, "Here I am comma at home comma alone period." It sounds weird, and it takes some getting used to, but it's a trick you'll need to use if you don't want to have to manually add all of the punctuation later. That brings up another good point: Make sure to proofread the text after it's been transcribed—this technology isn't perfect yet, so you will find typos.

Giving Your Computer a Voice

Talking to your computer is great, but unless it can respond, you'll be having a one-way conversation. In this section, you'll give your Mac a voice so it can respond to your voice commands, notify you of alerts that need your attention, and read selected text to you out loud. You'll also learn how to find and install voices that sound more realistic than any previously available.

Finding and Installing High-Quality Voices

OS X provides several high-quality voices in a variety of languages, but due to the enormous size of the files (approximately 300MB–500MB per voice), most voices aren't installed on your computer by default. If you plan on regularly using the text-to-speech feature, you'll want to download a high-quality voice. It will be much more realistic than the older voices, which sport the "spliced-together" sound typically associated with computer voices.

Here's how to download voices for your Mac:

1. From the **Apple** menu, select **System Preferences**.
2. Click **Dictation & Speech**.
3. Click **Text to Speech**.
4. From the **System Voice** menu, select **Customize**. The window shown in Figure 10-6 appears.
5. To play a sample of a voice, click the voice (do not select the checkbox) and then click **Play**.
6. To download a voice to your computer, select the checkbox next to the voice and then click **OK**.

After the voice downloads to your computer, you can select it from the System Voice menu.

If you ever want to permanently delete a voice from your computer, you'll need to drag the files and folders associated with the voice in */System/Library/Speech/Voices* to the Trash—deselecting voices in System Preferences doesn't delete them.

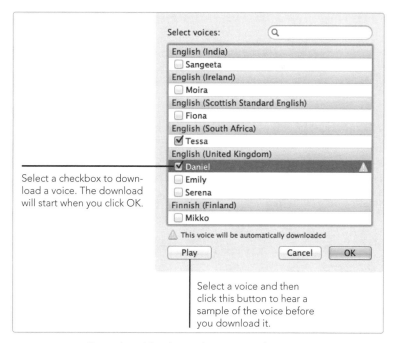

Select a checkbox to download a voice. The download will start when you click OK.

This voice will be automatically downloaded

Select a voice and then click this button to hear a sample of the voice before you download it.

FIGURE 10-6: *Download high-quality voices for your Mac.*

Customizing Text-to-Speech Settings

When do you want your computer to talk to you? That's the question you'll answer when you customize the text-to-speech settings in System Preferences. Some people appreciate the voice emanating from their computer; others find it annoying. Use trial and error to strike a balance between the convenient and the obnoxious.

Here's how to customize text-to-speech settings:

1. From the **Apple** menu, select **System Preferences**.
2. Click **Dictation & Speech**.
3. Click **Text to Speech**. The window in Figure 10-7 appears.
4. Select a voice from the **System Voice** menu.
5. (Optional) Select the **Announce when alerts are displayed** checkbox if you want your Mac to speak alerts displayed on the screen.
6. (Optional) Select the **Announce when an application requires your attention** checkbox if you want your Mac to verbally notify you when an open application needs you to perform an action.
7. (Optional) Select the **Speak selected text when the key is pressed** checkbox if you want your Mac to read selected text from any application. CONTROL-ESC is the default keyboard shortcut for this feature—click **Change Key** to modify the shortcut.

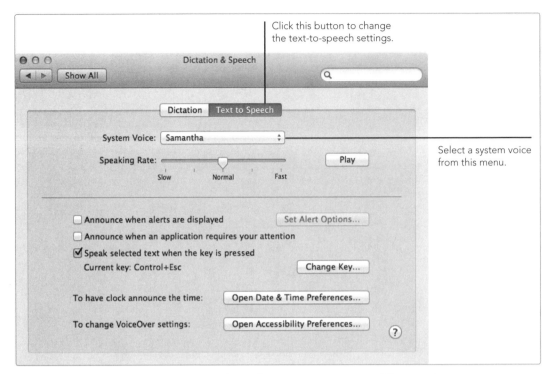

FIGURE 10-7: *Customize text-to-speech preferences to give your Mac a voice.*

The last feature—speaking selected text when the key is pressed—is really useful in certain circumstances. For example, you could have the computer read you a news article while you cook dinner.

Creating Custom Commands for Speech Recognition

You've learned how to use your Mac's built-in speech recognition and text-to-speech features. Those are pretty awesome by themselves, but now it's time to take things up a notch. You can create custom voice commands that will tell your Mac to perform the actions you designate.

All voice commands are stored in */Users/<username>/Library/Speech/ Speakable Items*, where *<username>* is your user account on the computer. The voice commands stored in that folder are universally available no matter which application is currently active; commands nested in */Users/<username>/Library/ Speech/Speakable Items/Application Speakable Items* are available only within their respective applications.

* **NOTE:** Your Library folder is hidden by default. To access it, switch to the Finder, hold down the OPTION key, and select *Library* from the *Go* menu.

You can use the AppleScript Editor to create new voice commands with AppleScript. For example, if you wanted to create a voice command for opening a new tab in Safari, you could type this into a new window in the AppleScript Editor:

```
tell application "System Events" to keystroke "t" using {command down}
```

This script tells your computer to press ⌘-T, which is the keyboard shortcut in Safari for creating a new tab. Save the script to */Users/<username>/Library/Speech/ Speakable Items/Application Speakable Items/Safari* and name it *Open new tab*. Now when Safari is the active application and you say, "Open new tab," a new tab opens in the web browser.

To make other custom voice commands, you can write new scripts in Apple-Script or save existing scripts to the Speakable Items folder. Just make sure the filename is the same as the voice command you want to speak. For example, if you want to say, "Do a silly dance," you would save the file with the name *Do a silly dance*.

Additional Ideas for Talking to Your Mac

The dictation option built into OS X is good, but there are other third-party dictation products available. For example, take a look at an application called Dragon Dictate (*http://www.macspeech.com/*, $$$). It's been around for a while, and you just might find that it's more effective.

PART 3

Automation

11 Automating Tasks with Macros

If there were a nerd merit badge for Mac mastery, the ability to create and use *macros*—automated workflows for doing work—would definitely be a requirement. Macros can save you time by automating tedious tasks, remove the possibility of human error when performing tasks, and—most importantly—make you look like a hero in the eyes of your friends (or your boss). In short, macros separate the experts from the beginners.

Not excited yet? Consider this: With Automator, you can drag and drop actions to build a sequential list of work to be performed by the applications on your Mac. You could use Automator to add images from your favorite websites to iPhoto, print a family directory from your contacts in Contacts, or convert text into a spoken audio file. The goal is to simplify your life by making your computer do more of the "heavy lifting." After all, there's no need to waste your time on boring work when your Mac can do it for you!

To help you get started, this project will show you how to use Automator to create a macro that automates the process of creating a disk image. Next, you'll use a third-party application called Keyboard Maestro to create powerful macros from scratch.

Project goal: Create macros to automate tasks on your Mac.

What You'll Be Using

To make your life easier by creating macros, you'll use the following:

    Automator

    Keyboard Maestro (*http://www.keyboardmaestro.com/*, $$$)

Creating a Macro with Automator

When you're looking to automate tasks on your Mac, Automator should be your first stop. This application's interface is foolproof—most people can figure out how to drag and drop actions to create workflows in a matter of minutes. It's not the most versatile application available, but it works for automating many basic tasks.

In this section, you'll use Automator to create a workflow capable of making a disk image with Disk Utility. A disk image is an archive file that acts like a disk—you double-click the file, and it mounts on your computer. For example, you could create a disk image to share photos with friends and family members. It's an easy way to create a single file that's simple to open—perfect for in-laws who aren't so computer savvy.

Building the Workflow

The first step is to open the Automator application and create a *workflow*, which is just a fancy name for a set of step-by-step tasks that can be performed with the applications on your Mac. You just drag actions into the workflow and rearrange them in the order you want Automator to execute them.

Here's how to create a workflow with Automator:

1. Open the Automator application. (It's in the Applications folder.)
2. From the **File** menu, select **New**. The window shown in Figure 11-1 appears.
3. Select **Workflow**. This is the file type you'll be using to create a macro in this project.

Choose a type for your document:

| Workflow | Application | Service | Print Plugin |

| Folder Action | iCal Alarm | Image Capture Plugin |

Workflow

Workflows can be run from within Automator.

Open an Existing Document...   Close   Choose

FIGURE 11-1: Automator allows you to create a variety of documents for automation. In this chapter, you'll be working exclusively with workflows.

4. Click **Choose**. The Automator window appears, as shown in Figure 11-2.
5. Locate the **Get Selected Finder Items** action and drag it to the workflow. This is the first action in our workflow.
6. Locate the **New Disk Image** action and drag it to the workflow, as shown in Figure 11-3. This is the second action in our workflow. It tells OS X to create a new disk image on your computer.

✳ **NOTE:** If you select the *Size Disk Image to fit contents* setting, the disk image will automatically scale to fit whatever files it needs to store. It's a great way to keep the disk image at exactly the right size.

7. Locate the **Set Folder Views** action and drag it to the workflow, as shown in Figure 11-4. This is the third action in our workflow. It sets the display properties for your disk image window.
8. Locate the **Open Finder Items** action and drag it to the workflow. This is the fourth and last action in our workflow (Figure 11-4). It opens the disk image in the Finder.

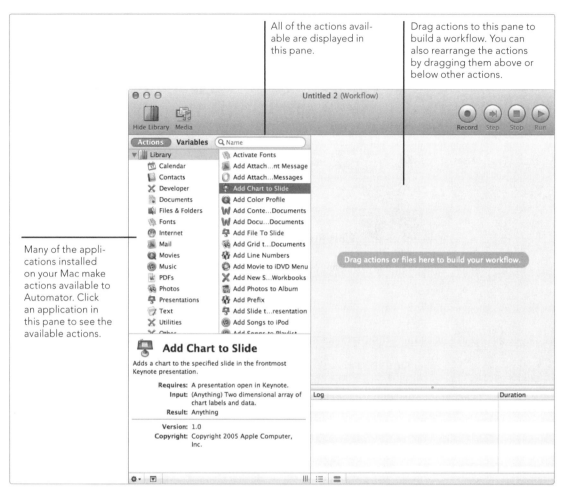

All of the actions available are displayed in this pane.

Drag actions to this pane to build a workflow. You can also rearrange the actions by dragging them above or below other actions.

Many of the applications installed on your Mac make actions available to Automator. Click an application in this pane to see the available actions.

FIGURE 11-2: *This is the Automator window. Drag actions to the workflow pane to create your macro.*

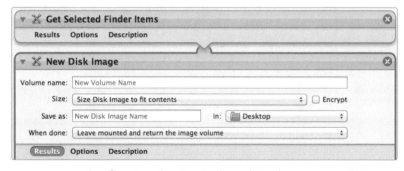

FIGURE 11-3: *Configuring the Get Selected Finder Items and New Disk Image actions*

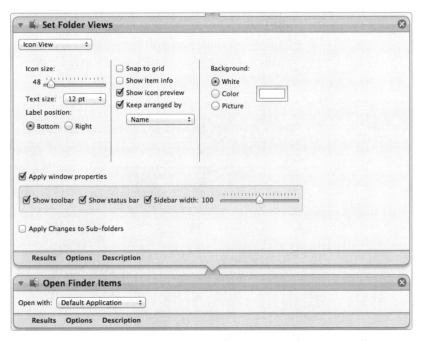

FIGURE 11-4: *Configuring the Set Folder Views and Open Finder Items actions*

9. From the **File** menu, select **Save**. The window shown in Figure 11-5 appears.

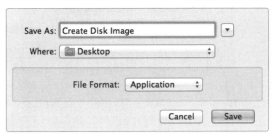

FIGURE 11-5: *Saving the macro*

10. Enter a name for the macro in the **Save As** field.
11. Change the File Format to **Application**.
12. Click **Save**.

Now you have a macro on your desktop that can be used to build disk images. The macro accepts files and folders as input, so you can drag things onto the macro to add them to a new disk image. You'll practice doing that in the next section.

Using the Macro

It's time to try using the macro to create a disk image. The process is easy. All you have to do is drag files and folders onto the macro to create the disk image. Here's how to use the macro:

1. Switch to the Finder.
2. Drag the files and folders that you want to add to the disk image onto the macro's icon.
3. The disk image appears in the Finder, as shown in Figure 11-6.

FIGURE 11-6: *The new disk image mounted on your computer*

You can share the disk image with family and friends or just leave it on your computer. And you can create as many disk images as you want. If you'd rather not drag files and folders to the macro, you could use the workflow as a folder action. That way, you'd be able to add files to a disk image by right-clicking on the files and selecting the action. For more information, see Chapter 14.

Using Macros with Keyboard Maestro

Using Automator is a great way to create macros, but it has a limited number of actions to choose from. A third-party application called Keyboard Maestro (*http://www.keyboardmaestro.com/*, $$$) provides more actions and options so you can create more flexible and advanced macros. In this section, you'll learn how to use this powerful application to use premade macros and create your own. You'll also learn how to create shortcuts to access your macros.

Enabling Existing Macros

Like Automator, Keyboard Maestro comes with an easy-to-use interface for building macros. But it also comes with a surprising number of macros—premade workflows that are available for use immediately. After you install the application, open it up and check out the available macros. You might want to enable some of them!

Here's how to enable existing macros:

1. Open the Keyboard Maestro application. The Keyboard Maestro Editor window appears, as shown in Figure 11-7.

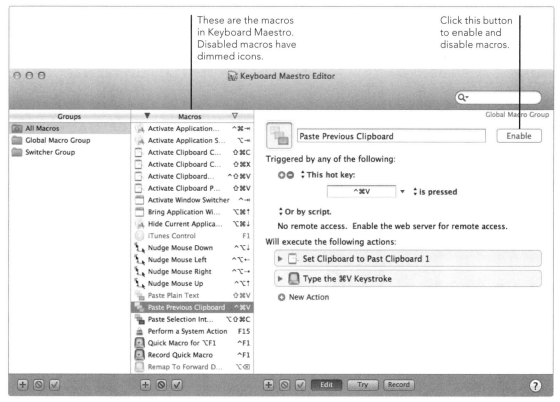

FIGURE 11-7: *Enabling macros in Keyboard Maestro Editor*

2. Select a disabled macro in the Macros pane. You can look at the icons to tell which macros are disabled—they have dimmed icons.
3. Click **Enable**. The macro is now enabled and ready to use.

Assigning Triggers

You've enabled some existing macros—now you need the ability to access them. To do so, you'll assign triggers to access the macro from outside of Keyboard Maestro. *Triggers* are keyboard shortcuts or any of 15 other options that can be used to execute a macro automatically or manually.

Here's how to assign triggers:

1. Open the Keyboard Maestro application.
2. From the Macros pane, select a macro. The window shown in Figure 11-8 appears.

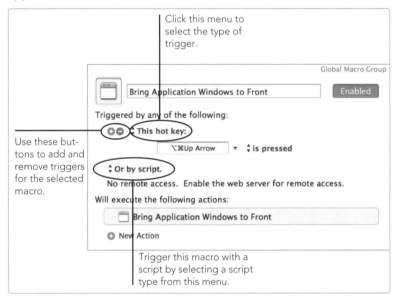

FIGURE 11-8: *Assigning triggers to macros in the Keyboard Maestro Editor*

3. Click the **+** button to add a new trigger.
4. Select a trigger type from the menu that appears, as shown in Figure 11-9.

Most trigger types require you to specify a modifier. For example, if you select the hot-key trigger, you'll need to enter the keyboard shortcut to execute the macro.

You can also generate code for scripts to trigger the macro in Keyboard Maestro. To do so, select a script from the **Or by script** menu and insert the generated code into your script.

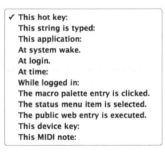

FIGURE 11-9: *Selecting a trigger type*

Creating a New Macro

The default macros that come with Keyboard Maestro are pretty good, but there's nothing quite like creating your very own macro. When you're ready to roll your own, you'll be pleasantly surprised to discover that Keyboard Maestro resembles the Automator interface—all you have to do is drag actions from one pane to another. It's easy!

Here's how to create a new macro:

1. Open the Keyboard Maestro application.
2. Click the **+** button under the Macros pane. The window shown in Figure 11-10 appears.

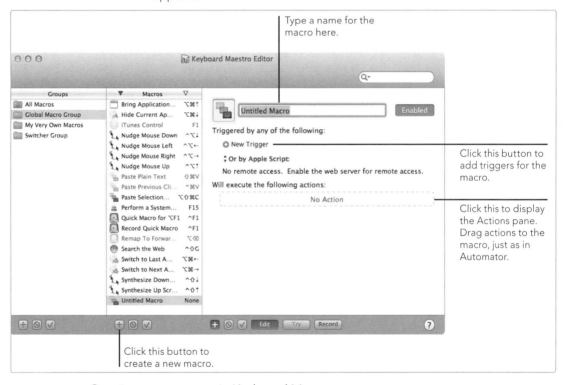

FIGURE 11-10: *Creating a new macro in Keyboard Maestro*

3. Enter a name for the macro.
4. Click the **+** button to create a new trigger. You can add more than one.
5. Click the **No Action** button to display the Actions pane. (It appears over the top of the Groups and Macros panes.)
6. Drag actions to the macro pane to create a workflow, just as in the Automator application.
7. When you're finished creating the macro, click **Edit** to take the editor out of edit mode.

Try executing the macro with the trigger you specified. You can make revisions to the macro by selecting it and clicking the Edit button.

Adding and Configuring Groups

Keyboard Maestro allows you to classify macros into *groups*. Groups are a good way to limit the power of certain macros. You can control the applications in which the macros in a group can be accessed and when the macros are activated. If nothing else, creating a group is a useful way to keep your custom macros separate from the default macros that come with the Keyboard Maestro application.

Here's how to use groups:

1. Open the Keyboard Maestro application.
2. Click the **+** button under the Groups pane to create a new group. The window shown in Figure 11-11 appears.

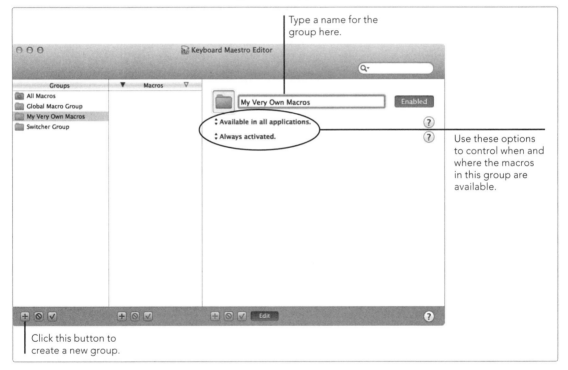

FIGURE 11-11: *Creating and configuring groups*

3. Type a name for the group.
4. From the **Available in all applications** menu, select an option to limit the applications in which these macros will be available. (Or just leave it set to **Available in all applications**.)

5. From the **Always activated** menu, select an option to limit when these macros will be available. For example, if you want the macro to be available globally from any application, leave it set to **Always activated**. If you plan on using the macro only occasionally, select one of the other options, such as **For One Action**.
6. Click **Edit** to take the group out of editing mode.
7. From the Groups pane, select **All Macros**.
8. To add macros to the new group, drag them from the Macros pane onto the new group.

You have created the new group. If you ever want to edit it, just select it and click the Edit button—you'll be able to make changes to the settings.

Disabling Macros

It's important to disable the macros in Keyboard Maestro that you no longer plan on using. Most of the macros have triggers, and you don't want to leave an enabled but useless macro lying around that you might accidentally trigger. Here's how to disable macros:

1. Open the Keyboard Maestro application.
2. From the Macros pane, select a macro.
3. Click **Disable**. The macro is now disabled.

If you'd like to leave the macro enabled but make it inaccessible, you can remove all of the triggers for the macro. If you do this, you won't be able to trigger the macro unless you use the Keyboard Maestro application.

Additional Ideas for Making Macros

You can have some great fun with macros. But don't stop there. You can combine Automator workflows with folder services to execute macros from contextual menus. For more information, see Chapter 14.

You can also combine macros with AppleScripts for completely automated solutions. It's beautiful to see the power of AppleScript combined with the simplicity of Automator. For more information about AppleScript, see Chapter 12.

12

Automating Tasks with AppleScript

Have you ever wanted to automate a task on your Mac—one that needs to be performed over and over again? For example, maybe as part of your job you resize images, apply a filter, compress the files, and then upload them to a website. You know your Mac is capable of automating work like this, but Automator is too limited and you're not sure what other options are available.

Enter AppleScript, one of the best-kept secrets on your Mac. AppleScript is a scripting language built into OS X that can automate practically any task or workflow, performing tasks and transferring data between applications. There is a catch—AppleScript can be difficult to learn and to adapt for your purposes. It's a true programming language.

This project will help you get started with AppleScript. You'll create your first script in the

AppleScript Editor application and then learn how to add interface elements, work with variables, use control structures to make your script intelligent, and launch your AppleScript. Finally, you'll learn about some great resources that will help you perfect your scripting skills.

Project goal: Create your first AppleScript.

What You'll Be Using

To automate your work with AppleScript, you'll use the following:

 AppleScript Editor

What Can You Do with AppleScript?

You just learned that AppleScript is capable of automating tasks on your Mac. But how can you put AppleScript to use in the real world—and not just with the examples presented in this project?

The first step is one of the hardest. You need to break down your desired task into component steps that AppleScript can perform, bit by bit. To do this, consider a common but tedious action you perform with your computer—like creating a document with Microsoft Word—and then think of the individual steps it requires. You open Word, create a new document, type some text, and then save the document to your hard disk. This is a *workflow*, something AppleScript excels at automating—if it knows the steps.

That's a simple example, of course. In the real world, an AppleScript might perform hundreds or even thousands of steps. That's why it's so important that you know all of the steps *before* you start creating the script. If it helps, try typing out all of the steps in sequential order. Don't worry: You only have to do this once.

The benefits of using AppleScript should be obvious. With a push of a button, you can run a script that quickly performs tasks without any human intervention. Plus, you remove the possibility of human error, which is always a potential problem when manually performing tasks with so many steps.

What's the Difference Between a Macro and a Script?

If you read Chapter 11, you might be wondering about the differences between Automator and AppleScript—or said another way, the differences between a *macro* and a *script*. As it happens, the two are similar, but in some situations you'll need to use AppleScript instead of Automator. Here are some of the notable differences:

▶ Automator has a limited number of actions available. If you can't find an action that does what you want, you're out of luck. AppleScript allows you to do almost anything with nearly any application.

- Scripts can perform different actions in different situations. For example, a script can perform Task A if Variable Z is present, or it can perform Task B if Variable Y is present. Automator actions run sequentially from start to finish—there's no way to build in logic for different variables and situations.

- Scripts take time to program, test, and implement. Automator actions can be created quickly and easily, and it's simple to start using them right away.

- The Automator application has an accessible interface that encourages experimentation. Most people—even beginners—can create macros in a matter of minutes. AppleScript is a scripting language that can take weeks to learn.

To summarize, Automator is easier and faster to use, but it has limited functionality. AppleScript has a substantial learning curve, but you can do a lot more with it. You might want to try using both, just to get the hang of them. Then when the time comes to pick one for a real-world task, you'll know which one to use.

Getting Started with the AppleScript Editor

First we'll write a simple script with the AppleScript Editor and run the script. Then you'll use the record feature so the AppleScript Editor can automatically create a script while you perform actions on your computer. Just remember, nobody becomes an AppleScript pro overnight!

Writing and Running Your First AppleScript

You'll use the AppleScript Editor application to write, edit, and run your scripts—it comes preinstalled with every Mac. This application is as basic as it gets. All you have to do is start typing in the main window and then click Compile and Run.

Your first AppleScript will do something simple but also fun and even useful: Tell your computer to say something. To expand on this script, you could create an AppleScript that automatically finds and reads the top news article on the *New York Times* website when you turn on your computer in the morning.

Here's how to write and run your first AppleScript:

1. Open the AppleScript Editor. (It's in the Utilities folder.) The window shown in Figure 12-1 appears.
2. In the main pane, type **say "Hello, World!"**. This is your first AppleScript!
3. Click **Compile**. The AppleScript Editor checks your syntax and prepares to run the script. One thing you'll notice is that the format of the script changes, as shown in Figure 12-2. Instead of plaintext, you'll see a nice, formatted script. A message will be displayed in the lower pane if errors are found in the script.

∗ *NOTE:* Clicking Compile isn't necessary, but it is a best practice that can help you find errors in your script before you run it.

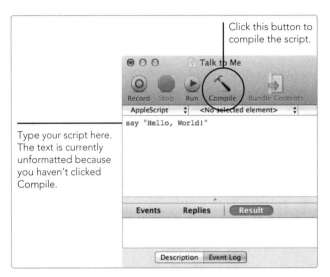

Click this button to
compile the script.

Type your script here.
The text is currently
unformatted because
you haven't clicked
Compile.

FIGURE 12-1: *AppleScript may be difficult to learn, but
the AppleScript Editor is not.*

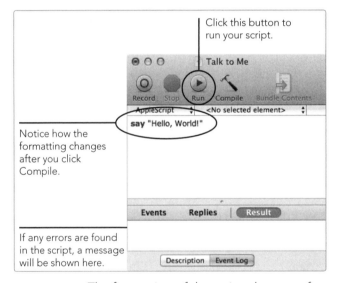

Click this button to
run your script.

Notice how the
formatting changes
after you click
Compile.

If any errors are found
in the script, a message
will be shown here.

FIGURE 12-2: *The formatting of the script changes after
you click Compile.*

4. Click **Run**. The AppleScript Editor executes your script—your computer
    should say "Hello, World!"

    Congratulations! You've just created and run your very first AppleScript.

Scripting with Natural Language

Were you amazed by how easy it was to create that script? All you had to do was type **say** and the AppleScript Editor knew that you wanted the computer to say something. The command corresponds to an imperative command—it's written the way you would tell somebody to do something. This is called *natural language programming* because you're writing scripts the same way you write or say anything else. This simple syntax sets AppleScript apart from most other programming languages.

Here are some other examples of natural language in AppleScript:

```
tell application "TextEdit" to quit
display alert "Don't do that!"
print page 10
```

The beauty of natural language programming is that most of the code doesn't need any explanation. We can all tell what these sample commands do when they're executed. Knowing this, you can guess many of the available AppleScript commands and easily research commands you aren't familiar with.

Learning AppleScript by Example

The record feature in the AppleScript Editor sounds great in theory, but it doesn't work very well in practice. Why not? Developers have to build support for this feature into their applications, and many of them don't. The feature is still worth mentioning, if only because it makes a great learning tool—you can perform actions and then see the corresponding AppleScript.

Here's how it works: Click the **Record** button, and the AppleScript Editor will watch what you do and record your every move in AppleScript, provided you're using a supported application. A sample result is shown in Figure 12-3.

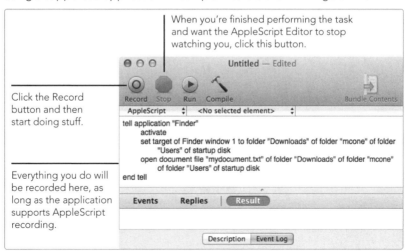

FIGURE 12-3: *The AppleScript Editor watches you perform actions and records the corresponding script.*

The best way to find out which applications support the AppleScript record feature is to just try using and recording them. Most actions performed in Apple's programs (like the Finder), at least, are recorded, and many of the applications developed by Bare Bones Software (*http://www.barebones.com/*) have great AppleScript support. (You'll learn how to access a dictionary of scripting actions available within third-party programs in the next section.)

Dabbling in Advanced AppleScript Concepts

Now that you know how to use the AppleScript Editor to create basic scripts, what's next? You can start learning advanced AppleScript concepts—the building blocks for writing complicated scripts capable of performing the most difficult and tedious tasks. In this section, you'll learn how to work with applications and variables, incorporate structures, and build interfaces.

Working with Applications

One of the first things you'll need to learn is how to use AppleScript with the applications on your computer. After all, most of the work you perform on your computer is with applications, so it makes sense that your AppleScript will also need to work with them. To perform multiple tasks within a single application, create a *block* by nesting commands, as shown below:

```
tell application "TextWrangler"
    activate
    make new text document
end tell
```

In this example, TextWrangler (*http://barebones.com/products/textwrangler/*, free) will execute the commands in the block. The first line, `tell application "TextWrangler"`, just tells the application to start listening for commands. The second line, `activate`, opens the TextWrangler application, if it is not already open. The third line, `make new text document`, opens a new document. And the last line, `end tell`, notifies TextWrangler that AppleScript is finished with it.

How do you know which commands to use to control an application? Use the AppleScript *dictionary* provided for most applications—it contains all of the commands for the application that can be used in your script. To access a dictionary, open the AppleScript Editor and select **Open Dictionary** from the **File** menu. Select an application from the list, and then the application's dictionary appears, as shown in Figure 12-4.

You'll quickly discover that the dictionaries make excellent reference guides. In fact, when you're first learning AppleScript, the dictionaries are your best friends. After you get the hang of things, you won't need to rely on them as much.

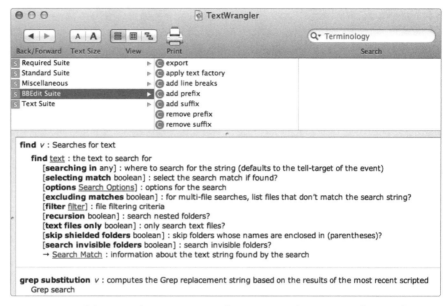

FIGURE 12-4: *Most applications provide scripting dictionaries listing the commands available to AppleScript.*

Working with Variables

Variables are something like virtual boxes capable of holding values or data that can be accessed by your script and the applications on your Mac. You can create variables in your script to store information or to transfer information from one application to another. For example, you could copy the text in a Microsoft Word document, put it in a variable, and then use the variable to paste the text into TextEdit.

Here are some simple examples of what you can do with variables:

▶ Store numbers: set variable to 1

▶ Store text: set variable to "this is the text"

▶ Store a list: copy {"hello", 8, "world"} to variable

As the geeks have probably figured out by now, variables in AppleScript are not strictly typed and do not need to be "declared" (that is, defined before you put anything in them). Variables can also take letters or numbers. There's a lot you can do with this flexibility.

Using Flow-Control Structures to Do Work

You can add *flow-control structures* to your scripts to handle different types of scenarios. For example, you might create a set of tasks to perform if variable A is present and a whole other set of tasks in case it's not present. Programmers call this flow control. If a traffic light is green, you drive through the intersection, and if it's red, you stop your vehicle.

There are many flow-control structures available. Here are some of the most common:

▶ **Conditional**   Perform the commands in the first block if the statement is true. Otherwise, use the commands in the second block.

```
if x is less than 5 then
    -- commands
else
    -- different commands
end if
```

▶ **Looping**   Repeat the commands in the block for the specified duration.

```
repeat with i from 1 to 100
    -- commands
end repeat
```

▶ **Error handling**   Try performing the commands in the first block. If there's an error, perform the commands in the second block.

```
try
    -- test these commands
on error
    -- perform other commands
end try
```

The flow-control structures for conditionals, loops, and error handling should be a good start for most beginners and intermediate AppleScript programmers. When you're ready to progress to advanced flow-control structures, use the resources listed at the end of this chapter.

Building a Simple User Interface

Sometimes you'll need to interact with your scripts. Maybe you want to see the *output*—a summary of what happened, what went wrong, or how much work was performed. Or maybe you want to be presented with a choice before running a script. You're in need of an interface.

Here are some of the most common interfaces available for your script:

▶ **Simple alert**   Use this to display information in a window with an OK button. (The input of the user clicking the button is not recorded.) It works well as a confirmation that the script completed.

```
display alert "The script executed successfully"
```

- ▶ **List** Use this when you need to provide your script with input. Multiple options are presented in a window—you're asked to select one and click **OK**. The result is shown in Figure 12-5.

```
set chosenListItem to choose from list {"1", "2", "3"} ¬
    with title "Name of the List" ¬
    with prompt "You need to do something!" ¬
    default items "2" ¬
    OK button name "OK" ¬
    cancel button name "Cancel" ¬
    multiple selections allowed false ¬
    with empty selection allowed
```

- ▶ **Advanced alert** When you need to provide your script with a simple "yes" or "no" answer, use the advanced alert. This displays a window with two buttons. The result is shown in Figure 12-6.

```
set resultAlertReply to display alert ¬
    "Alert Text" as warning ¬
    buttons {"Okay", "Cancel"} ¬
    default button 1 ¬
    cancel button 2 ¬
    giving up after 2
```

FIGURE 12-5: *Displaying a list of selectable options*

FIGURE 12-6: *An advanced alert*

You might be wondering how you use the values that are returned from the button clicks. The following code sample should give you one idea of how to use the input.

```
display alert "Do you want to do this?" buttons {"No", "Yes"}
set theAnswer to button returned of the result
if theAnswer is "Yes" then
    say "Thank you, I will proceed"
else
    say "The script execution has been canceled"
end if
```

The interface elements are definitely advanced and require testing to get them just right—make sure they work correctly before you start using them for real work!

Launching Your AppleScript

So you've written a couple of scripts. Now you're faced with a new problem: How do you launch them without having to open the AppleScript Editor and click Run? You have several options:

▶ Use the global OS X AppleScript menu. To turn it on, open the AppleScript Editor, select **Preferences** from the **AppleScript Editor** menu, click **General**, and then select the **Show Script menu in menu bar** checkbox. To add your scripts to the menu, select **Open User Scripts Folder** from the script menu in the menu bar and then drag your scripts to the folder.

▶ Add your scripts as login items. See Chapter 2 for instructions.

▶ Launch a script with a keyboard shortcut by using a third-party application called FastScripts (*http://www.red-sweater.com/fastscripts/*, free version available).

▶ Save a script as an application. Select **Save As** from the **AppleScript Editor** menu and then select **Application** from the **File Format** menu.

With all of these options available, you should be able to launch your scripts in a way that's convenient for you.

Additional Ideas for Creating and Using AppleScripts

No single chapter can do AppleScript justice. To really learn how to use AppleScript, you'll need to practice on your own, review other people's scripts, and use other resources.

Check out some of these resources for intermediate to advanced AppleScript programmers:

▶ Apple's Developer website (*http://developer.apple.com/*) has several free AppleScript tutorials available.

▶ MacScripter (*http://macscripter.net/*) has free tutorials on AppleScript and an open forum where users can post questions and answers.

▶ Doug's AppleScripts for iTunes (*http://dougscripts.com/itunes/*) has more than 400 free scripts available to interact with iTunes. It's a great resource!

▶ *AppleScript 1-2-3* by Sal Soghoian and Bill Cheeseman (Peachpit Press, 2009) is arguably the best book on AppleScript available. One of the authors worked at Apple for more than 11 years.

Remember, practice makes perfect. Experimentation is a great way to hone your AppleScript skills and practice what you know. Good luck!

13

Creating a Bluetooth Proximity Monitor

Ready to get up, stretch, and walk away from your computer? First you'll have to follow a checklist that has probably become second nature—pause iTunes, mute the volume, set your instant messenger applications to away, and lock the screen. It all had to be performed manually, until now.

The next time you step away from your computer, how about just taking your iPhone, smartphone, or iPad with you? With a *Bluetooth proximity monitor* running, your Mac will know the device has moved out of range and will run an AppleScript to perform a series of actions, like locking the screen and pausing iTunes. When you return, your Mac will run a different AppleScript to unlock your screen and start playing music again.

Since you'll be creating the AppleScripts in the project, you can make your Mac do anything you want when the proximity of the Bluetooth device changes. And you don't need an iPhone or iPad—any Bluetooth-enabled device can work with the Proximity application, including smartphones running the Android operating system.

Project goal: Turn your Mac into a proximity monitor capable of performing actions when a Bluetooth device moves into or out of range.

What You'll Be Using

To automatically tell your Mac when you step away and what to do when you leave, you'll use the following:

 Proximity (*http://code.google.com/p/reduxcomputing-proximity/*, free)

 AppleScript Editor

How Bluetooth Proximity Detection Works

Macs are capable of detecting Bluetooth devices up to 10 meters (33 feet) away. The Proximity application takes this factoid and makes it useful. By using your Mac's internal Bluetooth sensor, Proximity can run AppleScripts when the state of a connected Bluetooth device changes. There are two states for a device: in range and out of range. Proximity can run separate AppleScripts for each state, making this a great way to automatically perform a variety of actions on the Mac when you walk away from it and when you come back.

Setting Up the Bluetooth Proximity Monitor

If AppleScripts are the real substance of your Bluetooth proximity monitor, Proximity (*http://code.google.com/p/reduxcomputing-proximity/*, free) is the glue that holds everything together. You need to install and configure this application before you create the scripts that will be triggered as you go away and return.

Here's how to configure Proximity:

1. Open the Proximity application. The Proximity icon appears in the menu bar.
2. From the **Proximity** menu, select **Preferences**. The window shown in Figure 13-1 appears.
3. In the first field, enter a time in seconds to specify the interval at which Proximity will check for the Bluetooth device. This number should be as low as possible for fast detection and script execution. You don't want to get back to your desk and find that Proximity hasn't detected your device leaving yet!
4. Click **Change Device**. The Detect Bluetooth Device window appears.
5. Select a Bluetooth device from the list and then click **Select**. If you're trying to select an iPhone or iPad, you may need to open the Bluetooth settings to make it discoverable. (In iOS, tap **Settings**, then **General**, and then **Bluetooth**.)

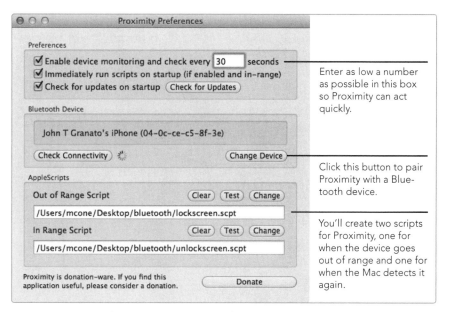

Enter as low a number as possible in this box so Proximity can act quickly.

Click this button to pair Proximity with a Bluetooth device.

You'll create two scripts for Proximity, one for when the device goes out of range and one for when the Mac detects it again.

FIGURE 13-1: *Configure Proximity's preferences for maximum effectiveness.*

After you create the scripts, you'll need to circle back around to Proximity to select them in the preferences.

Performing Actions Based on Bluetooth Proximity

Here comes the fun part. Open the AppleScript Editor application (it's in the Utilities folder) and create two new scripts—an *Out of Range* script, which will be triggered when you walk away, and an *In Range* script, which will be triggered when you return. Then start adding some of the code snippets provided below.

Of course, you don't have to add all of the code provided below, nor do you have to limit yourself to it. You can mix and match any of the actions you want—or add new actions of your own—to create custom scripts. Whatever you put in your scripts, it's a good idea to test them to make sure they do what you expect before adding them to Proximity.

Locking the Screen

One of the most obvious uses for Proximity is security related—it can lock the screen when you walk away and unlock it when you return. Protecting your computer from unauthorized access is a best practice, but sometimes it's hard to remember to start the screensaver before you walk away. Implementing this as part of a Bluetooth proximity monitor automatically engages this security control.

Put this in the *Out of Range.scpt* script to lock the screen (you or someone else can still unlock it without the Bluetooth device in proximity, but doing so requires a password):

```
tell application "System Events"
    tell security preferences
        set require password to wake to true
    end tell
end tell
try
    tell application "ScreenSaverEngine"
        activate
    end tell
end try
```

Now put this in *In Range.scpt* to unlock the screen when you return:

```
tell application "System Events"
    tell security preferences
        set require password to wake to false
    end tell
end tell

tell application "ScreenSaverEngine" to quit
```

Now screen locking is automated. Just remember to take your iPhone (or whatever Bluetooth device you're using) with you when you walk away from the computer, or your Mac will never know you've left.

Pausing iTunes

Pausing and resuming iTunes is another useful feature you can bake into your proximity monitor. When you add this code snippet, iTunes pauses your music when you walk away and then resumes playing when you come back.

Put this in *Out of Range.scpt* to pause playback:

```
tell application "iTunes" to pause
```

And then put this in *In Range.scpt* to resume iTunes when you return:

```
tell application "iTunes" to play
```

Pausing and resuming playback is just one example of how you can control iTunes with AppleScript. iTunes has excellent AppleScript support, so use your imagination to add other features. For example, you could tell iTunes that when you return, it should start playing a random album, download and play an hourly news podcast, or even change the iTunes equalizer settings. For more ideas, visit a website called Doug's AppleScripts for iTunes (*http://dougscripts.com/itunes/*).

Setting an Away Message

If you use Messages or Adium (*http://adium.im/*, free) for instant messaging, you can automatically display an away message when you leave your desk to let your friends know that you're not there.

Put this in *Out of Range.scpt* to set both Messages and Adium to "away" status:

```
tell application "Messages"
    set status to away
end tell
tell application "Adium" to go away with message "Out of Bluetooth range"
```

The out-of-range script now has two commands—one for Messages and one for Adium. Obviously, you'll want to replace `Out of Bluetooth range` with the Adium away message of your choice.

Put this in *In Range.scpt* to change your status in Messages and Adium to "available":

```
tell application "Messages"
    set status to available
end tell
tell application "Adium" to go available
```

Walking away from your computer is now a quick way to end an annoying conversation, just as in real life!

Adding the Scripts and Testing Everything

Now that you have the scripts, it's time to select them in Proximity. Here's how:

1. From the **Proximity** menu, select **Preferences**. The window shown earlier in Figure 13-1 appears.
2. To select an *Out of Range Script*, click **Change** and select the AppleScript file you want to run.
3. To select an *In Range Script*, click **Change** and select the appropriate AppleScript file.
4. You can test the scripts by clicking **Test**. If the scripts don't work the way you expect, make changes and test them again.

Now it's time for the real test. Try turning off the Bluetooth device. When your computer recognizes that the device has disappeared, Proximity will execute the out-of-range script. Then turn the Bluetooth device back on—Proximity will execute the in-range script. If Proximity doesn't work as quickly as you were expecting, try lowering the time setting in Proximity's preferences.

Additional Ideas for Creating a Bluetooth Proximity Monitor

You might be wondering what happens in a worst-case scenario. If you go to lunch and lose your iPhone, what's going to happen when you get back to your desk? Well, Proximity won't be able to trigger the in-range script, but you'll still be able to deactivate your screensaver with your password. So it's no big deal if you lose your Bluetooth device—this proximity stuff isn't very serious security. For practical security advice, see Part 6.

The possibilities for a Bluetooth proximity monitor are virtually endless. You're limited by your scripting abilities, but even if you aren't a scripting whiz kid, you can still do quite a bit. For example, you can download some scripts off the Mac OS X Hints website (*http://hints.macworld.com/article.php?story=201107190007230*) to create an alarm for your laptop with an application called iAlertU (*http://sourceforge .net/projects/ialertu/*, free). Just install the scripts and then walk away from your computer with your Bluetooth device. Your computer will be protected by iAlertU—if anybody messes with your Mac, it will start emitting a loud alarm.

Home automation is another intriguing possibility. If you positioned your Mac close enough to your garage or front door and connected it to a home automation app like Indigo (*http://www.perceptiveautomation.com/indigo/*, $$$), you could do things like turn a television off when you leave the house and turn the lights on when you get home.

14

Automating File and Folder Actions

All environments—virtual or otherwise—need to have basic upkeep performed on a regular basis. At home you wash the dishes, mow the grass, and change your car's motor oil. On your computer, you need to empty the Trash when it's full, clean out the downloads folder when there are too many old documents, and occasionally perform specific actions on a group of files, like rotating images or resaving them in a new format.

Boring chores like this are a drag. Fortunately, on your computer at least, there are tools that can help you automate repetitive tasks. The folder actions service built into OS X makes it easy to apply AppleScripts or

Automator workflows to any file dropped into a folder on your computer. And a third-party preference pane called Hazel gives you a slew of powerful options you can apply selectively to files in a particular folder.

Project goal: Create a folder action and use Hazel to automate computer upkeep.

What You'll Be Using

To automate routine chores, you'll use the following:

   Automator

   Hazel (*http://www.noodlesoft.com/hazel.php*, $$)

Using OS X Folder Actions

The OS X *folder actions* service can automatically perform a variety of actions on files that are dropped into a folder you designate. When you enable folder actions, you'll attach one or more scripts or Automator actions to the folder. Several default scripts come with every Mac, and you can create your own and download contributed scripts on the Internet.

What can folder actions help you do? You can batch-process images into a standard file type like JPEG or PNG, receive a notification when a new file is added to a folder, import songs to iTunes, and more.

Here's how to use a folder action to change pictures to PNG format:

1. Create a new folder and name it. The folder in this example is named *My Fancy Action Folder*.
2. Right-click the folder and select **Services ▸ Folder Actions Setup**. The window shown in Figure 14-1 appears.
3. Select a script to attach as a folder action and click **Attach**. For this example, we'll select **Image— Duplicate as PNG.scpt**. The window shown in Figure 14-2 appears.

FIGURE 14-1: *Select a script to attach as a folder action.*

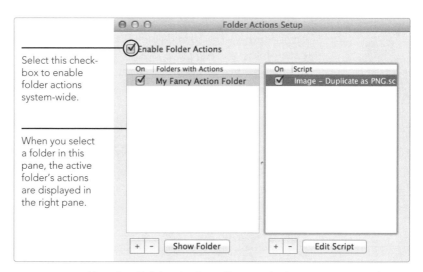

Select this check-box to enable folder actions system-wide.

When you select a folder in this pane, the active folder's actions are displayed in the right pane.

FIGURE 14-2: *Use the Folder Actions Setup window to manage the folder actions.*

4. You can add additional folder actions to the folder by selecting it in the left pane, clicking the **+** button under the right pane, and selecting another script. Close the Folder Actions Setup window when you're finished—you have now designated folder actions.

5. Test the folder action by dropping an image into the folder. The script converts the image to PNG format and creates two folders within the top-level folder—one for original images and the other for images in PNG format, as shown in Figure 14-3.

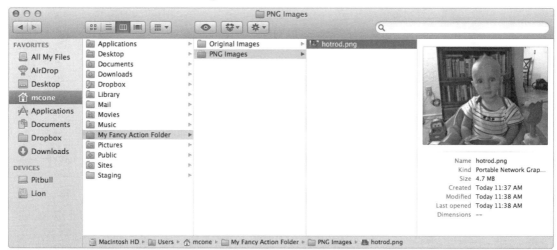

FIGURE 14-3: *Photos dropped into* My Fancy Action Folder *are converted to PNG format and saved in a folder called* PNG Images, *and the original files are saved in a folder called* Original Images.

There are a couple advantages—or disadvantages, depending on your perspective—to using folder actions. First, folder actions need to be enabled on any folder you want to attach scripts to. Once you enable folder actions, the attached scripts will be applied to every file dropped into the folder. If you are proficient at scripting, you can use Automator workflows or AppleScripts to create your own folder actions.

Using Automator to Create Folder Actions

The default scripts for folder actions aren't as flexible or powerful as you might want. Fortunately, Automator—the application you learned how to use in Chapter 11—makes creating folder actions relatively easy.

In Automator, you'll string together *actions* to create advanced folder actions. Remember, actions are common tasks that can be performed with the applications on your Mac. First you add actions and customize the variables. Then when you run the folder action, Automator interfaces with the applications to perform the tasks. Not all software developers create Automator actions for their applications, but many do.

For the purposes of this example, let's say you want to create a folder action that uploads files to a web server and then changes the label color so you know that the files have been uploaded. (Panic's Transmit FTP client provides the upload action.) Anyone who has a photo album on their blog might find this action useful—new photos are automatically uploaded to the website when you drag the files into the folder.

Here's how to use Automator to create the upload file folder action:

1. Open the Automator application. The window shown in Figure 14-4 appears.
2. Select **Folder Action** and then click **Choose**. The Automator window appears.
3. To upload the file to the server in this example, use the **Upload** action provided by Panic's Transmit FTP client (*http://www.panic.com/transmit/*, $$$). Add the action and specify the server's connection information or select a favorite that you've saved in Transmit.
4. To change the file's label color, use the **Label Finder Items** action. Select the color you want to label uploaded files. That completes our workflow—the finished product is shown in Figure 14-5.
5. Select **File ▸ Save**.
6. Enter a name for your folder action and then click **Save**. Your new folder action is now available for selection from the Folder Actions Setup window, as shown in Figure 14-6.

If you ever want to edit this workflow, select the script in the Folder Actions Setup window and then click **Edit Script**.

* *NOTE:* **In case you're wondering how to turn an AppleScript into a folder action, you just save it as a script in this folder:** */Library/Scripts/Folder Actions*. **The script will then be available for selection in the Folder Actions Setup window.**

Select the
Folder Action
document type.

FIGURE 14-4: *After opening Automator, select Folder Action and click Choose.*

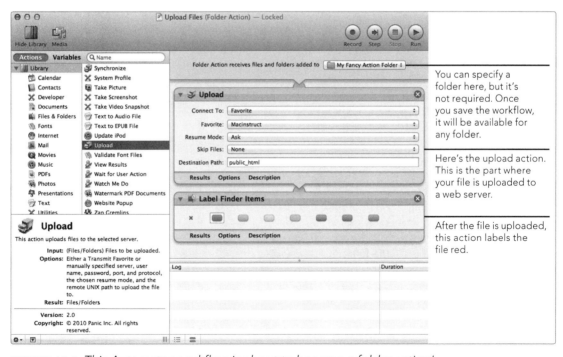

You can specify a folder here, but it's not required. Once you save the workflow, it will be available for any folder.

Here's the upload action. This is the part where your file is uploaded to a web server.

After the file is uploaded, this action labels the file red.

FIGURE 14-5: *This Automator workflow is about to become a folder action!*

FIGURE 14-6: *The new Automator workflow is now available when you open folder actions.*

Using Hazel to Perform File and Folder Actions

Folder actions pack a powerful automation punch, but they're not flexible enough for every purpose. After all, it's a real pain having to use Automator or AppleScript to automate even the most basic tasks. And folder actions are blunt tools that are applied to every file dropped into a folder—you can't selectively apply actions to individual files.

Fortunately, a more flexible version of folder actions is available in the form of third-party preference pane Hazel (*http://www.noodlesoft.com/hazel.php*, $$). (A free trial is available.) Hazel is user friendly, totally customizable, and even more powerful than folder actions. After you install Hazel, you can access it from System Preferences.

Hazel's interface is straightforward and easy to navigate, as shown in Figure 14-7. As with folder actions, you can select folders and add rules. Hazel comes with a couple of sample rules to get you started, but it's easy to create your own.

Hazel's rules interface, shown in Figure 14-8, is where the preference pane really shines. Here you can create *if-then* statements to apply rules to only some of the files in the folder.

You start by identifying the conditions under which the rule should be applied and then set the actions that should be performed. (Hazel can perform multiple actions in a single rule.) You can perform a host of actions on files, in addition to attaching AppleScripts and Automator workflows.

Hazel's options can be overwhelming at first, and it can be hard to know what kind of rules to make. The next couple of sections in this chapter provide concrete examples of rules that you can start using immediately.

Folders under Hazel's purview are displayed in the sidebar. You can add and apply different rules to each folder.

Rules for the selected folder are shown here. Enable a rule by selecting the checkbox.

Use these buttons to add, remove, and edit rules for the selected folder.

Use these buttons to select and remove folders; preview the files and folders that will be affected by rules; and import, export, and run rules.

FIGURE 14-7: *The Hazel interface allows you to add rules to folders.*

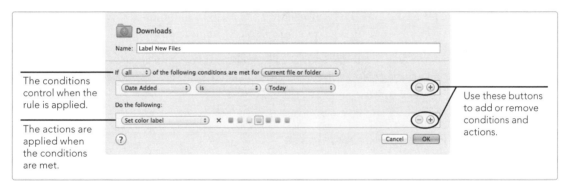

The conditions control when the rule is applied.

The actions are applied when the conditions are met.

Use these buttons to add or remove conditions and actions.

FIGURE 14-8: *Building a new rule in Hazel. This rule applies green color labels to all of the files added to the Downloads folder today.*

Taking Out the Trash

One of Hazel's best features is its ability to automatically remove files from the Trash after a specified period of time or when a maximum size threshold is met. Yes, that's right—you'll never have to manually empty the Trash again. Just click the Trash button in Hazel and configure the options shown in Figure 14-9.

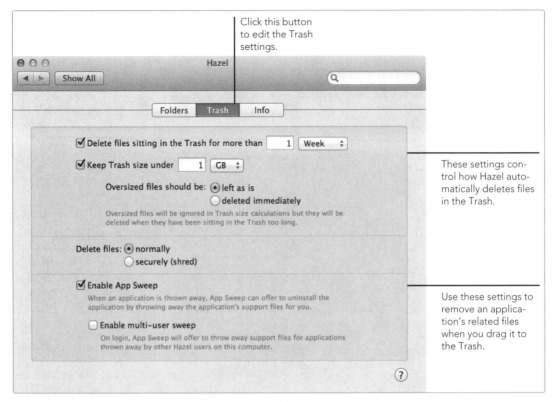

FIGURE 14-9: *Hazel takes out the Trash on your Mac automatically.*

When you throw away applications, Hazel can find and delete an application's support files at the same time. Select the **Enable App Sweep** checkbox to turn on this feature. See Chapter 5 to learn more about deleting an application's support files.

Purging Old Downloads

If you're like most users, you download files from websites and forget about them. Those files accumulate in your Downloads folder over a period of weeks or months and create a big mess.

Hazel can take care of these old files automatically by removing them with a rule that you can "set and forget." Start by creating a condition that identifies all files and folders that have not been added in the last four weeks, or whatever time period you're comfortable with, and then create an action to move the files and folders to the Trash, as shown in Figure 14-10.

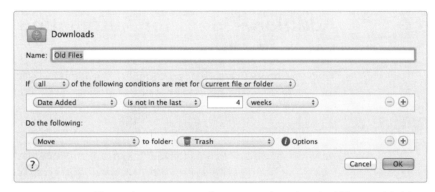

FIGURE 14-10: *This rule automatically moves downloaded files and folders more than four weeks old to the Trash.*

You can also daisy-chain rules to create a system-wide workflow. For example, if you use the instructions in the last section to configure the automatic emptying of the Trash and set this rule to move old downloads to the Trash, you'll have created an automated workflow that moves old downloads to the Trash after four weeks and then deletes them after one week.

Archiving Folders

Let's say that you need to compress folders full of files that you no longer have to read or edit but still need to keep for your records—for example, a folder with tax documents filed last year. You could create a new folder to hold the archives and then create the rule shown in Figure 14-11. All of the files dropped into the folder are archived and renamed to add the date and extension to the filename.

You can edit the rename pattern by clicking the text field—a window appears and allows you to add, edit, or delete the variables in the current pattern.

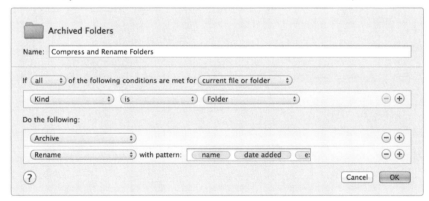

FIGURE 14-11: *This rule compresses folders and renames them to add the date they were archived.*

Additional Ideas for Automating File and Folder Actions

It can take hours to create good folder actions and Hazel rules that work the way you want them to. So before you start making your own folder actions or Hazel rules, it's a good idea to search the Internet for similar actions or rules that others have already created and shared.

Use the websites referenced in Chapters 11 and 12 to find free Automator workflows and AppleScripts for your folder actions. For ideas for Hazel rules, take a look at the Noodlesoft forums (*http://www.noodlesoft.com/forums/*)—they have an entire section for user-contributed rules.

15

Triggering Location-Based Actions

If you use a laptop, you probably already know that different system settings are better for different locations. In a café, for instance, you might lock the keychain and use a VPN to protect your Mac from hackers. At home, you might dim your Mac's display and disable the screensaver password.

When you start working in a different location, changing the appropriate settings is important to maintain the security, usability, and functionality you've come to expect from your Mac.

All of these changes to location-specific settings had to be performed manually—until now. Sidekick automates the process of switching your Mac's settings by detecting your current location and then applying the customized rules and settings that you specify. It can even execute AppleScripts to perform sophisticated configuration changes. You don't have to push a button!

Project goal: Set up actions and triggers based on location.

What You'll Be Using

To customize your Mac for wherever you are, you'll use the following:

 Sidekick (*http://oomphalot.com/sidekick/*, $$)

 AppleScript Editor

Understanding Location-Based Actions

When manually changing settings, it's easy to forget to do things. You might, for example, forget to enable essential security settings—a small mistake that can lead to big problems. Using automated location-based actions is a best practice that saves you time and alleviates potential headaches.

Figure 15-1 illustrates how location-based actions work.

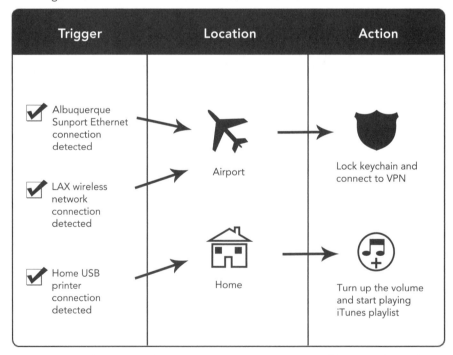

FIGURE 15-1: *The trigger, location, and action process of location-based actions*

An environmental variable, or *trigger*, switches your Mac to a different location and automatically executes actions you designate for that location. Setting up the initial configuration can be tricky. You'll start by adding locations (known as *places* in Sidekick) and actions, and then you'll set up triggers for the different places.

Getting Started with Sidekick

Sidekick is a utility that runs in the background—no icon is displayed in the Dock. To interact with the application, use the menu bar icon, as shown in Figure 15-2. After you add places, you'll be able to use this Sidekick menu to manually select a place if Sidekick doesn't automatically select it. To access the Sidekick interface, select **Configure** from this menu.

When you first install Sidekick, it automatically adds itself as a login item. (For more information about login items, see Chapter 2.) Having Sidekick start at login ensures that the location switching will occur automatically.

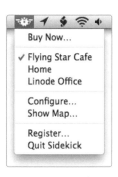

FIGURE 15-2: *The Sidekick menu is available by clicking the menu bar icon.*

Adding Places

To get started, you'll need to add places. *Place* in Sidekick is a bit of a misnomer. Places can correspond to physical locations, of course, but it's better to think of places as collections of actions that apply to certain kinds of physical locations. For example, if you work in multiple cafés and use the same actions at all of them, you would create one *café* place and then add multiple triggers for that place— there's no need to add every café as a separate place. (In "Setting Up Triggers" on page 152, you'll add street addresses to trigger a place.)

Here's how to add a place:

1. From the **Sidekick** menu, select **Configure**. The window shown in Figure 15-3 appears.
2. Click the **+ Add Place** button below the sidebar to add a place. The new place appears in the sidebar.
3. You can edit the name by clicking the place in the sidebar and typing a new name. (Remember, the name does not need to correspond to a physical location.)
4. (Optional) Pinpoint the place's location on the map. There are three ways to do this. You can type the address in the **Add Address** box, click the button to the right to pinpoint your current location based on the wireless network you are connected to, or click the pin button and drag it to a location on the map. Doing any of these creates a trigger based on location—something you'll learn more about later in this project.

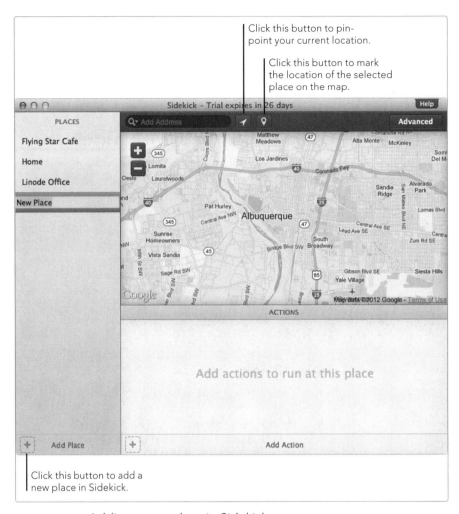

Click this button to pin-point your current location.

Click this button to mark the location of the selected place on the map.

Click this button to add a new place in Sidekick.

FIGURE 15-3: *Adding a new place in Sidekick*

Repeat these steps for every place—or type of place—you frequent. Some common examples include home, work, and school.

Configuring Actions

Actions are the changes to system and application settings that will be triggered when you start working in a place. Sidekick provides a number of preconfigured actions that allow you to do things like change your status in the Messages application, run a command in the Terminal, or change the Desktop picture. You can also perform system tasks, like change screensaver settings, connect to a server, set the default printer, and lock the keychain.

Here's how to add an action:

1. From the sidebar, select a place.
2. Click the **+ Add Action** button, as shown in Figure 15-4.
3. Select an action from the menu. Depending on the action you select, you may have to enter additional information to configure it.

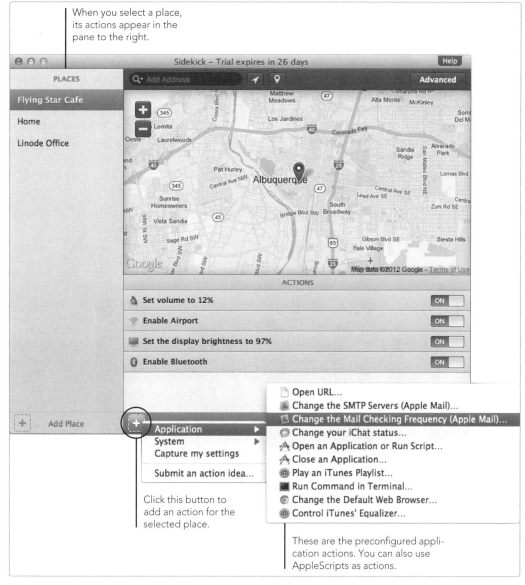

FIGURE 15-4: *Adding actions for the Flying Star Café—which the author highly recommends if you ever visit Albuquerque*

Repeat the procedure to add additional actions—you can add as many as you want. When you're finished, try selecting the place from the Sidekick menu to see if the actions execute.

Setting Up Triggers

Now that you've added places and actions, you need to tell Sidekick when to trigger the actions for those places. You'll use these triggers to associate a place type (such as Café) with a particular location (such as Starbucks, your neighborhood coffee shop, and so on). The more triggers you configure, the better Sidekick will work for you.

You can identify three variables as triggers: addresses (physical location), networks, and connected devices.

✳ *NOTE:* **Sidekick uses location services to pinpoint your physical location, so you'll need to use the network or a connected device for locations that do not have a wireless network.**

Here's how to add a trigger to Sidekick:

1. From the **Sidekick** menu, select **Configure**.
2. From the sidebar, select a place.
3. Click **Advanced**. The window shown in Figure 15-5 appears.

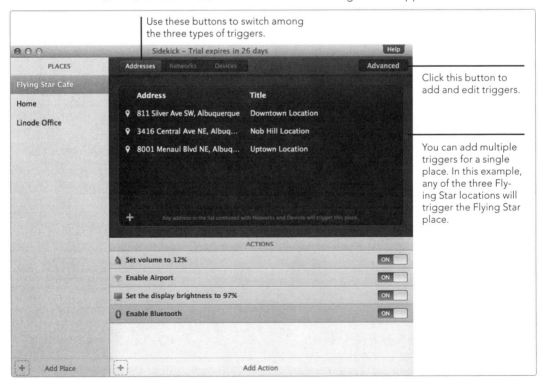

FIGURE 15-5: Creating triggers based on addresses, networks, and connected devices

4. Click **Addresses** and then click the **+** button to add triggers for street addresses. An address may already be shown if Sidekick was able to determine your location based on the wireless network you were connected to when you created the place.

5. Click **Networks** and then click the **+** button to add triggers for Ethernet and wireless networks. Wireless networks require a name, and you can optionally add an IP address for either Ethernet or wireless networks if the network router assigns an IP address to your computer.

6. Click **Devices** and then click the **+** button to add triggers for any device that is currently connected to your computer. For example, if you connect your MacBook to a second display when you're at home, you could use that display as a trigger for the "Home" place.

Repeat the procedure to add additional triggers—you can add as many as you want. Once you've added triggers, Sidekick starts silently monitoring networks and connected USB devices. When a change is detected that links to a different place, the place is switched, and the actions for that place are automatically executed.

Manually Switching Places

When using triggers to switch places isn't practical, or if you just find yourself in a new coffee shop, you can manually switch between places by using the Sidekick menu in the menu bar. By using this menu, you can use Sidekick to switch a desktop Mac's settings at different times of day or to switch between various computing configurations, like work and gaming modes. For example, you could set work mode to connect you to the servers and printers at work and gaming mode to turn off the screensaver and set your iChat status to away.

Using AppleScripts as Actions

You may have noticed that Sidekick doesn't provide a ton of preconfigured actions. Fortunately, you can use AppleScripts as actions—a powerful feature that allows you to further customize your location settings. (For more information about AppleScript, see Chapter 12.)

To better understand how you can use AppleScript with Sidekick, imagine you want to connect to a VPN while at your Café place. (You can read more about VPNs in Chapter 29.) In this example, pretend you already use WiTopia's personalVPN (*http://www.witopia.net/*, $), which comes with the Viscosity VPN application for OS X. To connect to the VPN with Sidekick, you need to create an AppleScript that launches Viscosity and initiates a VPN connection.

Here's how to create an AppleScript action and trigger it when you switch to the Café location:

1. Open the AppleScript Editor application.
2. Type the following text into the editor window, as shown in Figure 15-6:

```
tell application "Viscosity" to connect "us - Atlanta, GA"
```

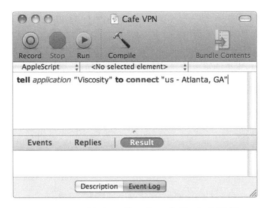

FIGURE 15-6: *Using the AppleScript Editor to create an advanced action for Sidekick*

3. Save the AppleScript.
4. From the **Sidekick** menu, select **Configure**.
5. From the sidebar, select the Café place.
6. Click the **+ Add Action** button.
7. Select **Open an Application or Run Script…**.
8. Select your AppleScript and click **Save**.

Your Mac will connect to the VPN the next time the Café place is invoked.

Of course, this is just one example of how you can use AppleScript to create your own actions. If you're a scripting pro, Sidekick can do just about anything with the applications on your Mac. The possibilities are endless!

Additional Ideas for Triggering Actions

You can download and install plug-ins to integrate Sidekick with a number of third-party applications, like Adium and 1Password. Each plug-in contains actions for an application that can be triggered based on place. Check out the plug-in library on Sidekick's website (*http://oomphalot.com/sidekick/*).

Sidekick isn't the only application that can trigger actions based on location. MarcoPolo (*http://www.symonds.id.au/marcopolo/*, free) provides more triggers than Sidekick, but its interface is confusing and it is no longer being updated.

PART 4

Managing Your Life

16

Managing Your Email

Email is a powerful form of communication. It's fast and free and practically universally available—everyone has an email address these days. But with power comes problems, and email has plenty. Incoming messages can be distracting, for one thing. Another challenge is successfully managing the messages you receive to ensure that you can find them in the future. And how do you best preserve the thousands of messages you've accumulated over the years?

In this project, you'll learn how to tune the Mail application to process email exactly the way you want. You'll also use third-party applications to process email with keystrokes, to tag messages, and to archive email for the future. By the time you're finished, you'll have taken control of your inbox.

Project goal: Set up rules, mailboxes, and third-party applications to manage email.

What You'll Be Using

To make sure your email is an asset—not a liability—you'll use the following:

 Mail

 MailTags (*http://www.indev.ca/MailTags.html*, $$)

 Mail Act-On (*http://www.indev.ca/MailActOn.html*, $$)

 MailSteward (*http://www.mailsteward.com/*, $$$)

Taming the Mail Application

This project assumes that you're using the Mail application included with OS X to send and receive email. There's no reason *not* to be using this app—its interface is easy to understand, and it has some powerful features. In this section, you'll learn how to use some of Mail's lesser-known features to better manage your email.

Controlling How Often Mail Checks for Email

A constant barrage of new email can be distracting. To minimize email-related interruptions and stay sane, you can adjust Mail's preferences to check for email less often—like every 30 or 60 minutes—or stop it from checking automatically at all. This can be a way to increase your productivity without ignoring people altogether.

Here's how to change when Mail checks for new email:

1. Open the Mail application.
2. From the **Mail** menu, select **Preferences**. The window shown in Figure 16-1 appears.
3. From the **Check for new messages** menu, select a time interval.

If you choose **Manually**, you'll have to check for messages by clicking the Get New Messages button. This is a good way to prevent information overload, since you'll only receive new email messages after clicking the button. On the other hand, you might forget to check your email and miss an important message.

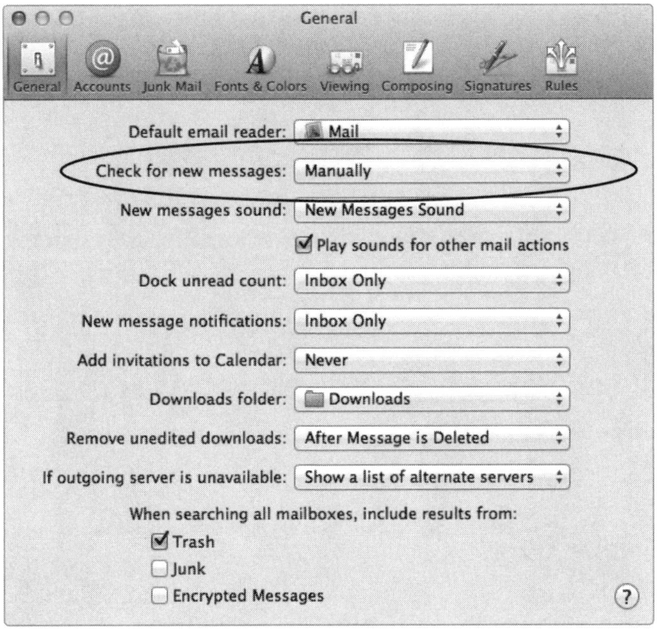

FIGURE 16-1: *Change when Mail checks for new messages to prevent email overload.*

Using Rules to Filter Incoming Messages

If you've ever wished that you could automatically move messages that meet certain criteria to special mailboxes, you're in luck. *Rules* are custom sets of instructions that can scan your incoming email and automatically put it where you want it. For example, you could create a rule to move all the email messages from your parents into a mailbox you created for just their messages, as you'll learn below.

Here's how to create a rule to filter messages:

1. Open the Mail application.
2. Create a new mailbox for your parents' messages by selecting **New Mailbox** from the **Mailbox** menu.
3. From the **Mail** menu, select **Preferences**.
4. Click **Rules**. The window shown in Figure 16-2 appears.
5. Click **Add Rule**. The window in Figure 16-3 appears.
6. Enter a name for the rule in the **Description** field.
7. For this example—remember, we're filtering messages from our parents— we need to add a condition that activates the rule when we receive a message from our parents. Select **From**, **Contains**, and then the name or email address of a parent.
8. Now add an action that Mail will perform if the conditions are met. For this example, select **Move Message** and then select the mailbox you created to store parental email.
9. Click **OK**.

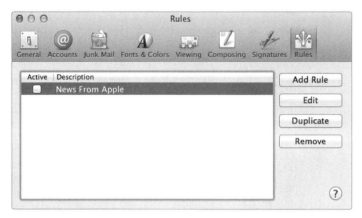

FIGURE 16-2: *All of Mail's rules are listed here.*

Use these buttons to add and remove conditions.

Use these buttons to add and remove actions.

FIGURE 16-3: *Add conditions and actions to be performed if the conditions are met.*

Going forward, all of the email your parents send will be stored in the mailbox you designated. (Existing messages in your inbox are not affected.) You can click the **+** buttons to add other conditions and actions.

What else can you do with rules? If you subscribe to mailing lists, you could create separate folders for the messages from those lists. Or if you wanted to prioritize the messages from your boss, you could flag all of her messages. You can even forward all incoming messages from a certain sender to another email address.

Use your imagination to create your own powerful email rules using the many conditions and actions available. The goal is to create a set of rules capable of prioritizing incoming messages and bringing the important ones to your attention.

Creating a Smart Mailbox

If you find yourself frequently searching for messages, consider creating a *smart mailbox*—a container for messages that match certain criteria. You can think of a smart mailbox as a "saved search" that's capable of finding specific types of messages again and again, whether they're in your inbox or not. Smart mailboxes are similar to rules, but there is a key difference. Rules can apply actions to messages—they're great for *doing* things to messages, like moving them to a different mailbox or forwarding them to a different email address. Smart mailboxes, on the other hand, just help you find messages.

Here's how to create a smart mailbox:

1. Open the Mail application.
2. From the **Mailbox** menu, select **New Smart Mailbox**. The window shown in Figure 16-4 appears.

FIGURE 16-4: *Build a Smart Mailbox by adding conditions to limit the messages that will be displayed.*

3. Click the **+** button to add a new condition.
4. Configure a condition by selecting options from the menus.
5. Click **OK** to create the Smart Mailbox. The Smart Mailbox appears in the sidebar, as shown in Figure 16-5.

Now you can access your smart mailbox. It should already contain messages, if any meet the criteria you specified. (Unlike rules, smart mailboxes collect messages that you've already received.) If you ever want to change the conditions of the smart mailbox, just right-click it and select **Edit Smart Mailbox**.

FIGURE 16-5: *You can access Smart Mailboxes from the sidebar.*

Categorizing Email with Tags

To create an effective set of email organization principles for the future, most people look at the messages they've received in the past. Since most email originates again and again from the same senders, this approach makes sense. But you can't anticipate everything. Bosses come and go, new mailing lists are launched, and new friends are made while others fade into obscurity. For these reasons and others, categorizing messages with *tags* is very useful.

Using tags to categorize content has gained popularity in recent years. For example, if you have a blog, you may have tagged blog posts to appear in certain categories, such as "work" or "family." An application called MailTags (*http://www.indev.ca/MailTags.html*, $$) takes the concept a step further by allowing you to assign keywords, project names, colors, priorities, and notes to any email message. Once you have email tagged, it's easy to find messages in certain categories. Once you've used MailTags for a while, you'll wonder how you ever got by without it.

Tagging Messages

MailTags integrates seamlessly with the Mail application. When you install the application, Mail's interface will just be slightly modified to allow tagging.

Here's how to tag messages with MailTags:

1. Install MailTags, if you haven't already. A free 30-day trial is available.
2. Open the Mail application.
3. Open an email message. You'll notice that there's a new + button on the right side of the message, as shown in Figure 16-6—that's MailTags.
4. Click the **+** button. The pop-up window shown in Figure 16-7 appears.

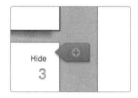

FIGURE 16-6: *Click the + button to add tags with MailTags.*

FIGURE 16-7: *Tagging email messages with MailTags*

5. Enter tags for the email message. Keywords are the most common type of tag, but you can also use a color or project name. You can even use MailTags to set a reminder in the Calendar application.

* **NOTE:** MailTags allows freestyle tagging, which means you can come up with your own keywords. Just start typing a word and then press RETURN when you're finished.

You've just tagged your first email message!

Creating Effective Tags

MailTags makes it easy to tag messages—a bit *too* easy. Take some time to think about the tags you need and why you need them. The whole point of this exercise is to make your life easier, not more difficult. Remember, tagging messages should help you find them again weeks, months, or years down the road. If you start creating a bunch of keywords without thinking about how you'll use them, you could wind up with five keywords for messages from one recipient—not helpful at all.

Coming up with descriptive tags and using them consistently takes practice. I recommend tagging messages in one of two ways. Categorize by sender, such as using "family" as a keyword for messages from your brother and sister. Or categorize by message type, such as using the color yellow for all messages related to the high-priority projects you're working on.

Finding Tagged Messages

MailTags is fully integrated into Mail's search. To find messages you've tagged in the past, just type a keyword or a tag into Mail's search field, as shown in Figure 16-8. For example, to find messages that you've tagged with the "work" keyword, type **work** into the field and then select the **work** keyword from the menu.

FIGURE 16-8: *Searching by keyword tags*

By the way, searching for messages is a good way to tell whether or not your tagging skills are effective. If you can't find a message, you may need to revisit the tags you're using. Ask yourself periodically if there's something you could be doing to categorize messages in a more effective manner.

Processing Email with Keystrokes

The tools and skills discussed so far will be of great benefit to all readers, no matter how many messages they send and receive. But if you send and receive massive amounts of email—100 or more messages a day—you'll need even more help. Mail Act-On (*http://www.indev.ca/MailActOn.html*, $$) is a third-party tool that was created for heavy-duty users. Install this, and you can tag and move messages using nothing but your keyboard—it's a real efficiency booster.

Using Mail Act-On

While this tool can help your productivity, it can also take some getting used to. If you're like most people, you're accustomed to managing email with your mouse. You drag and drop messages from one folder to another, and if you use MailTags, you're used to clicking around in that interface as well. Mail Act-On lets you do that stuff with the keyboard.

Here's how to get started with Mail Act-On:

1. Install Mail Act-On, if you haven't already. A free 30-day trial is available.
2. Open the Mail application.
3. Select a message in your inbox.
4. Press F1. (Many users will need to press both the F1 and FN keys.) The menu shown in Figure 16-9 appears.
5. To select one of the options displayed in this menu, press the corresponding key on the keyboard.
6. Depending on the option you select, you may need to make other selections. For example, if you wanted to move the message to a folder, you would press M and then use the arrow keys to select a folder.

FIGURE 16-9: *The Mail Act-On screen*

Give it a couple of days to grow on you, and you might find that Mail Act-On is a good fit for your email management needs.

Configuring Keystrokes

Once you get the hang of Mail Act-On, you'll want to do even more with it. The biggest stumbling block is that main menu. Most of the time, you'll know exactly what you want to do with the message you selected. Having to press F1 to invoke the main menu and then having to press another key to select an option is a real drag.

Fortunately, there's a way to bypass the main menu. If you memorize the keys mapped to each menu item, you can jump right to the option you want. Here's how to access and configure the menu keys for Mail Act-On:

1. Open the Mail application.
2. From the **Mail** menu, select **Preferences**.
3. Click **Mail Act-On**.
4. Click **Menus**. The window shown in Figure 16-10 appears. Notice that the menu keys for each menu are displayed in the table.
5. Select a menu item to configure its preferences.

Now you're ready to roll without the main menu. To get started, press a menu key (like F3 to move a message to another folder). See? Things go a lot faster now.

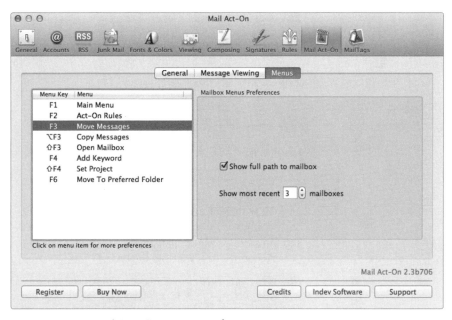

FIGURE 16-10: *Mail Act-On menu preferences*

Archiving Email

If you have thousands of messages just sitting in Mail, you might have a problem. See, the Mail application wasn't designed to store or search through tens of thousands of messages. That's why it's best to let a third-party application called MailSteward (*http://www.mailsteward.com/*, $$$) take care of your age-old email. It packs all of your messages into one file that can be easily stored on an external hard drive or backed up to a server. Plus, the MailSteward interface makes it easy to search for old messages, if the need arises.

Setting Up MailSteward

To get started with MailSteward, you'll need to create a database file and configure the settings for the archive. The database file is where MailSteward will keep all of your email, so store it in a safe place.

Here's how to set up MailSteward:

1. Download and install the MailSteward application, if you haven't already. A free version is available that holds up to 15,000 messages.
2. Open the MailSteward application. The window shown in Figure 16-11 appears.

FIGURE 16-11: *Working with data-bases in MailSteward*

3. Click **New** to create a new database file. A save dialog appears.
4. Enter a name for the database and click **Create**. The database file is created, and the settings window appears.
5. Click **Accounts**. The window shown in Figure 16-12 appears.

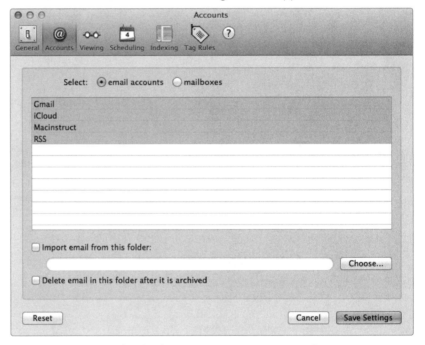

FIGURE 16-12: *Specify which accounts you want to archive.*

6. By default, MailSteward automatically selects all of your email accounts in Mail for archiving. If you don't want to archive email from a certain account, click it to deselect it.

7. Click **Indexing**. The window shown in Figure 16-13 appears.

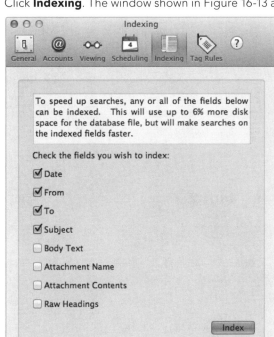

FIGURE 16-13: *Selecting fields to index will speed up archive searches.*

8. Select the fields you want MailSteward to index. Selecting at least a couple of these fields will make your life a whole lot easier when you have to search for old email. I recommend that you select **Date**, **From**, **To**, and **Subject**.
9. Once you're finished configuring the settings, click **Save Settings**.

Good work—you've created the database file and configured the settings. Now you're ready to tell MailSteward to copy your email into the database. (This is called *creating the archive*.)

Creating the Archive

When you create an archive with MailSteward, it collects email sent and received between certain dates and stores it in the database. You could create several archives—one for each year, for example—or just create one big archive for all of your messages. Note that MailSteward does not delete messages from the Mail application.

Here's how to create an archive in MailSteward:

1. Open the MailSteward application. The MailSteward window appears, as shown in Figure 16-14.
2. Click **archive**. The dialog shown in Figure 16-15 appears.

FIGURE 16-14: *The MailSteward window*

FIGURE 16-15: *Archive all of your email or only some of it.*

3. Set dates to archive only the email sent and received between certain dates. Or, to archive all of your email, leave all of the fields set to **All**.
4. Click **Archive**. MailSteward starts copying your email to the database.

The process can take several minutes, depending on the number of email messages you're archiving. Repeat the process to create other archives. With the paid version of MailSteward, you can archive as many messages as you want.

Finding Messages in the Archive

An email archive doesn't do you any good if you can't find any of the messages stored in it. Fortunately, MailSteward has a great interface for searching and browsing messages. You can also use the interface to save or delete messages.

Here's how to find messages in a MailSteward archive:

1. Open the MailSteward application.
2. Click **Browse** in the MailSteward window. The window shown in Figure 16-16 appears.

Now you can scroll through all of the messages in the archive. You can also print, save, delete, export, and forward messages. To search for messages, click **search**, either in this window or in the main MailSteward window.

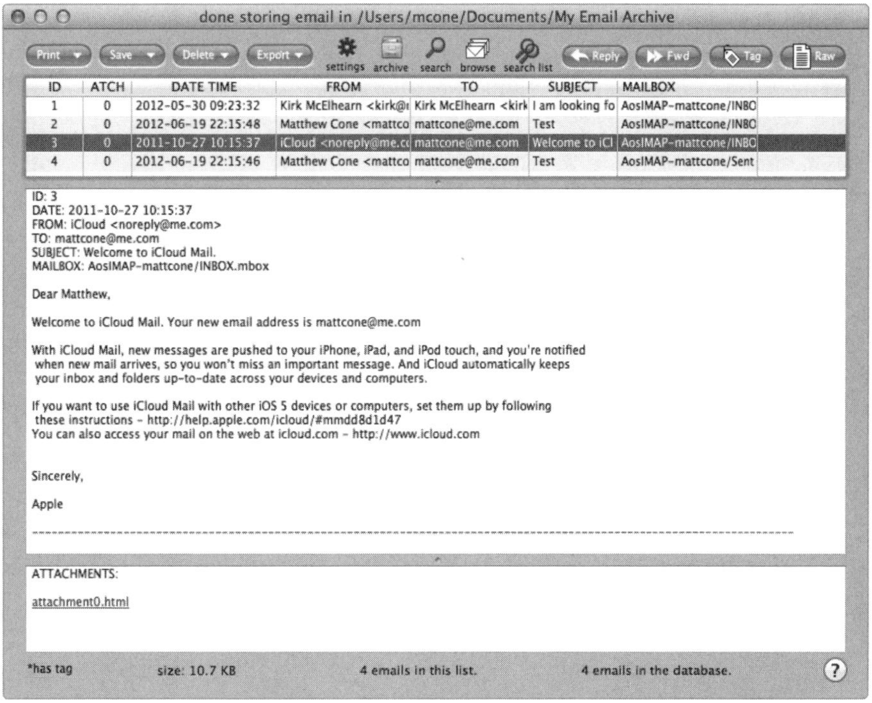

FIGURE 16-16: *Using the MailSteward interface to read archived messages*

Additional Ideas for Managing Your Email

If you're a Gmail user (*http://www.gmail.com/*, free), you should know that Gmail has many of the features discussed in this chapter, like tags. (They're called "labels" in Gmail.) To take advantage of Gmail's organization features on your Mac, check out an application called Sparrow (*http://sprw.me/*, $).

Finally, here are some words of advice: When pondering solutions for managing your email, keep in mind that no one magic bullet can make managing your email easy. Experiment with tagging, keystrokes, and archiving until you find the combination of tools that works for you.

17 Killing Spam

Few words can conjure up images of replica watches, hot stock picks, and vulgar herbal supplements the way *spam* does. Junk email has clogged up inboxes since the early '90s, and the problem has only gotten worse. Some experts estimate that spam now comprises 92 percent of all email sent.

Spam filters are effective at protecting against this digital onslaught. Once configured, a good filter can automatically remove up to 98 percent of the junk mail from your inbox. Consider the alternative—manually sifting through 100 messages just to find 8 good ones—and the spam filter's value is apparent.

Two options are presented in this project: using the client-side spam filter built into the Mail application or relying on Gmail to provide server-side spam filtering before email is downloaded to your computer. Both options have advantages and disadvantages, but as a general rule of thumb, individuals who send and receive email from more than one device (like a smartphone or tablet) will want to use server-side spam filtering. Skip ahead to "Filtering Spam on a Server with Gmail" on page 176 for that solution.

Project goal: Filter spam before it reaches your inbox.

What You'll Be Using

To avoid seeing spam, you'll use the following:

 Mail

Gмail   Gmail (*http://www.gmail.com/*, free)

Filtering Junk Mail in the Mail Application

Apple's Mail application includes a junk mail filter that can automatically identify and delete spam. Configuring this feature is a three-part process. The first step is enabling the filter and learning how it works. Next comes training the filter to make it more accurate at identifying spam and legitimate email messages. Finally you'll turn on automation to let the Mail application automatically move or delete messages marked as spam.

It's important not to skip steps. Initially, the Mail application won't be able to correctly identify which messages are spam. Automating the filter before you've properly trained it could be a recipe for disaster—legitimate email messages could be marked as spam and deleted!

Enabling the Junk Mail Filter

The junk mail filter is turned off by default. When you turn this feature on, the Mail application starts scanning incoming mail for spam. Those messages that contain content that matches certain rules—keywords in the body of the message, for example, or known bad senders—are marked as spam.

Here's how to enable the junk mail filter in the Mail application:

1. Open the Mail application.
2. Select **Preferences ▸ Mail**.
3. Click **Junk Mail**. The window shown in Figure 17-1 appears.
4. Select the **Enable junk mail filtering** checkbox.
5. Select **Mark as junk mail, but leave it in my Inbox**. This is the best option to select when getting started with the Junk Mail feature. You'll see which messages get marked as spam and have an opportunity to train Junk Mail to be more accurate.
6. Select the three checkboxes under **The following types of messages are exempt from junk mail filtering**. These options help ensure that valid email messages are not marked as spam.

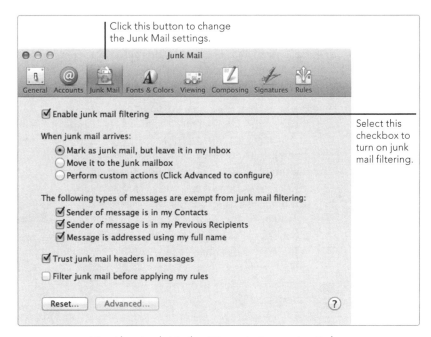

Click this button to change the Junk Mail settings.

Select this checkbox to turn on junk mail filtering.

FIGURE 17-1: *Use the Junk Mail settings to tag potential spam messages and perform actions on them.*

7. Select **Trust junk mail headers in messages**. This can improve the accuracy of junk mail filtering by allowing the Mail application to use any headers added by your service provider's email server.

8. Close the preferences window.

    Now when you receive email, Mail highlights spam messages in brown and labels them with a mailbag icon, as shown in Figure 17-2. (Junk mail filtering does not act on messages that are already in your inbox.)

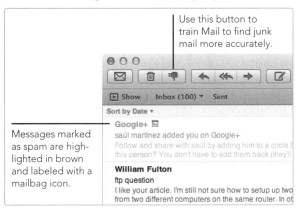

Use this button to train Mail to find junk mail more accurately.

Messages marked as spam are highlighted in brown and labeled with a mailbag icon.

FIGURE 17-2: *Spam is clearly labeled so you can spot it easily.*

Unless you get a lot of email, it might take a couple of days to receive enough messages to proceed to the training. Wait until you have at least 20 messages—both spam and legitimate—before you proceed to the next section.

Training Mail to Filter Spam Accurately

It might seem silly to leave spam messages in your inbox, but you'll likely find that the junk mail filter isn't totally accurate, at least not initially. Some legitimate messages may be marked as spam, and some spam messages may appear legitimate. To help the junk mail filter correctly identify spam, you need to train it by clicking the thumbs-up and thumbs-down buttons on the toolbar, as shown in Figure 17-3.

When you select a message that is not marked as spam, the thumbs-down button appears. Click that button to mark the message as spam. Likewise, when you select a message that is marked as spam, the thumbs-up button appears. Click that thumbs-up button to mark the message as legitimate.

FIGURE 17-3: *Just like in the real world, thumbs-down is bad and thumbs-up is good.*

This serves two important purposes. First, you need to label email messages correctly for your records—there should never be legitimate email marked as spam in your inbox. Clicking the buttons also helps train the junk mail filter to recognize spam and legitimate email more accurately in the future.

Every time you click one of the buttons, you're helping the junk mail filter learn good and bad recipients, headers, and text in the body of the message. Eventually the junk mail filter will be accurate enough that you'll no longer need to manually change the status of messages. At that point, you can automate the junk mail filter to process spam and whisk it out of your inbox.

Taking Off the Training Wheels

When you're confident in the Mail application's ability to correctly tag spam messages (and *not* tag legitimate messages as spam), it's time to automate junk mail filtering so it automatically removes spam from your inbox. Depending on the action you select, spam messages won't be permanently deleted—they'll just be moved out of your inbox and into a separate folder where you can review them if you suspect that a legitimate message was marked as spam.

Here's how to automate the junk mail filter:

1. Open the Mail application.
2. Select **Preferences ▸ Mail**.
3. Click **Junk Mail**. The window shown in Figure 17-4 appears.
4. Select **Perform custom actions**. This provides much more flexibility than the **Move it to the Junk mailbox** option, which only moves spam to a Junk folder.
5. Click **Advanced**. The window shown in Figure 17-5 appears.
6. In the top part of the window, set the conditions required for performing the actions.

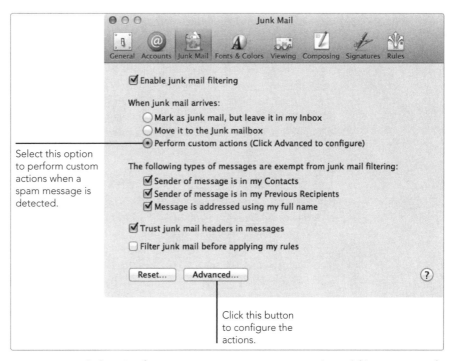

Select this option to perform custom actions when a spam message is detected.

Click this button to configure the actions.

FIGURE 17-4: Select Perform custom actions *to get junk mail filtering out of training mode.*

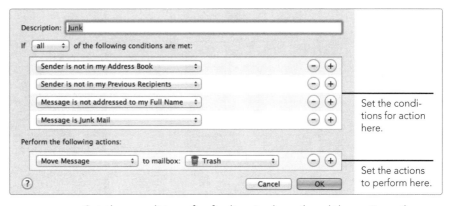

Set the conditions for action here.

Set the actions to perform here.

FIGURE 17-5: Set the conditions for finding junk mail and the actions that should be performed when it is discovered.

7. In the bottom part of the window, set the action(s) that should be performed when the conditions are met. In this example, all spam messages are moved to the Trash, but you can set the action to whatever you want.

8. Click **OK**.

9. Close the preferences window.

From now on, Mail moves all incoming messages marked as spam to the Trash. (Just as when you enabled the junk mail filter, these new settings apply only to new messages, not the existing messages in your inbox.)

If you're completely confident in the Mail application's spam-filtering abilities, you can create an action that automatically deletes spam when it's detected. This can be risky, however. Since junk mail filtering is rarely 100 percent accurate, you're bound to delete some legitimate messages. Of course, that may be a risk you're willing to live with, depending on your tolerance for spam.

Filtering Spam on a Server with Gmail

Filtering spam on your Mac is a *client-side* solution that requires you to download all email from the server and filter it using rules on your computer. This approach has some drawbacks. If you use other devices—like the iPhone or iPad—to send and receive email, you'll need to install and configure spam filters on those devices, too, as illustrated in Figure 17-6. Plus, most client-side spam filters aren't all that accurate, even after they've been trained by users.

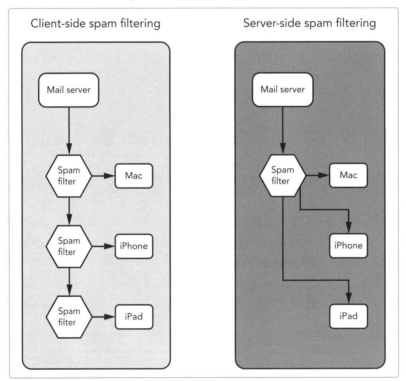

FIGURE 17-6: *For people who use multiple devices, server-side spam filtering is preferable to client-side filtering.*

Server-side spam filtering kills junk mail before you even see it on your computer. The difference between this and client-side filtering is that the spam filter is implemented on the mail server instead of your personal device.

Server-side spam filtering is ideal for several reasons. You don't have to train the filter, for one thing. Gmail, Google's free email service, has for years relied on millions of users to train its spam filter. At this point, it's about 98 percent accurate and certainly one of the best server-side spam filters available. And because the filtering occurs on the server, there's nothing to configure on your Mac or other devices. Just add your Gmail account to the email client, and you'll start receiving spam-free email.

What about all of your other email accounts—the ones from other service providers that you started using years ago? Not to worry. Gmail can automatically download messages from up to five other email accounts and apply its built-in spam filter to *all* of your email. And because you can also use Gmail to send messages from the other email accounts, your friends and family won't know the difference. You don't even need to tell them your new Gmail address. For the purposes of this project, Gmail is just a server-side spam filter for your existing email accounts.

Adding Your Email Accounts to Gmail

As you might expect, implementing server-side spam filtering starts with creating a Gmail account and adding your other email accounts to Gmail. When you sign up for a Gmail account, you get a new email address and several gigabytes of storage space on Google's servers.

After you create the account, you'll need to configure Gmail to download messages from your other email accounts. (Gmail can only download messages from POP3 email accounts at this time.) In Gmail-speak, this is known as *adding email accounts*. Gmail automatically downloads messages and filters spam from the email accounts you've added.

Here's how to add your email account to Gmail:

1. Log in to Gmail (*http://www.gmail.com/*, free) or create a new Gmail account specifically for filtering spam. Creating a new Gmail account is recommended. It's free!
2. Click the gear icon in the top-right corner. From the menu, select **Settings**, as shown in Figure 17-7.
3. Click **Accounts**. The screen shown in Figure 17-8 appears.
4. Click **Add a POP3 mail account you own**.
5. Enter your email address and click **Next Step**. The screen shown in Figure 17-9 appears.
6. Enter the username, password, and POP server for your email account.

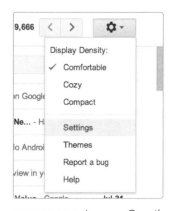

FIGURE 17-7: *In your Gmail account, select Settings from the gear menu.*

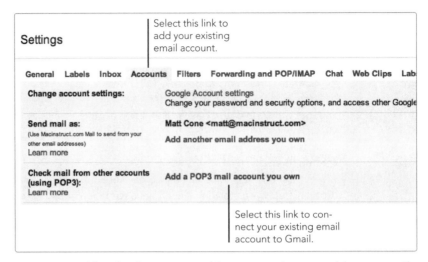

FIGURE 17-8: *Use the Accounts and Import settings to add your email account.*

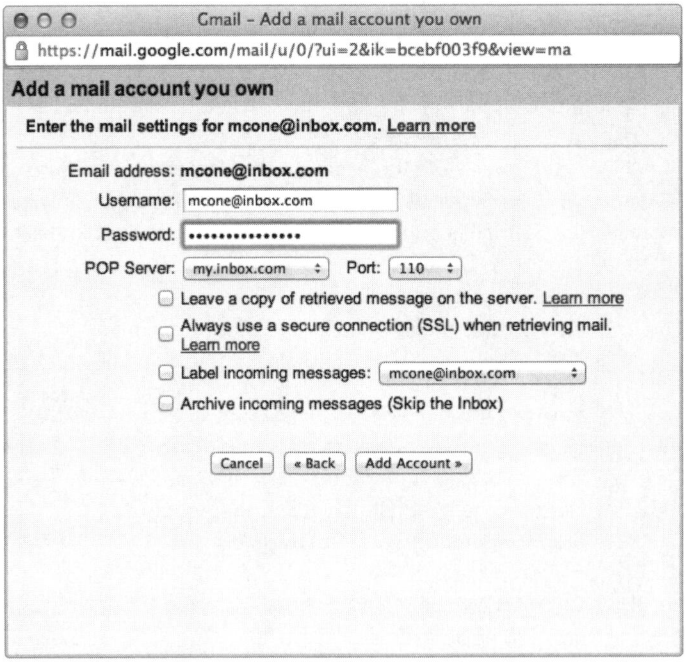

FIGURE 17-9: *Enter the settings for your email account.*

✻ **NOTE:** Gmail does a decent job of automatically detecting the POP server and port, but you might have to change the settings to work with your service provider's mail server. When in doubt, contact your email service provider to obtain the correct information.

7. Click **Add Account**. Your email account is added to Gmail.
8. Gmail allows you to send messages from the email account. This can be helpful if you frequently use an iPhone, iPad, or other device to send email. Select **Yes** to allow Gmail to send messages from the email account or **No** to disable this feature.
9. Click **Finish**. Gmail adds your email account, as shown in Figure 17-10.

Check mail from other accounts (using POP3): Learn more	mcone@inbox.com Last checked: 33 minutes ago. View history Check mail now Add a POP3 mail account you own

FIGURE 17-10: *The email account appears in the Accounts and Import settings.*

Gmail periodically checks your email account for new mail automatically. Any new messages are downloaded to your Gmail account.

Since Gmail allows you to add up to five email accounts, this is a great opportunity to create a central email account for all of the email accounts you use. Then you'll be able to use Gmail to send and receive email from all of your accounts.

Enabling IMAP Access

Now you can use the Gmail website to send and receive messages from your email accounts. But it's just not as convenient as using the native email clients for Mac, iPhone, and iPad. Ideally, once you configure all of the settings, you'll never have to log in to the Gmail website again.

You can ditch Gmail's website entirely by enabling IMAP. Enabling IMAP access allows your Mac, iPhone, iPad, and other devices to send and receive email from your Gmail account using third-party email clients. Gmail also allows you to enable POP download, which is an option required for some email clients, but it's better to use IMAP whenever possible. (One important distinction between POP and IMAP is that Mail does not download messages from the IMAP server to your computer—all of the messages are stored on the server only.)

Here's how to enable IMAP access:

1. Log in to Gmail.
2. Click the gear icon in the top-right corner. From the menu, select **Settings**.
3. Click **Forwarding and POP/IMAP**.
4. In the **IMAP Access** section of the web page, select **Enable IMAP** and **Auto-Expunge off**, as shown in Figure 17-11.
5. Click **Save Changes**. IMAP access is now enabled.

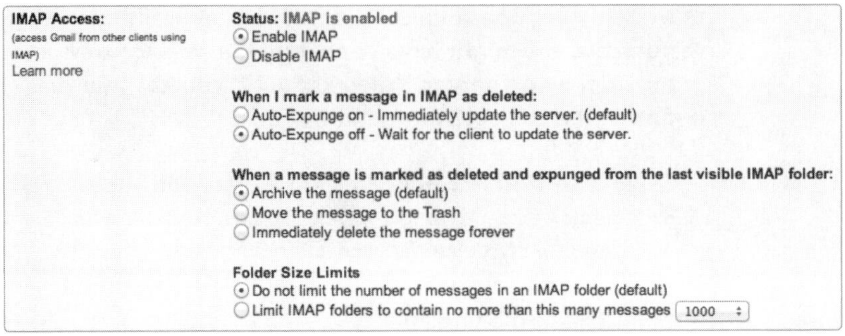

FIGURE 17-11: *Turn on IMAP to access email from all of your devices.*

In the next section, you'll learn how to connect your Gmail account to the Mail application. If you'd like to use your Gmail account with other email clients and devices, check out the link at the bottom of the Forwarding and POP/IMAP settings—you'll find instructions on connecting Gmail to a variety of applications and devices.

Using the Mail Application to Read Your Gmail

This is the easy part. Gmail is already filtering all of the spam from your email account—all you have to do is kick back and read the email on your Mac. Connecting your Gmail account to the Mail application is the final step.

Here's how to use the Mail application to read your Gmail:

1. Open the Mail application.
2. Select **Preferences ▸ Mail**.
3. Click **Accounts**. The window shown in Figure 17-12 appears.
4. Click the **+** button.
5. Enter your name, Gmail email address, and password.
6. Click **Create**. The Mail application connects to Gmail, verifies your username and password, and displays a summary screen.
7. Click **Create** again to add the Gmail account to the Mail application.

After you close the preferences window, Mail connects to Gmail and starts displaying your email in the inbox. You can sort through the spam if you want by selecting the Spam folder on the sidebar, as shown in Figure 17-13.

If you enabled the Mail application's junk mail filter by following the instructions in "Filtering Junk Mail in the Mail Application" on page 172, you might want to turn that feature off now. Sure, you could leave it enabled, but why bother? Gmail is already filtering all of the spam and probably doing a more effective job of it!

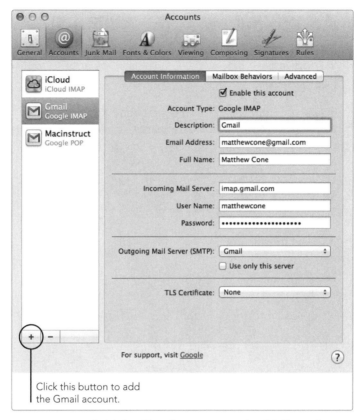

Click this button to add
the Gmail account.

FIGURE 17-12: *Add the Gmail account to the Mail application for easy email access on your Mac.*

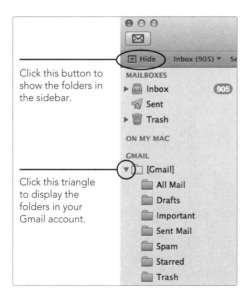

Click this button to
show the folders in
the sidebar.

Click this triangle
to display the
folders in your
Gmail account.

FIGURE 17-13: *See the folders within your Gmail account.*

Additional Ideas for Killing Spam

There are other client-side spam filters for OS X. SpamSieve (*http://c-command .com/spamsieve/*, $$$) is one of the most popular, and for good reason. This application interfaces with many email applications and uses an advanced filtering method for greater accuracy. SpamSieve's configuration is similar to Mail's junk mail filter, but training takes less time and is more accurate.

Those who use Gmail will quickly discover that it provides many benefits other than spam filtering. For example, you can create rules that process email at the server, rather than on your computer. This could be a real advantage if you keep receiving, say, large email messages with embedded media files and you'd prefer to delete the messages on the server instead of downloading them to your computer and deleting them there.

18

Creating Quick and Easy Alerts

Sometimes doing the simplest things with your Mac can seem difficult. For example, it's not immediately clear how to set a basic alarm that will remind you that your tea water is probably boiling in five minutes. Sure, you could use Calendar or Reminders to create these kinds of reminders, but it's not a quick or easy process.

Setting basic reminders—the ones too small for Calendar or Reminders but too important to forget—is best left to a couple of third-party applications. You can use the free application Pester to quickly set simple alerts, and the more advanced application Alarms displays a cool to-do list of reminders at the top of your screen and flashes a menu bar icon when it's time to do something. Both applications can help you quickly enter tasks and track them to completion.

Project goal: Use third-party applications to quickly and easily create alerts on your Mac.

What You'll Be Using

To set alerts with ease, you'll use the following:

 Pester (*http://sabi.net/nriley/software/*, free)

 Alarms (*http://www.mediaatelier.com/Alarms/*, $$)

Creating Basic Alerts

When you need to set an alarm for the smallest reminder, turn to Pester (*http://sabi.net/nriley/software/*, free). Just open the application, type a message that will appear on the screen when the alarm goes off, set a time for the alarm to go off, and then click **Set**, as shown in Figure 18-1. Pester does the rest, lying in wait until the time comes to alert you. By default, Pester bounces the Dock icon, displays the message and time on your screen, and plays the system alert sound. (The alerts can be changed, as you'll learn in "Configuring Alerts" on page 185.)

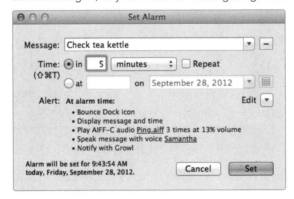

FIGURE 18-1: *Pester makes creating a basic reminder a snap.*

Setting Repeating Alarms

You can also set alarms to repeat at certain intervals. For example, if you had a cold and needed to remember to take cough medicine every four hours, you would set the time to 4 hours and select the **Repeat** checkbox. Unfortunately, Pester doesn't have the scheduling prowess of Calendar; you can't create a reminder and then set it to repeat on the third Wednesday of every month.

Configuring Alerts

A reminder won't do you any good if you can't see or hear the alarm. That's why it's important to customize the way Pester notifies you when an alarm goes off. There are several options.

Here's how to configure the alerts for an alarm in Pester:

1. Open the Pester application.
2. In the Set Alarm window, click the triangle button next to **Edit**. The window shown in Figure 18-2 appears.

FIGURE 18-2: *Pester provides many alert options—there's no way you'll miss this one!*

3. Select one or more checkboxes to turn on different alerts. You can set Pester to display a message on the screen, play an alert sound, speak a message, bounce the Dock icon, or display a Growl notification—or all of the above.
4. After you've enabled one or more alerts, click **Set** to set the alarm. Pester will display (or sound) the alerts when the alarm goes off.

You may find that different situations require different types of alerts. If you plan to be using your Mac when the alarm is scheduled to go off, you can get by with setting one of the notification alerts—you'll see it on the screen. If you might be away from your Mac when the alarm is scheduled to go off, consider turning up your Mac's volume and setting one of the audio alerts so you can hear it.

Creating Advanced Alerts

Pester is great for setting an occasional alarm, but it's not designed to manage lots of different alarms at once. To set a series of alarms, or for help managing your to-do list, try using an application called Alarms (*http://www.mediaatelier.com/Alarms/*, $$).

Using the Alarms Timeline

When you click the Alarms menu bar icon, an unobtrusive timeline slides down at the top of the screen—you use this for alarm entry and management, as shown in Figure 18-3. When it's time to do something, Alarms flashes its menu bar icon and plays a sound until you mark the task complete.

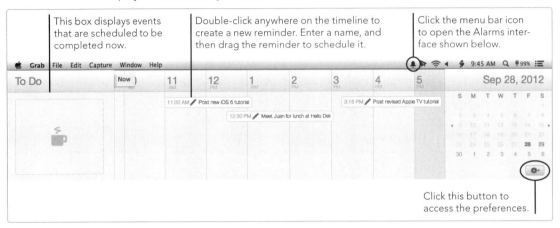

FIGURE 18-3: *Click the Alarm menu bar icon to display a timeline of reminders at the top of your screen.*

Here's how to create reminders with Alarms:

1. Open the Alarms application.
2. Click the **Alarms** menu bar icon. The timeline display slides down.
3. If you're creating a reminder for a day other than today, select a day from the calendar on the right.
4. Double-click anywhere on the timeline to create a new reminder. A text field appears.
5. Enter the reminder and press RETURN. The reminder appears on the timeline.
6. To schedule the reminder for a particular time, drag it to the appropriate place on the timeline.

When an alarm goes off, the reminder appears in the To Do list on the left. At that point, you can mark the reminder complete by clicking the checkmark, or you can reschedule it by dragging it back onto the timeline.

Synchronizing Alarms with Calendar and Contacts

In many ways, the Alarms application infringes on Calendar's territory. If you find yourself using the reminders in Alarms to complement Calendar, you might consider synchronizing Alarms with Calendar so that the reminders you create in Alarms are also displayed in Calendar. You can also configure Alarms to display any birthdays you've stored in Contacts.

Here's how to synchronize Alarms reminders with Calendar and Contacts:

1. Open the Alarms application.
2. Click the **Alarms** menu bar icon. The timeline display slides down.
3. Click the gear button in the lower-right corner and then select **Preferences** from the menu. The window shown in Figure 18-4 appears.

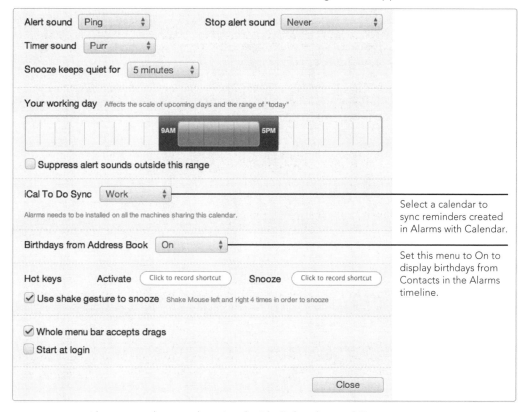

FIGURE 18-4: *Alarms can be synchronized with Calendar and Contacts.*

4. Select a calendar from the **iCal To Do Sync** menu. This ensures that all of the reminders you create in Alarms will automatically appear in the calendar you have selected.
5. Set the **Birthdays from Address Book** menu to **On**. This ensures that all of the birthdays stored in Contacts will appear in Alarms as reminders on those days.
6. Click **Close**.

Alarms will now synchronize reminders with the selected calendar and display birthdays from Contacts as reminders.

Additional Ideas for Reminders

Pester and Alarms can handle any and all of your simple alarms and reminders with ease. Of course, if you plan to create more sophisticated reminders and events, just use Reminders or Calendar. Or, better yet, use something better than Calendar, like Fantastical (*http://flexibits.com/*, $$) or BusyCal (*http://www.busymac.com/busycal/index.html*, $$$), two advanced calendar applications that take reminder scheduling to the next level. They even synchronize with online calendar services, like Google Calendar, which means you can access the events you create from your iOS or Android devices.

19 Managing Your Music

When it was first released back in 2001, iTunes was dedicated entirely to music. There wasn't a store for buying music, renting movies, or downloading podcasts back then. And there weren't any iPods, iPhones, or iPads to connect yet—let alone any applications for those devices. But over time, iTunes was modified to handle all of these things and more, effectively transforming the music application into what it is today: a confusing and cluttered media management center.

If you're ready to "get back to the music" and beef up your music management skills, you'll need more than just iTunes know-how. You'll need to enlist the help of several third-party tools and services that are designed to help you manage your music effectively. These tools will help you upgrade your music, create shortcuts for iTunes controls, add missing metadata, use multiple iTunes libraries, and even store your music in the cloud to make it accessible on your other computers and iOS devices. By the end of this project, you'll have put the "tunes" back in iTunes.

Project goal: Store your music in the cloud, upgrade your iTunes music, create shortcuts for iTunes controls, add missing metadata for songs, and start using multiple iTunes libraries.

What You'll Be Using

To manage your music effectively, you'll use the following:

 iTunes

 CoverSutra (*http://sophiestication.com/coversutra/*, $)

 TuneUp (*http://www.tuneupmedia.com/*, $$$)

 PowerTunes (*http://www.fatcatsoftware.com/powertunes/*, $$)

Getting Started with iTunes Match

iTunes Match is Apple's cloud music service. For a small yearly fee ($24.99), all of your music will be stored on iCloud's servers and made accessible to the other computers and iOS devices you are signed in to. You can download and stream your music from iCloud at any time.

Signing Up for iTunes Match

The first step is to sign up for iTunes Match, if you haven't already. You'll use your Apple ID to sign in and authorize the charge, and then iTunes will take care of the rest. All of the songs on your computer will be analyzed and *matched* to songs on the iCloud servers. The songs that can't be matched will be uploaded to Apple's servers from your computer.

Here's how to sign up for iTunes Match:

1. Open the iTunes application.
2. From the sidebar, select iTunes Match, as shown in Figure 19-1.
3. Click **Subscribe for $24.99 Per Year** and follow the instructions.
4. Once you've subscribed, iTunes analyzes the songs on your computer to determine which tracks are already available in iCloud and which tracks need to be uploaded. A message will be displayed when the process is complete.

Now that you've signed up and uploaded your music, you're ready to take advantage of some cool features.

FIGURE 19-1: *The iTunes Match window*

⁂ **NOTE:** You cannot use iTunes Match if you have more than 25,000 tracks in your iTunes library. See "Managing iTunes Libraries" on page 198 for instructions on breaking a big library up into separate, smaller libraries.

Upgrading Your Music

One of the best iTunes Match features has nothing to do with storing your music in the cloud: You can upgrade the matched music in your library to higher-quality, DRM-free songs—even those low-quality tracks you downloaded from Napster all those years ago. (Not all songs are available to be matched.) Upgrading is free with your iTunes Match subscription—you should definitely take advantage of it! This is a great option for people who imported a lot of music from CDs at lower-quality bit rates.

Here's how it works: First you'll create a smart playlist to find all of the songs that can be upgraded. Then you'll delete those songs from your computer and download them from iCloud. The new files will have higher bit rates for better sound, and they'll be free of copyright protection controls.

Here's how to upgrade your music with iTunes Match:

1. Open the iTunes application.
2. Select **File ▸ New Smart Playlist**. The window shown in Figure 19-2 appears.
3. Set the first rule to **Bit Rate is less than 256 kbps**.

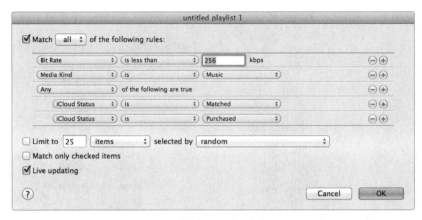

FIGURE 19-2: *Create a smart playlist to find the songs that can be upgraded with iTunes Match.*

4.   Click the **+** button to add a new rule.
5.   Set the second rule to **Media Kind is Music**.
6.   Hold down OPTION and click **+** to create a conditional rule.
7.   Set the third rule to **iCloud Status is Matched**.
8.   Click the **+** button to add a new rule.
9.   Set the fourth rule to **iCloud Status is Purchased**.
10.   Click **OK**. The playlist of upgradable songs appears in the sidebar.
11.   Select the playlist you just created.
12.   Select all of the songs in the playlist.
13.   Press OPTION-DELETE. A window appears asking if you want to delete the songs from your iTunes library. Click **Delete**. (Do *not* select the *Also delete these songs from iCloud* checkbox.) If iTunes asks if you want to move the files to the Trash, click **Move to Trash**.
14.   Since the songs are still on Apple's servers, they still appear in the playlist. Select all of the songs, right-click the list, and then select **Download**.

iTunes will download all of the songs in the playlist to your computer. When you get them back, they'll have bit rates of 265Kbps and no DRM protection. The DRM-free bit is exciting—it means that you can *finally* play all of your music on non-Apple devices and with third-party music software.

Streaming Your Music to Other Computers

Away from home and working on another computer that has iTunes installed? Log in to iTunes Match to access all of your music stored in iCloud. Here's how:

1.   Open iTunes.
2.   Select **Store ▸ Turn on iTunes Match**.
3.   Log in with your Apple ID. iTunes accesses your music in iCloud and makes it available for streaming on the computer.

This is an easy way to access your music at work without bringing your iPhone or iPod. The music is streamed from the iCloud servers. To download songs to the computer you're currently working on, select the songs, right-click them, and then select **Download**. The songs will download to the computer.

Controlling iTunes with Shortcuts

One major obstacle to managing your music effectively is the iTunes interface. It's a hassle to switch to iTunes, select a playlist or search for an artist, and then choose a song. Wouldn't it be nice if there were a more effective way to access iTunes? Enter an application called CoverSutra *(http://sophiestication.com/ coversutra/, $)*.

In addition to making your music more accessible, CoverSutra is jam-packed with small, beautiful interface elements that making listening to music fun. For example, a small window pops up any time you press the play or pause button (F8) on the keyboard, just to let you know what happened. And if you have the setting enabled, a notification with the artist, album, and song name is displayed at the top of the screen when the song changes.

Getting Started with CoverSutra

Once you open CoverSutra, it places an icon on your menu bar. Click the icon to reveal a Spotlight-like search box for your music. (You can also set a keyboard shortcut for this menu—more on that in the next section.) Start typing an artist or song name, and search results will start appearing in real time, as shown in Figure 19-3. Just select a song to start playing it in iTunes.

FIGURE 19-3: *Use CoverSutra to search your iTunes library from your menu bar.*

It doesn't take long to realize that this is very possibly the only interface you'll need to access your music. If CoverSutra is something you'd like to have available all of the time, open the settings to add it as a login item or just configure it to open when you open iTunes. It can also log the music you play in iTunes to the Last.fm recommendation service.

Configuring Shortcuts in CoverSutra

Perhaps CoverSutra's most exciting feature is its ability to map keyboard shortcuts to common iTunes functions. For example, you can create shortcuts for turning repeat and shuffle on and off, rating songs at a certain star level, and changing the sound level in the iTunes application. You can also set shortcuts for previous track, play and pause, and next track—shortcuts that are already mapped to F7, F8, and F9 on most Mac keyboards but can be reassigned with CoverSutra. Finally, you can also set shortcuts for the CoverSutra interface.

Here's how to configure shortcuts in CoverSutra:

1. From the **CoverSutra** menu, select the gear icon and then select **Preferences**.
2. Click **Shortcuts**. The window shown in Figure 19-4 appears.

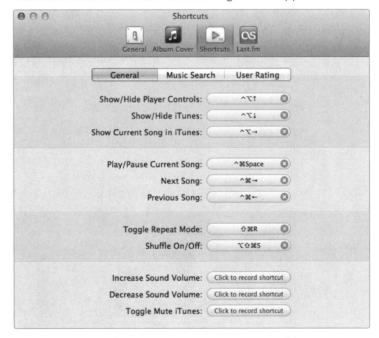

FIGURE 19-4: *Set shortcuts in CoverSutra to quickly interact with iTunes.*

3. To edit a shortcut, click a box and then press the keys you want to use to activate that feature.

Notice that there are three tabs full of shortcuts: General, Music Search, and User Rating. The music search shortcuts control the CoverSutra menu bar interface, and the user rating shortcuts allow you to assign a rating to the current song. Setting user rating shortcuts is useful, because music can be sorted in iTunes by the ratings you've assigned. If you can get into the habit of rating songs while they're playing, you'll collect valuable metadata.

Using the CoverSutra Player

Between CoverSutra's menu and the keyboard shortcuts, most people should be able to control music playback without using iTunes at all. But if you still feel the itch to use an interface, CoverSutra has one more trick up its sleeve: the CoverSutra player. This mini interface lets you move forward and backward between songs, play and pause the music, turn on shuffle and repeat, and rate the current song, as shown in Figure 19-5.

FIGURE 19-5: *The CoverSutra player*

There are a couple of ways to access the player. You can hold down OPTION and click the CoverSutra menu, or you can assign a keyboard shortcut. (It's the first shortcut listed under the General tab: Show/Hide Player Controls.) The interface isn't tremendously helpful, but if you assign a keyboard shortcut to it, it's still faster than switching to iTunes.

Adding Missing Metadata

Are some of the songs in your iTunes library missing *metadata*? You use this descriptive information—song title, artist name, album name, etc.—to find and sort the music on your computer every day. You wouldn't be able to tell one track from another without it!

Unfortunately, most of us have at least a couple of tracks that are missing metadata. And if you've ever imported CDs to your library, some of your music is probably missing cover art. The iTunes Match service allows you to fix metadata, but it works only for music sold in the iTunes Store.

You can manually fix metadata—track by track, album cover by album cover—but there's a third-party application that automates the process. TuneUp (*http://www.tuneupmedia.com/*, $$$) is displayed next to iTunes whenever you open it, ready and waiting to fix your bungled tracks. In this section, you'll learn how to use TuneUp to fix mislabeled songs and add missing cover art.

Fixing Mislabeled Songs

A mislabeled song is missing its song title, artist name, or album name metadata—or it has the incorrect data stored in those fields.

Here's how to fix mislabeled songs:

1. Open iTunes and then open the TuneUp application. The TuneUp pane appears next to the iTunes window. If this is the first time you've opened the application, you will need to create a free account to log in to the TuneUp servers.

2. From the TuneUp window, click the **Clean** tabs, as shown in Figure 19-6.

3. Select the mislabeled songs in your iTunes library. Mislabeled songs are often missing the artist and album names, as shown in Figure 19-7.

4. Drag the mislabeled songs to the TuneUp window. TuneUp analyzes the songs and returns possible matches for the songs, as shown in Figure 19-8.

FIGURE 19-6: *The TuneUp interface*

√	Name	Time	Artist ▲	Album
√	ACDC – For those abou...	5:46		
√	Blink 182 – Man Overb...	2:47		
√	Britney Spears – Hit Me...	3:30		
√	Chordettes – Mr Sandm...	2:27		

FIGURE 19-7: *Examples of mislabeled songs*

If TuneUp correctly matched all of the tracks, click Save All to save the new metadata to all of the tracks.

Click this button to save the metadata for an individual track.

FIGURE 19-8: *TuneUp analyzes the mislabeled songs and returns possible matches.*

5. (Optional) Check the results in the TuneUp window. Does the information look correct? If so, click **Save All** to save the new metadata for all of the songs.

6. (Optional) If TuneUp found correct information for just some of the songs, click the **Save** button on the individual tracks that are correct to save that metadata.

TuneUp isn't perfect—it won't be able to find the metadata for every track ever recorded. If it can't find the metadata for one of your tracks, you'll need to fix the metadata manually. To do so, select the track in iTunes, select **File ▸ Get Info**, click the **Info** tab, and fill in the missing information. Click the **Artwork** tab to add cover art.

Adding Missing Cover Art

Getting album cover artwork is one of the best parts of buying new music. And on this count, the iTunes Store has you covered—all of the songs you purchase from the iTunes Store come with cover art. But what about the older tracks on your computer or the ones you imported from CDs? Those tracks might not have cover art.

TuneUp can help you add the missing covers. It looks at your tracks and finds the artwork online, allowing you to save the art into the tracks. Here's how to do it:

1. Open iTunes and then open the TuneUp application. The TuneUp pane appears next to the iTunes window. If this is the first time you've opened the application, you will need to create a free account to log in to the TuneUp servers.

2. From the TuneUp window, click the **Cover Art** tab. TuneUp analyzes your library and finds the albums' missing cover art, as shown in Figure 19-9.

3. (Optional) If all of the cover artwork looks correct, click **Save all** to save the artwork for all albums to your computer.

4. (Optional) To save artwork for a specific album only, click the **Save** button next to the album.

TuneUp will save the artwork to the tracks. If you have an iOS device, like an iPhone or iPad, be sure to sync so that the artwork is transferred to the device.

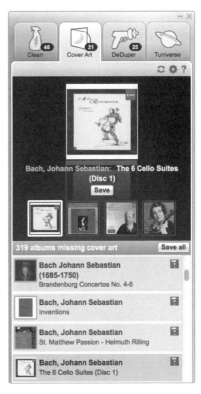

FIGURE 19-9: *Use TuneUp to spruce up your music library with cover artwork.*

Managing iTunes Libraries

You might not know this, but iTunes organizes all of your music with a database called a *library*. The library, an XML file, lists all of the songs you have stored on your hard drive, as well as any of the playlists you've created. Unfortunately, iTunes does not allow you to create multiple libraries, something that can be useful if you have lots of music on your computer.

The PowerTunes application (*http://www.fatcatsoftware.com/powertunes/*, $$) lets you take the power back by rearranging your music in new and better ways. You can create new libraries, duplicate a library, and copy songs from one library to another. You can also move your iTunes music folder to a different location—for example, to free up additional space on your startup disk by moving all of your music to an external drive.

Adding Existing Libraries

When you first open PowerTunes, you'll need to tell it about the iTunes libraries that are currently on your computer. Once the libraries are in PowerTunes, you'll be able to duplicate them, merge them, or copy songs to or from other libraries. Here's how to add existing libraries to PowerTunes:

1. Open the PowerTunes application.
2. Click **Add Library**. The Open dialog appears.
3. Select your existing iTunes library. By default, the file is stored in */Users/ <username>/Music/iTunes/iTunes Library.itl*. The library appears in the PowerTunes window, as shown in Figure 19-10.
4. Repeat these steps to add any other iTunes libraries currently on your computer.

FIGURE 19-10: *Your iTunes library in PowerTunes*

Now that your libraries are in PowerTunes, you can perform some more advanced tasks, like copying music between them or duplicating them—all of which is described in the coming sections.

Creating a New Library

You can only have one library open in iTunes at a time, so why would you want to create a new one? To better organize your music. If you're a DJ, you could create different libraries for the different types of music on your computer or even for different types of parties or situations. And if you're a home user with more than 25,000 tracks in your library—the maximum number of songs allowed by iTunes Match—it might be a good idea to start organizing your music into smaller, separate libraries.

Here's how to create a new iTunes library:

1. Open the PowerTunes application.
2. Click **New Library**. The window shown in Figure 19-11 appears.

FIGURE 19-11: *PowerTunes provides several options for creating new libraries.*

3. Enter a name for the new library. By default, the library will be stored in the path listed—click **Custom location** to store it somewhere else, like on an external drive.
4. To create a completely new media folder for this library, select **Create new media folder**. (This option is recommended.) You can set the new library to use an existing folder by selecting one of the other options.
5. Click **Create Library**. PowerTunes creates the new library and displays it in the PowerTunes sidebar, as shown in Figure 19-12.

You can click the button next to a library to open it in iTunes. This is a fast way to switch libraries in iTunes. Another option is to select a library manually by holding down the OPTION key when opening iTunes.

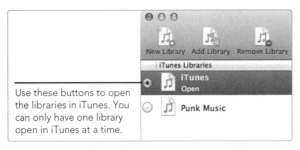

Use these buttons to open the libraries in iTunes. You can only have one library open in iTunes at a time.

FIGURE 19-12: *Click the button next to a library to open it in iTunes.*

Duplicating a Library

Duplicating a library is a good way to create a brand-new library with all of your existing music. Once the new library is created, you can start deleting music in PowerTunes—all of the music will still be available in your original library. Here's how to duplicate a library:

1. Open PowerTunes.
2. From the sidebar, select the library you want to duplicate.
3. Select **File ▸ Duplicate Library**.
4. In the dialog that appears, type a name for the new library.
5. Click **Create Library**. PowerTunes will copy all of the media in the original library to the new library.

    The new library will appear in the PowerTunes sidebar.

Copying Songs from One Library to Another

Now that you have multiple libraries, you might be wondering how to transfer music from one library to another. With PowerTunes, it's as easy as selecting songs and then dragging them onto a new library, as shown in Figure 19-13. Since the songs are being copied (not moved), they'll appear in both libraries. You can still delete songs from a library the old-fashioned way by opening iTunes, selecting songs, and then pressing DELETE.

FIGURE 19-13: *Drag songs to copy them from one library to another. In this example, 16 songs are about to be copied to the Punk Music library.*

Merging Libraries

The great thing about PowerTunes—and creating new iTunes libraries in general—is that you can always get things back to the way they used to be. The *merge libraries* feature combines two or more libraries into one. This is also a useful option when transferring your music from an older computer to a new one.

Here's how to merge iTunes libraries:

1. Open the PowerTunes application.
2. Select **Library ▸ Merge Libraries**. The dialog shown in Figure 19-14 appears.

FIGURE 19-14: *Select the libraries you want to merge into a single library.*

3. In the left pane, select the libraries you want to merge.
4. In the right pane, select the library you want to copy the songs into. By default, PowerTunes copies the songs to a new library, and in some cases, that may be the only option available.
5. Click **Continue**. PowerTunes merges the libraries into the library you selected.

The merged library will appear in the PowerTunes sidebar.

Moving Your Media Folder to a Different Location

Here's a common scenario: Your startup disk is almost out of space, and you're looking to move some files to an external drive. Moving your iTunes media folder—all of your music, movies, and other media—should be one of your first steps. PowerTunes makes it as easy as selecting a destination folder.

Here's how to move your media folder to a different location:

1. Open the PowerTunes application.
2. Select **Library ▸ Move/Copy Media Folder**. The Save dialog appears.
3. Select a destination folder for your media.
4. (Optional) Select the **Copy media folder instead of moving** to make a backup of your media folder.
5. Click **Save**. PowerTunes moves your media folder to the new location.

Now your media files are stored in the new location. The transition should be seamless—iTunes won't even know the difference!

Additional Ideas for Managing Your Music

If you own a MacBook Air or another computer with a solid-state drive, you might be pinched for space on your hard disk. You can ditch your music by signing up for iTunes Match, uploading your music to iCloud, and then deleting the songs from your computer. All of your music will be stored on the iCloud servers and available for streaming while you're connected to a wireless network. It's not quite as convenient as having all of your music on your computer's hard drive, but it sure frees up a lot of space. And if you're not in love with iCloud, check out the competing online music offerings from Google (*http://play.google.com/*) and Amazon (*http://amazon.com/cloudplayer/*).

PART 5

Internet and Networks

20

Creating Your Own Safari Extension

You already know that you can add features to Safari by installing *extensions*. Apple maintains a gallery full of free extensions that can do things like remove advertisements, change the look and feel of a particular website, and display news in a custom toolbar. But you can also create your own Safari extensions for personal pleasure or mass dissemination—for free. All you need is some basic knowledge of HTML, CSS, or JavaScript.

Use this project to get a piece of the action. Rather than coding from scratch, you'll use Tabinet,[1] an open source Safari extension that was featured in Apple's Safari Extension

1. You can download Tabinet here: *https://github.com/movesmyers/Tabinet/*.

Gallery, as a framework for your very own extension. Tabinet saves all of your browser tabs so you can open them later. Of course, you can do a lot more with Safari extensions once you get the hang of creating them.

Project goal: Create a Safari extension that places a button on your toolbar that opens a website when clicked.

What You'll Be Using

To make browsing easier with a Safari extension, you'll use the following:

 Safari

 Safari Developer Program (*http://developer.apple.com/programs/safari/*, free)

Understanding Safari Extensions

Extensions can add a number of features to the Safari web browser, as shown in Figure 20-1. Some popular extensions place buttons on the toolbar, open new windows and tabs, change the way websites look by injecting CSS and JavaScript, add contextual menu items, or add custom extension bars that allow users to interact with web services. Extensions can include all of these features or just some of them.

FIGURE 20-1: Safari extensions can add features and change the way websites look.

The extension you create in this project will only add two toolbar buttons that save and reopen a set of tabs. Although other extensions can give you more features, adding too many features can annoy users. A good rule of thumb is to keep your extensions as unobtrusive as possible—you don't need to add an extension bar *and* a toolbar button, for example.

What happens behind the scenes after a user installs the extension? It waits for the user to do something and then communicates with websites, the web browser, and itself to perform actions like opening websites and injecting CSS code into a website.

For security and stability reasons, Safari keeps extensions isolated from everything else—a practice known as *sandboxing*. Apple doesn't want users worrying about whether or not an extension will collect their personal information or crash their computer every time they click an extension's toolbar button. To communicate in this secure environment, extensions send messages through *proxies*, as shown in Figure 20-2.

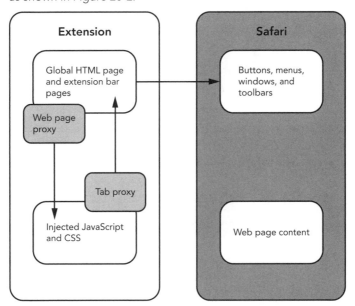

FIGURE 20-2: *Safari extensions are sandboxed for security and stability reasons.*

You'll learn more about the nitty-gritty details later in this chapter, when you're assembling the nuts and bolts of the extension. Just remember later, when you're trying to get the elements of your extension to talk to everything else, that your extension has to use proxies to communicate.

Getting Started

Before you delve into the process of creating the extension, you'll need to lay the groundwork. Get started by registering for the Safari Developer Program, generating a certificate, and enabling the developer menu in the Safari application.

Registering for the Safari Developer Program

Visit Apple's website and register for the Safari Developer Program (*http://developer .apple.com/programs/safari/*). Registration is free of charge and hassle-free—you'll use your Apple ID, the same credential you use to access the iTunes Store.

Why do you need to register for the developer program? For one thing, a signed certificate from Apple is required to validate your identity and protect your extension from unauthorized modification. Registration also provides access to documentation and code samples on Apple's website—definitely useful if you go on to develop more advanced extensions after you complete this project.

Generating a Certificate

Apple takes the security of Safari extensions seriously. It requires all developers to generate a certificate before installing, distributing, or updating Safari extensions. This credential is much stronger than a username and password combination—it's like a digital driver's license issued by Apple.

Here's how to generate a certificate for your Safari extension:

1. Visit the Developer Certificate Utility website: *http://developer.apple.com/certificates/safari/*. Scroll down to the Safari Developer Program section of the web page, as shown in Figure 20-3.
2. Click **Create Certificates**.

FIGURE 20-3: *Use the developer certificate utility to create a certificate for your Safari extension.*

3. Click **Add Certificate**. The Safari Extension Certificate Assistant window appears, as shown in Figure 20-4.
4. To create a Certificate Signing Request (CSR) for Apple, open the Keychain Access application. (It's in the Utilities folder.)

Generate a Certificate Signing Request

To request a Safari Extension Certificate, you first need to generate a Certificate Signing Request (CSR) utilizing the Keychain Access application in Mac OS X Leopard.

Launch Keychain Access
In the Applications folder on your Mac, open the Utilities folder and launch Keychain Access.

- Within the Keychain Access drop down menu, select Keychain Access > Certificate Assistant > Request a Certificate from a Certificate Authority
- In the Certificate Information window, enter the following information:
  - In the User Email Address field, enter your email address
  - In the Common Name field, create a name for your private key (eg. John Doe Dev Key)
  - In the Request is group, select the "Saved to disk" option
- Click Continue within Keychain Access to complete the CSR generating process

Cancel   Go Back   Continue

FIGURE 20-4: *Follow the instructions to request a certificate with Keychain Access.*

5.   From the **Keychain Access** menu, select **Certificate Assistant** and then **Request a Certificate From a Certificate Authority**. The dialog shown in Figure 20-5 appears.

6.   Enter your email address in the **User Email Address** field.

7.   Enter your name in the **Common Name** field.

8.   Select **Saved to disk** and **Let me specify key pair information**. Click **Continue**.

9.   A save dialog appears. Enter a name for the file and select a folder in which to save it. Click **Save**.

10.   In the next window, set **Key Size** to 2048 bits and **Algorithm** to RSA. Click **Continue**.

11.   Save the Certificate Signing Request to your hard disk.

12.   Back in your web browser, click **Continue** in the Safari Extension Certificate Assistant window. The window shown in Figure 20-6 appears.

13.   To upload the CSR to Apple's website, click **Choose File** and select the CSR on your hard disk. Click **Generate**.

14.   The Apple website generates your signed certificate—the process should take only a few seconds.

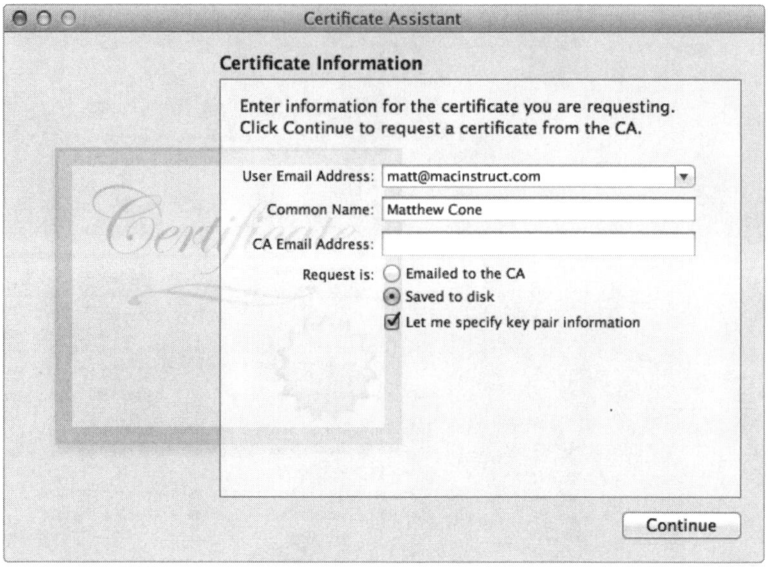

FIGURE 20-5: *Use Keychain Access to generate a Certificate Signing Request.*

Submit Certificate Signing Request

The creation of a CSR will prompt Keychain Access to simultaneously generate a public and private key pair. Your private key is stored on your Mac in the login Keychain by default and can be viewed in the Keychain Access application under the "Keys" category.

Select the Certificate Signing request (CSR) file that you saved to your disk.

Choose File Certificate...ningRequest

Cancel   Go Back   Generate

FIGURE 20-6: *Upload the CSR to Apple's website.*

15. After Apple has generated your certificate, click **Continue**. A list of your signed certificates appears. (Unless you're an active developer, you'll see only one certificate in the list.)
16. Click **Download**. The signed certificate downloads to your computer.
17. Double-click the certificate to install it on your computer. You can verify that the certificate has been installed by opening it in Keychain Access, as shown in Figure 20-7.

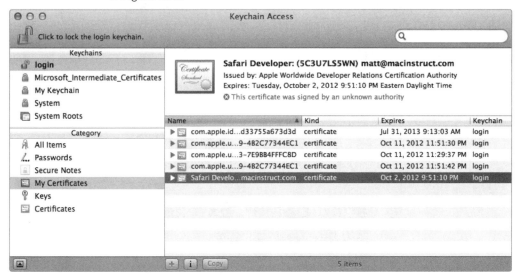

FIGURE 20-7: *Your signed certificate for the Safari Developer Program is stored in Keychain Access.*

Now that you've generated a certificate signed by Apple and installed it on your computer, you're ready to develop your first Safari extension.

Enabling the Safari Developer Menu

You'll create Safari extensions with Safari Extension Builder—a developer interface built into Safari. To access Extension Builder and a slew of other developer tools, you'll first have to enable Safari's Develop menu, which is hidden by default.

Here's how to enable Safari's Develop menu:

1. Open the Safari application.
2. From the **Safari** menu, select **Preferences**.
3. Click **Advanced**. The dialog shown in Figure 20-8 appears.
4. Select the **Show Develop menu in menu bar** checkbox.
5. Close the Preferences window.

Now you'll see the Develop menu in the menu bar—it's between the Bookmarks and Window menus.

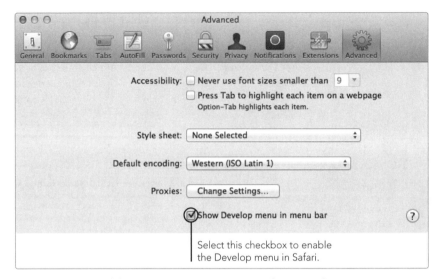

Select this checkbox to enable
the Develop menu in Safari.

FIGURE 20-8: Enable the Develop menu in Safari's preferences.

Creating a Safari Extension

We're now ready to develop the Safari extension itself. As an example, we'll use Tabinet, an open source extension that was featured in Apple's Safari Extension Gallery. The developer, Rick Myers, created Tabinet to address one of his pet peeves: Safari's inability to save and restore tabs on demand.

Tabinet fixes this problem by placing two buttons on Safari's toolbar. You can click one to save your tabs, and then click another one to restore the tabs. The tabs can be restored even after you quit and reopen Safari. Since Rick thoughtfully made his extension available to the public, we can view the source code and compile it ourselves.

First, you'll configure the extension settings in Safari, just to let the application know the extension is there. The extension won't do much at first, but you'll add bits and pieces to its functionality in the following sections.

Configuring the Extension Settings

It's time to open Extension Builder and create a new extension. Extension Builder allows you to add elements and link files, images, and other resources to the extension. In this section, you'll create the extension and configure some of the settings.

* **NOTE:** Not all of the fields available in Extension Builder need to be filled. I'll show you which ones are absolutely necessary for this project.

Here's how to create the Safari extension by using Tabinet as a framework:

1. If you haven't already downloaded the Tabinet source files, do that now. You can find them here: *https://github.com/movesmyers/Tabinet/*. Remember where you save them.
2. Open the Safari application.
3. From the **Develop** menu, select **Show Extension Builder**.
4. Click the **+** button in the lower-left corner and then click **New Extension**. You'll be prompted to save the extension. Remember where you save it— you'll need to access the directory later. The dialog shown in Figure 20-9 appears.

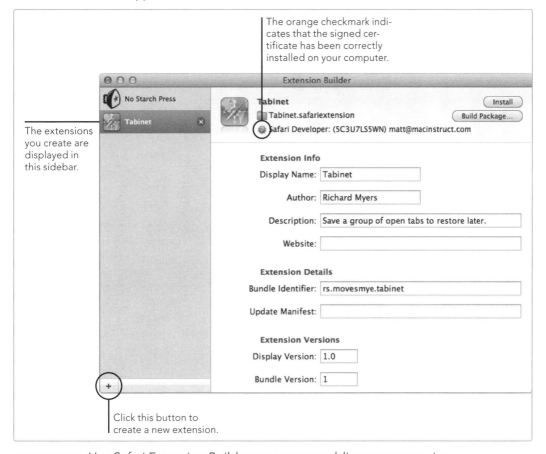

FIGURE 20-9: Use Safari Extension Builder to start assembling your extension.

5. In the Finder, open the *Tabinet* folder that you downloaded. Copy the *Icon* folder in the *Tabinet* folder to the extension folder you just created.

6. Back in Safari, enter a name for your extension in the **Display Name** field, enter your name in the **Author** field, and enter a description of the extension in the **Description** field. If you have a website, enter that in the **Website** field.
7. From the **Access Level** menu, select **All**.
8. Select the **Include Secure Pages** checkbox.
9. From the **Database Quota** menu, select **100 MB**. This reserves some space on the hard drive for the extension to store things.

Now it's time to add the two toolbar items for Tabinet, one for saving the tabs and the other for restoring them:

10. Scroll down to the Toolbar Items section. Click **New Toolbar Item**. The pane shown in Figure 20-10 appears.

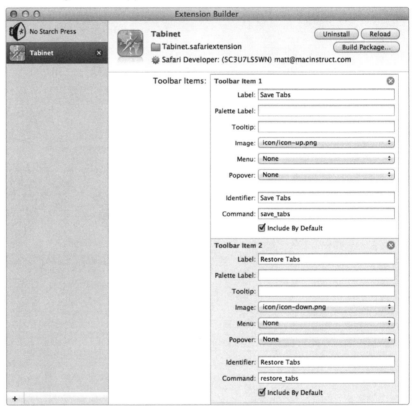

FIGURE 20-10: *Create toolbar buttons for Tabinet.*

11. Enter **Save Tabs** in the **Label** field. This is the name that will be shown if the toolbar overflows.
12. From the **Image** menu, select *icon/icon-up.png*. This is the icon that will be displayed on the toolbar.

13. Enter **Save Tabs** in the **Identifier** field. This is used to differentiate the extension's button from a script.
14. Enter **save_tabs** in the **Command** field. Later, a script will use this to detect when the toolbar button is clicked.
15. Click **New Toolbar Item** to add the other toolbar item.
16. Enter **Restore Tabs** in the **Label** field.
17. From the **Image** menu, select *icon/icon-down.png*. This is the icon that will be displayed on the toolbar.
18. Enter **Restore Tabs** in the **Identifier** field. This is used to differentiate the extension's button from a script.
19. Enter **restore_tabs** in the **Command** field. Later, a script will use this to detect when the toolbar button is clicked.

That's it for now. Keep the Extension Builder open so you can select the extension's image—something you'll create in the next section.

Making the Global Page

Remember the diagram in Figure 20-2 that shows how your extension talks to the browser and web pages? Now that you've created the framework for the extension and an icon for the toolbar button, it's time to make the "glue" that holds all of the parts together. You'll create a *global page* and insert a script capable of saving tabs and restoring them when the respective buttons are clicked.

The global page is simply an HTML document that contains hidden extension elements. For this project, you'll just put a simple script in the global page. The first part of the script performs actions when you click the Save button. The tabs are stored in a database on your Mac's hard disk. The second part of the script handles the restoring. When you click the Restore button, all of the tabs will be retrieved from the database and then opened.

Here's how to make the global page:

1. Open a text editor application, like TextWrangler (*http://www.barebones .com/products/textwrangler/*, free).
2. Create a new document and enter the script shown below.

```
<!DOCTYPE HTML>

<script>

function saveTabs(event) {
    if (event.command === "save_tabs") {
        tabs = event.target.browserWindow.tabs;
        var q = 0;
        for (var x in tabs) {
            q++;
            localStorage.setItem(q, tabs[x].url);
        }
        return;
        }
    }
```

```
function restoreTabs(event) {
    if (event.command === "restore_tabs") {
        var newWin = safari.application.openBrowserWindow();
        var numKeys = localStorage.length;
        for(i=1;i<numKeys+1;i++) {
            var url = localStorage.getItem(i);
            if (i==1) {
                var newTab = safari.application.activeBrowserWindow.activeTab;
            }
            else {
                var newTab = safari.application.activeBrowserWindow.openTab();
            }
            newTab.url = url;
        }
        localStorage.clear();
        return;
        }
    }

safari.application.addEventListener("command", saveTabs, false);
safari.application.addEventListener("command", restoreTabs, false);

</script>
```

3. Save the document as *global.html* in the extension's directory.
4. Back in the Extension Builder window, select *global.html* from the **Global Page File** menu.

Now it's time to design the buttons!

Designing the Buttons

Tabinet comes with two images for the buttons, and to use them, you just move them to the extension directory and select them in Extension Builder.

But it's easy to make an icon for any toolbar button. Create a 16 × 16 pixel image with black artwork and a transparent background, name the image *icon.png*, and save it in the extension's directory. When you install the extension later, the icon(s) will appear on the toolbar, as shown in Figure 20-11.

FIGURE 20-11: *Tabinet's buttons appear on the toolbar.*

If you make your own icon, it might take some trial and error to get the icon exactly right. You can also play around with different sizes and shapes of artwork to create an effective visual element.

Installing and Building the Extension

Now that you've finished creating the extension, it's time to install it in Safari. In the Extension Builder window, click **Install**, as shown in Figure 20-12. Your extension buttons should now be visible on the toolbar—click them to save and restore your tabs.

FIGURE 20-12: *Create a toolbar button for your extension.*

You can also export your extension to share it with others. Click the **Build Package** button in the Extension Builder window to save your extension as a self-contained executable.

Additional Ideas for Creating Your Own Safari Extension

Those who want to create more advanced extensions should invest some time in reading Apple's documentation. It's free, comprehensive, and a real help for anyone ready to delve into the advanced intricacies of extension building.

Another thing to think about for more advanced projects is version control. Some professional developers keep the source code for their extensions in version control systems (like Subversion or Git), apply the software development life cycle methodology to fix bugs and add features, and release updates on a regular basis.

21

Turning Websites into Applications

Websites are so powerful these days that many people don't find a need for much traditional software. Instead, they regularly use *web applications*—as some companies have started calling their websites—to read email, create documents, store information, track personal tasks, and keep in touch with friends and family. The problem with using websites to perform this kind of work is your computer's web browser. Managing all of those windows is a pain, and web browsers can crash and take all of your windows—and unsaved work—with them. Wouldn't it be great if you could avoid browser pitfalls by visiting your favorite websites in self-contained applications?

With an application called Fluid, you can. Fluid lets you create an application, called a *site-specific browser (SSB)*, specifically designed for accessing a single website. Instead of opening a web browser, entering a URL, and logging in to the website, you can use the website in a dedicated window. Fluid lets you create as many SSBs as you want.

Project goal: Create an SSB and customize the display settings.

What You'll Be Using

To avoid dealing with a browser when you visit your favorite sites, you'll use the following:

 Fluid (*http://fluidapp.com/*, free or $ for extra features)

Creating Site-Specific Browsers

Fluid makes it easy to create site-specific browsers. Just open the application, provide some basic information—like the website's URL and name—and the SSB is created and stored in your Applications folder. You can put the SSB's icon in the Dock, add it as a login item (see Chapter 2), and share it with other users on your Mac.

Here's how to create a site-specific browser with Fluid:

1. Open the Fluid application. The window shown in Figure 21-1 appears.

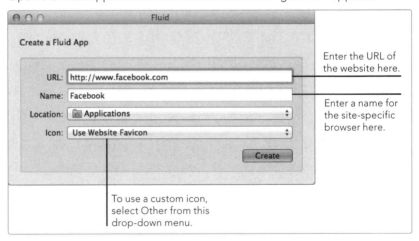

FIGURE 21-1: *Creating a new site-specific browser with Fluid*

2. Enter the address of the website in the **URL** field.
3. Enter a name for the site-specific browser in the **Name** field.

4. To save the site-specific browser in a location other than the Applications folder, select **Other** from the **Location** menu.

5. To use an icon other than the website's favicon—the icon displayed in the address bar of a web browser when you visit the site—select **Other** from the **Icon** menu.

✽ *NOTE:* **For hundreds of free custom icons for a variety of websites, check out the Fluid group on Flickr (*http://www.flickr.com/groups/fluid_icons/*).**

6. Click **Create**. The window shown in Figure 21-2 appears.

FIGURE 21-2: A site-specific browser is ready to be launched.

7. Click **Launch Now** to open your new site-specific browser. The website appears, as shown in Figure 21-3.

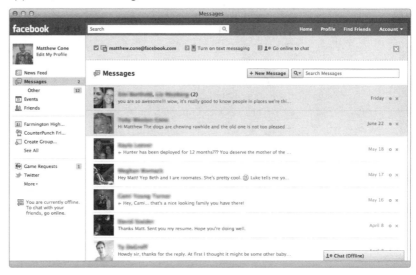

FIGURE 21-3: By default, site-specific browsers hide address bars, backward or forward buttons, and search boxes. If you miss those items, you can display them by selecting Show Status Bar from the View menu.

Now your SSB is available as an application in your Applications folder (or the location you specified when you set it up). Just double-click the icon to open the website, or you can drag the icon to the Dock for easy access, as shown in Figure 21-4.

SSBs created with Fluid are sandboxed, which means that website cookies for SSBs are stored independently of those stored by web browsers. For example, you could log in to an SSB for Facebook and then open a web browser and log in to Facebook with a different account.

FIGURE 21-4: *Drag and drop SSB icons onto the Dock for easy access. For some websites, Fluid can display notifications of unread messages on the SSB's icon, shown here on the Gmail icon.*

Pinning a Site-Specific Browser to the Menu Bar

Having an SSB in the Dock not good enough? If you purchased a Fluid license, try using the *pin to status bar* feature to place the SSB's icon in the menu bar. After you pin the SSB, click the icon in the menu bar to display the website window and then click the icon again to hide the window. This feature is perfect for news or social networking websites that you might want to monitor frequently. It works best for smaller windows, so try using a mobile version of the website for the SSB.

Here's how to pin an SSB to the menu bar:

1. Open the SSB.
2. From the application menu (which is the name of your SSB), select **Pin to Status Bar**. A message appears asking if you really want to pin the SSB.
3. Click **OK**. After the SSB closes and reopens, the icon is displayed in the menu bar, as shown in Figure 21-5.

Note that pinning the SSB removes the icon from the dock—you'll be able to access the SSB only from the menu bar. You can resize the SSB window and move it anywhere on the screen you like. I move the window right under the menu bar for easy access.

To unpin the SSB, right-click the icon in the menu bar and select **Unpin App from Status Bar**.

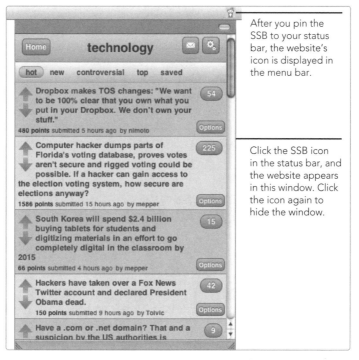

After you pin the SSB to your status bar, the website's icon is displayed in the menu bar.

Click the SSB icon in the status bar, and the website appears in this window. Click the icon again to hide the window.

FIGURE 21-5: Pin an SSB to your status bar for ready access to your favorite websites. This works best when the website's window is small, like this compact version of the Reddit website.

Customizing Display Settings

Most people create an SSB and just leave it at that, but the paid version of Fluid provides two powerful features that allow you to modify the way a website looks and functions. In this section, you'll apply *user styles* and *user scripts* to customize your SSB by overriding a website's default cascading style sheets (CSS) and implementing new functionality with scripts. This means that you can do things like hide advertisements and rearrange links on a sidebar.

* **NOTE:** User styles and user scripts aren't exclusive to Fluid. Some web browsers—like Safari, Firefox, and Chrome—also have extensions that allow you to utilize user styles and user scripts.

Modifying Site-Specific Browsers with User Styles

You can change the way a website looks by replacing the default CSS with your own user style. To understand how this works, it's best to think about a website as the sum of two distinct parts: content and presentation. The content is all of the information you can see, like text and pictures. The presentation layer is a set of instructions that tells web browsers how to assemble and display the content. As shown in Figure 21-6, content can be filtered through the user style in the presentation layer to create the website you see in the SSB.

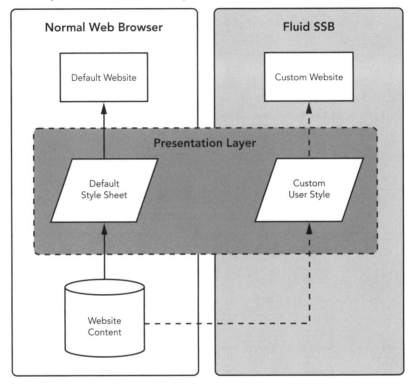

FIGURE 21-6: *User styles override a website's CSS to create a custom look and feel.*

You can create your own user styles by writing CSS, but it's easier to use some of the free styles that have been published online. Try searching *http://userstyles.org/* for user styles that can be applied to your favorite websites. This example utilizes the *Google Reader Symphonia Final 2* user style[1] to modify an SSB for the Google Reader RSS website (*http://www.google.com/reader/*).

Here's how to modify an SSB with a user style:

1. Open the SSB.
2. From the **Window** menu, select **Userstyles**. The window shown in Figure 21-7 appears.
3. Click the **+** button in the lower-left corner.

---

1. The Google Reader Symphonia Final 2 user style is available at *http://userstyles.org/styles/56339/google-reader-symphonia-final/.*

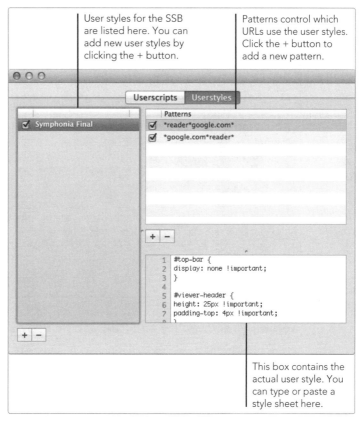

User styles for the SSB are listed here. You can add new user styles by clicking the + button.

Patterns control which URLs use the user styles. Click the + button to add a new pattern.

This box contains the actual user style. You can type or paste a style sheet here.

FIGURE 21-7: *Adding user styles with Fluid's Userstyles window*

4. Rename the user style by clicking once on the new line in the sidebar and typing a name.

5. Change the example pattern by clicking once on the new line in the **Patterns** box and typing a new pattern.

✱ **NOTE:** The pattern should match the URL you created for the website. For example, if you created an SSB for Facebook, use *facebook.com* as the pattern. The asterisks are wildcards that apply the user style to URLs with anything on either side of *facebook.com*.

6. Type or paste the user script into the box in the lower-right corner.

7. Close the Userstyles window.

8. From the **View** menu, select **Reload Page**. The SSB reloads the web page and applies the user style.

You'll know right away whether the user style worked or not—the difference can be quite striking. In fact, depending on the user style you selected, it can seem like you're looking at an entirely different website.

> ### Cleaning Up User Styles for Fluid
>
> Many of the published user styles have been designed to work with web browsers other than Fluid, so you'll need to edit the user styles to get them to work in Fluid. For example, to make the Google Reader Symphonia Final 2 user style work, you'll need to remove the following code from the beginning of the user style:
>
> ```
> @namespace url(http://www.w3.org/1999/xhtml);@-moz-document
> url-prefix("http://www.google.com/reader/view/"),url-prefix("https://
> www.google.com/reader/view/") {
> ```
>
> The key is removing the browser-specific elements from the beginning of the style so that you're pasting the CSS only. When you get to the first CSS element, which is #top-bar in the Google Reader Symphonia Final 2 user style, as shown in Figure 23-7, you can stop deleting.

Adding Functionality to Site-Specific Browsers with User Scripts

User scripts add features and functionality to your SSB. Unlike user styles, which modify the website's CSS in real time, user scripts are JavaScripts that are installed after the website loads. The new functionality is superimposed on the existing website, as shown in Figure 21-8.

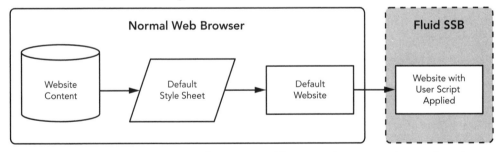

FIGURE 21-8: *User scripts add new features and functionality to a website after the site loads in the SSB.*

You can find thousands of free user scripts on *http://userscripts.org/*. Try using the "fluid" tag to find user scripts specifically designed for Fluid (*http://userscripts.org/tags/fluid/*). This example utilizes the *Grooveshark for Fluid* theme[2] to add notifications and Dock icon music controls to an SSB for the free Grooveshark music website (*http://www.grooveshark.com/*).

---

2. The Grooveshark for Fluid user script is available at *http://userscripts.org/scripts/show/87090/*.

Here's how to add functionality to SSBs with user scripts:

1. Open the SSB.
2. From the **Window** menu, select **Userscripts**.
3. Click the **+** button in the lower-left corner.
4. Rename the user script by clicking once on the new line in the sidebar and typing a name.
5. Change the example pattern by clicking once on the new line in the **Patterns** box and typing a new pattern.

* **NOTE:** **You may need to use asterisks as wildcard characters again, as described in "Modifying Site-Specific Browsers with User Styles" on page 223.**

6. Type or paste the user script into the box in the lower-right corner.
7. Close the Userscripts window.
8. From the **View** menu, select **Reload Page**. The SSB reloads the web page and applies the user script.

FIGURE 21-9: *Right-click the Grooveshark SSB icon for new play, pause, and previous song controls provided by the user script.*

Now notifications are displayed when Grooveshark starts playing another song. And when you right-click the Grooveshark SSB icon in the Dock, you'll see new music controls, as shown in Figure 21-9.

Don't stop with one user script! You can add as many as you like, and *http://userscripts.org/* has thousands of scripts for hundreds of websites.

Additional Ideas for Turning Websites into Applications

Site-specific browsers have many potential uses. For example, you could create SSBs to limit access to a particular website, like your company's job application website. A Fluid SSB would be great on a kiosk machine designed to allow potential employees to apply for jobs. Or you could use SSBs in a school lab to limit access to only a few websites.

22

Storing Files in the Cloud

By now, you've probably heard about the *cloud*. Maybe you've even used a cloud service like iCloud to store and share documents, photos, and music. But recent changes have made these Internet-based services much more practical— especially for anyone who uses multiple computers and handheld devices. This project will show you how to get the most out Apple's iCloud and another popular cloud service, Dropbox.

If you're unfamiliar with the cloud—which is just a buzzword for storage space on the Internet—here's how it works. First you sign up for an account with a service provider like Apple or Dropbox. Most providers have a free plan that can be upgraded for a small monthly or yearly fee if you find you need more space.

Then you'll connect the account to your computers and devices so that all of them can access the files and information stored in your cloud account. It's a great feeling to know that you can access your files anywhere, at any time, from any device.

Project goal: Store files in the cloud and access them with all of your computers and devices.

What You'll Be Using

To access your files from anywhere, you'll use the following:

 iCloud (*http://www.icloud.com/*, free for 5GB)

 Dropbox (*http://www.dropbox.com/*, free for 2GB)

Using iCloud to Store Files

iCloud automatically and seamlessly synchronizes certain files and information among all of your Apple devices. If you add a contact in Contacts, it automatically appears on your iPhone. And if you take a picture with your iPad, it shows up in iPhoto without you having to do anything. But you don't have much control over what is stored in your iCloud account. For example, you can't store documents you create in Microsoft Word in iCloud—you'll need to use Dropbox for that.

iCloud is Apple's latest attempt at creating an Internet storage and synchronization solution. If you've been a Mac user for a while, you might remember Apple's previous attempts at cloud services: iTools, .Mac, and Mobile Me. Many people used those services, but they were never all that popular, and they never worked the way that Apple expected them to. iCloud also has its fair share of bugs and glitches, but it's still a useful service for those who own more than one Apple computer or device.

Getting Started with iCloud

To get started, you need to link your Apple ID to iCloud on your Mac. Then you'll configure the files and settings you want to synchronize with iCloud. After everything uploads from your computer to iCloud, you'll be able to sign in to your iCloud account from all of your other computers and devices.

Here's how to get started with iCloud on your Mac:

1. From the **Apple** menu, select **System Preferences**.
2. Click **iCloud**.
3. Create an account if you haven't already and then sign in to iCloud. The window in Figure 22-1 appears.
4. Select the checkboxes of accounts and file types you want to synchronize with other devices. (Note that Back to My Mac and Find My Mac are actually services that integrate with iCloud. For more information about Back to My Mac, see Chapter 23.)

FIGURE 22-1: *Sign in to iCloud and select the types of files to synchronize with other devices.*

Now you'll need to wait a couple of minutes for iCloud to upload all of the information from your Mac to the iCloud servers. Then you can sign in to your iCloud account on your other Macs and iOS devices, like an iPhone or iPad. There's even an iCloud application for Windows PCs!

Using iCloud with Applications

Once you turn on iCloud, the entire process of synchronizing the files and settings you've selected is supposed to be automated. In practice, it's not always that simple. Your own experience may vary, but chances are good that you'll need to manually configure at least some of Apple's applications to work with iCloud.

Take iPhoto, for example. Photo Stream is the iCloud service that stores all of the pictures you've taken over the past 30 days and transfers them to your iOS devices. However, to fully turn on Photo Stream, you'll need to enable it in iPhoto's preferences. Select all of the checkboxes in the Photo Stream pane to enable this feature, as shown in Figure 22-2.

FIGURE 22-2: *To enable Photo Stream, select all the checkboxes in iPhoto preferences.*

Other applications may need similar tweaking for iCloud. For example, if you want to synchronize your contacts in Contacts but find that they aren't moving from your Mac to your iOS devices, check the Contacts preferences to verify that the iCloud account is enabled for that application.

Using Dropbox to Store and Synchronize Files

Dropbox is a third-party cloud service and Mac application that addresses one of iCloud's major shortcomings—it doesn't let you drag files to a folder and have them automatically upload to your cloud account. The Dropbox folder on your Mac is physically stored on your hard disk, but all of the contents are also uploaded to the Dropbox servers. Any computer or handheld device linked to your Dropbox account can access these files.

With iCloud, the emphasis is on synchronizing files and settings. Dropbox simply provides a centralized location for the most important files on your computer. It may be a better option for those who need to store and access certain types of files. You can share the files on your Dropbox with others and access your files from its website. Even if you use only one computer and don't own an iPhone or iPad, Dropbox makes a fine backup solution for your documents.

Getting Started with Dropbox

To get started, you'll need to download Dropbox (*http://www.dropbox.com/*, free for 2GB), register for an account, and install the application on your computer. Dropbox will make a couple of changes to your Mac. The application's icon appears in the menu bar, and the Dropbox folder appears in the sidebar of Finder windows, as shown in Figure 22-3. You probably won't use the menu bar icon much, but it's a good way to see if Dropbox is open and uploading your files.

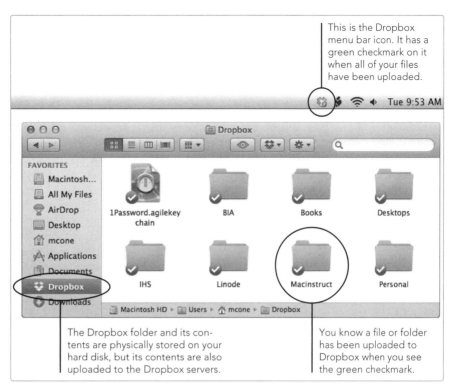

This is the Dropbox menu bar icon. It has a green checkmark on it when all of your files have been uploaded.

The Dropbox folder and its contents are physically stored on your hard disk, but its contents are also uploaded to the Dropbox servers.

You know a file or folder has been uploaded to Dropbox when you see the green checkmark.

FIGURE 22-3: *Drag and drop files and folders into the Dropbox folder and use the menu bar icon to control Dropbox.*

Now you can drag and drop files and folders on the Dropbox folder. Everything will be stored on your Mac and uploaded to the Dropbox servers—you know a file or folder has been uploaded when the green checkmark is displayed on the icon. Dropbox continues to monitor the files in the folder for changes. If you rename a folder or modify a file, Dropbox automatically updates the files and folders on its servers.

Sharing Dropbox Folders with Others

Dropbox lets you share folders with coworkers, friends, and family members. It's an ideal way to provide access to files that are too big to email or just give others access to a bunch of files in one your Dropbox folders. Plus, you can upload photos to a password-protected page on the Dropbox website by dragging and dropping them into a special folder.

Here's how to share the folders in your Dropbox with others:

1. From the **Dropbox** menu, select **Launch Dropbox Website**. Your Dropbox folders appear in the default web browser.
2. Select a folder and then click **Invite to folder**, as shown in Figure 22-4.

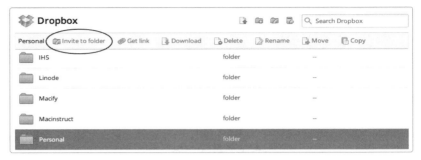

FIGURE 22-4: *Click Invite to folder to share a folder.*

3.   The share dialog appears, as shown in Figure 22-5. Enter the email addresses of the people you want to have access to the folder. You can optionally add a personal message that will be emailed to the individuals.

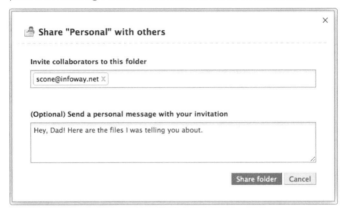

FIGURE 22-5: *Enter email addresses to give access to the folder to selected people.*

4.   Click **Share folder**. Dropbox emails the collaborators with instructions on how to access the folder you selected.

If you want to stop sharing a Dropbox folder, here's how to do it:

1.   From the **Dropbox** menu, select **Launch Dropbox Website**. Your Dropbox folders appear in the default web browser.
2.   Select the shared folder and then click **Shared folder options**, as shown in Figure 22-6.
3.   The dialog shown in Figure 22-7 appears. Click **Unshare this folder** to stop sharing the folder with all of the collaborators.

You should know about two folders in your Dropbox that are permanently shared. The *Photos* folder is designed specifically for pictures. Photos that you drop into this folder will appear on a page on Dropbox's website that you can share

FIGURE 22-6: *Use the Dropbox website to stop sharing folders.*

FIGURE 22-7: *Changing the sharing options for the selected folder*

with others. The *Public* folder holds stuff that is available to anyone and everyone on the Internet. Copy the URL of this folder on the Dropbox website and email it to others or publish it on your website. This is an ideal place to store files that you want to share with lots of people. For example, you could store your resume in this directory and send the link to potential employers.

Cool Things You Can Do with Dropbox

So far, you've barely scratched the surface of Dropbox's potential. What else can you do with this cloud service? A lot—here are some ideas to get you started:

▶ Connect your computers and devices to your Dropbox account. There are client applications for iOS, Windows, and Android operating systems. Plus, you can access all of the files by logging in to the Dropbox website (*http://www.dropbox.com/*).

- Use Dropbox Camera Upload to automatically upload pictures stored on your camera or smartphone to Dropbox. Just install the Dropbox application, connect the camera or smartphone to your Mac, and follow the instructions that appear on your screen. From now on, all of your photos will automatically be uploaded to Dropbox when you connect the device to your Mac.

- Use DropDAV (*http://www.dropdav.com/*, $5 per month) to allow other applications to access Dropbox without the Dropbox client application. This service works especially well with the iWork suite on iPad.

- Email files to your Dropbox by using the Send to Dropbox service (*http://sendtodropbox.com/*, free). Just visit the website, log in with your Dropbox username and password, and start emailing files—they appear in your Attachments folder.

- Create folders in Dropbox and then create *symbolic links* to those folders in OS X. (Symbolic links are a little like aliases, in that they point to a different folder. The difference is that symbolic links actually fool OS X and applications into thinking that the symbolic links are folders instead of shortcuts.) This is a great way to trick your Mac into thinking that the folders are on your Mac when they're really in your Dropbox. It works especially well with folders commonly used by applications like Apple's Mail. For example, you could store all of your email on Dropbox and access it on multiple Macs with the Mail application.

＊ **NOTE: To create symbolic links, open the Terminal application and type `ln -l ~/Dropbox/*folder* ~/*pathtothefolderinOSX*`, changing the folder and path names, of course.**

Use your imagination to take advantage of all of Dropbox's potential. There's a lot you can do with this service!

Additional Ideas for Storing Files in the Cloud

The cloud is still relatively young—new services are emerging all of the time. iCloud and Dropbox are currently two of the best services for Mac users, but that can change fast. For example, Google Drive works like Dropbox and provides users with 5GB of free storage—3GB more than Dropbox. Keep your eyes peeled for new and better ways to integrate cloud storage into your lifestyle.

23

Accessing Your Mac Remotely

When you can't take your Mac with you but still need to access all of the files and data stored on it, Apple's free Internet storage and connectivity service, iCloud, provides a great solution. An iCloud feature called *Back to My Mac* lets you access your computer from any other Mac connected to the Internet. Once you have this set up, it's easy to access the files stored on your home computer from the office, or vice versa.

There are two ways to access your Mac remotely. You can enable *file sharing* to access the specific files and folders you configure for sharing. Access can be controlled on a user-by-user basis. If you give individual users *read and write* access, they can modify files; if you give them just *read access*, they can access files but can't change them.

Screen sharing lets you access your Mac's desktop on another Mac or Windows PC. When used with file sharing, it's a complete remote access solution that allows you to do anything to your Mac from anywhere in the world. You can open applications, edit system settings, create documents, and do anything else you could do while sitting in front of your Mac.

Project goal: Use a Mac connected to the Internet to access your Mac remotely.

What You'll Be Using

To access your Mac remotely, you'll use the following:

 System Preferences

 iCloud (*http://www.icloud.com/*, free)

Preparing Your Mac for Remote Connections

The first step is to prepare the Mac in your home or office—the one you will be connecting to remotely—for remote connections. Just sign in to your iCloud account or create a new one and then turn on the appropriate OS X sharing services. This allows the Mac to share folders and the screen.

Here's how to prepare your Mac for remote connections:

1. From the **Apple** menu, select **System Preferences**.
2. Click **iCloud**.
3. Sign in to iCloud or create an account if you haven't already. The dialog in Figure 23-1 appears.

FIGURE 23-1: *Turn on Back to My Mac in the iCloud preferences.*

4.   Select the **Back to My Mac** checkbox.
5.   Click **Show All**.
6.   Click **Sharing**.
7.   Select the **Screen Sharing** checkbox. This feature allows you to use your Mac virtually from another computer. The dialog shown in Figure 23-2 appears.

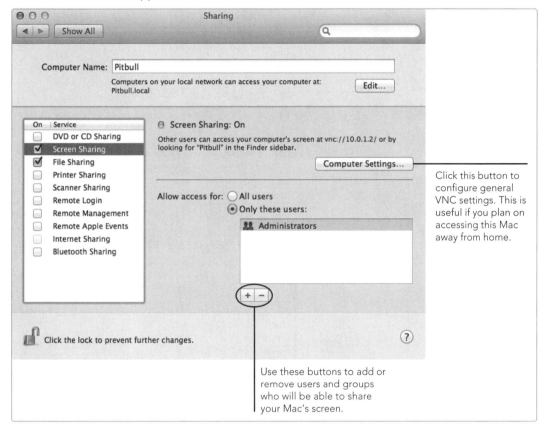

FIGURE 23-2: *Turn on the Screen Sharing feature to access your Mac's desktop from another computer.*

8.   (Optional) If you plan to access this computer from a Windows PC, click **Computer Settings**, select the **VNC viewer may control screen with password** checkbox, enter a password, and then click **OK**.
9.   You can control who can access your computer remotely by selecting **Only these users** and clicking the **+** and **–** buttons to add and remove users on your computer. By default, all of the administrators on your computer will be able to access it remotely.

10. Select the **File Sharing** checkbox. This feature allows you to browse and open the files in the shared folders on your Mac, as well as copy them to another computer. The window shown in Figure 23-3 appears.

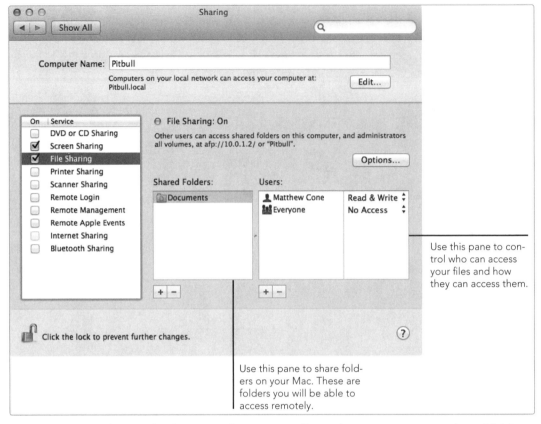

FIGURE 23-3: Configure File Sharing preferences to allow other users to access shared folders.

11. Use the Shared Folders pane to add folders and make them accessible to users who are remotely connected to your computer. If you don't know what you'll need to access, or if you need access to everything, it's a good idea to share your whole hard disk, just in case.

12. You can control who can access the shared files on your computer by clicking the **+** and **–** buttons to add and remove users on your computer. By default, all of the administrators on your computer will be able to access the shared files remotely.

13. Close System Preferences.

Of course, this Mac needs to be powered on and awake to accept any kind of remote connection. Before you leave on your trip, review Chapter 6 and verify that this Mac's energy settings allow it to remain powered on and awake for however long you will need to connect to it.

Connecting to Your Mac Remotely

Now that you've set everything up on the computer you want to access remotely, you need to configure some settings on the Mac you'll be using on the road. The first step is to sign in with your iCloud account so it can automatically locate and connect to the remote Mac. Then you'll learn how to browse the shared files and folders and access the remote Mac's desktop.

Preparing to Connect

Here's something important to know—you need to sign in to *both* computers with your iCloud account. Apple's servers automatically perform the rest of the magic behind the scenes. This is how one Mac is able to locate the other one, no matter where they are in the world.

Here's how to prepare your portable Mac to connect:

1. From the **Apple** menu, select **System Preferences**.
2. Click **iCloud**.
3. Sign in to iCloud.
4. Select the **Back to My Mac** checkbox.
5. Close System Preferences.

Now all you have to do is find a high-speed connection to the Internet. Screen sharing uses a lot of bandwidth!

Accessing Shared Files and Folders

Open a new Finder window to access the shared files and folders on your Mac from another Mac connected to the Internet. As shown in Figure 23-4, the remote Mac is displayed in the sidebar of the Finder window in the Shared section. All of the shared files and folders are available when you select the remote Mac.

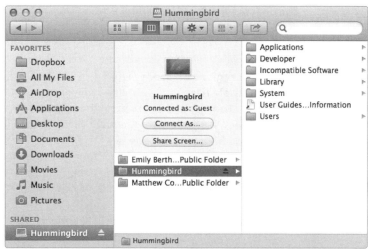

FIGURE 23-4: If you enabled File Sharing, all of your shared folders are available in the Finder window.

Now you can open the files or even copy them to the Mac you're currently using. And if you gave yourself read and write access, you can also delete files or add new ones.

Sharing Your Mac's Screen

When accessing shared files and folders isn't enough, you can share your Mac's screen. Using this feature when you're away from the office—or just in another room at home—puts your Mac's desktop in a window on the computer you're currently using. You can open applications, edit system settings, create documents, and do anything else you could do while sitting in front of your Mac.

Here's how to access your Mac's screen when you're away from home:

1. Open a new Finder window.
2. From the sidebar, under the **Shared** section, select the remote Mac.
3. Click **Share Screen**. The window shown in Figure 23-5 appears.

FIGURE 23-5: *To share the Mac's screen, log in as a registered user or enter your Apple ID and password.*

4. Select **As a registered user** to log in as a user on the computer. Or select **Using an Apple ID** to log in with the same account you're using with iCloud.
5. Enter your username and password in the **Name** and **Password** fields.
6. Click **Connect**. If another user is currently logged in to the computer, the dialog shown in Figure 23-6 appears.
7. Click **Share Display** to prompt the current user to share the screen. (The current user must approve access, so that option won't work if there's no one in front of the computer.) Or, to start a new session, click **Log In**—it's guaranteed to work every time, and the session of the current user will not be interrupted. The window shown in Figure 23-7 appears.

FIGURE 23-6: Select an option to connect to the remote Mac.

FIGURE 23-7: Sharing the screen of the remote Mac

Now it's just like you're sitting in front of your Mac. Go ahead—try opening some applications and editing some documents. As long as you have a fast connection to the Internet, screen sharing should feel like home away from home!

Additional Ideas for Accessing Your Mac Remotely

It's a good idea to do some real-world testing of your setup. You need to know you can access your Mac *before* you hit the road—it's too late to troubleshoot and fix problems once you're at the airport.

Thinking about trying other remote access solutions? It's hard to beat the sheer convenience of iCloud and Back to My Mac. Apple has taken all of the guesswork out of server software, port forwarding, and dynamic DNS—Back to My Mac just *works*. If you're feeling adventurous, though, take a look at the next chapter to learn how to access the remote Mac with an FTP application. Running an FTP server will allow you to access any of the files on the remote Mac, but you'll still have to configure port forwarding and dynamic DNS.

If you'd like to connect to your Mac from a Windows PC, you'll need to use a VNC client like TightVNC (*http://www.tightvnc.com/*, free). It's a good idea to configure port forwarding and dynamic DNS if you plan on going this route.

24

Turning Your Mac into a Web and FTP Server

You probably know that websites are stored on *web servers*—special computers that deliver files every time you visit a URL like *http://google.com/*. But you might not know that your Mac can act as a web server for your own personal or professional website. Turning your Mac into a web server is easy—just enable the server software baked into OS X. And if the built-in software isn't powerful enough, you can use an open source solution stack to make serving a database-driven website as easy as double-clicking an application.

There are several reasons why you might want to do this. If you're learning HTML or a programming language, you could turn your

Mac into a private development environment for experimentation purposes. If you work in a home or an office, you could set up a wiki page for people to share information and collaborate on projects. Or if you're a freelance designer, you could publish a public portfolio for clients.

Of course, your personal Mac probably won't cut it as a full-fledged production web server—that usually requires colocating your computer in a special facility. But for local development environments and small websites for friends and family members, your Mac makes the perfect server.

Project goal: Host a website on your Mac and access it from a friend's house.

What You'll Be Using

To make your Mac into a web server, you'll use the following:

 System Preferences

 MAMP (*http://www.mamp.info/*, free)

 Lighthouse (*http://codelaide.com/blog/products/lighthouse/*, $$)

 DynDNS (*https://www.dyn.com/dns/*, $$)

Understanding Web Servers

A dedicated web server is a fundamentally simple device. It's a computer that stores files and sends them to people who ask for them. An administrator's goal is to keep the server running and maintain the availability and integrity of the stored data. When it comes to your Mac, you'll want to make sure that your website is accessible even while the machine is performing other tasks for you.

To maintain a website, you'll need to install and enable server software to make the website accessible. Then you'll need to configure some third-party utilities to ensure that other people can access your Mac. This means changing your router's configuration and using dynamic DNS to link your Mac to a permanent host name.

The end result—your Mac acting as a personal web server—is very similar to a commercial web server. As long as your Mac is turned on and connected to the Internet, people can access the website hosted on your Mac by navigating to the URL of the website.

Configuring Server Software

There are two ways to host websites on your Mac. To host a static website, you can use the Apache web server included with OS X. To host a database-driven website, like a WordPress or Drupal website, you should install and configure a solution stack.

Starting Apache

The Apache web server is perfect for hosting static websites that consist primarily of HTML files and images. Once you turn on Apache, OS X will allow others to access the websites on your Mac. To start Apache, open the Terminal application (it's in the Utilities folder) and enter the following command:

```
sudo apachectl start
```

If you ever decide you want to stop serving web pages with your Mac, you can stop Apache by entering the following command:

```
sudo apachectl stop
```

It can take a couple of seconds for Apache to start. Once it does, you can move your website into /Library/Web Server/Documents. (To access the Library/ directory, switch to the Finder, hold down the OPTION key, and then select **Library** from the Go menu.) Remember, this solution is ideal for static HTML pages and files—PDF, Word, text—that you want to share with a small audience. If you need to host a content management system like WordPress, skip to "Using a Solution Stack" on page 247.

Now you can view your website with Safari by visiting *http://localhost/*. It's currently accessible to anyone connected to your local area network in your home or office—users will have to type the IP address of your computer into their web browser's address bar to view it. In "Using Dynamic DNS" on page 252, you'll learn how to make this website accessible to people outside of your home network with a memorable URL.

Using a Solution Stack

Sometimes Apache just isn't enough. To host a database-driven website on your Mac, you'll need to use a solution stack like MAMP (*http://www.mamp.info/*, free). This open source application bundle includes Apache, MySQL, and PHP—everything you need to set up a professional hosting environment on your Mac.

Just launch the MAMP application to get going. The Apache and MySQL servers start automatically, and a web page appears with the MySQL root password and links to administration tools like phpMyAdmin. MAMP comes preconfigured as a development environment, but you can edit MAMP's settings to turn it into a live web server.

Here's how to configure MAMP's settings:

1. If you started Apache as described in the previous section, stop it now. MAMP comes with its own version of Apache—you won't need to run another instance.
2. Double-click the MAMP application. The window shown in Figure 24-1 appears.
3. Click **Preferences**.

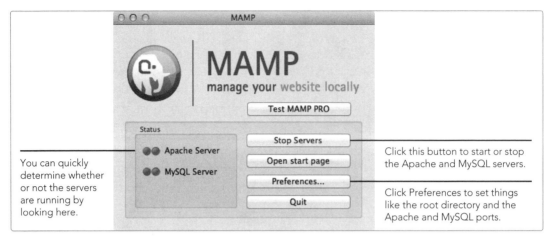

You can quickly determine whether or not the servers are running by looking here.

Click this button to start or stop the Apache and MySQL servers.

Click Preferences to set things like the root directory and the Apache and MySQL ports.

FIGURE 24-1: *The MAMP control panel*

4. Select the **Ports** tab and then click **Set to default Apache and MySQL ports**. This ensures that Apache is available on port 80 and MySQL on port 3306.

✳ *WARNING:* **If you set MySQL's port to 3306, you should change the default root password to protect your databases. Open the Terminal application and type this command:**

```
/Applications/MAMP/Library/bin/mysqladmin -u root -p password NEWPASSWORD
```

Replace *NEWPASSWORD* **with your new password. If you plan on using php-MyAdmin, edit the phpMyAdmin configuration file (*/Applications/MAMP/bin/phpMyAdmin-X.X.X/config.inc.php*) and update the MySQL password.**

5. Select the **Apache** tab and then click **Select** to set the document root. By default, the document root is set to */Applications/MAMP/htdocs*.
6. Click **OK** to save the changes. MAMP will automatically restart the servers and use the new settings.

Now MAMP is running. Move your website's files into the root directory (*/Applications/MAMP/htdocs*) and upload your database to MySQL with phpMy-Admin to make your database-driven website available to others. You can view your website with Safari by visiting *http://localhost/*.

The Apache, MySQL, and PHP configuration files are stored in the MAMP directory in the Applications folder. If you need to edit the Apache configuration file, for example, you can find it in */Applications/MAMP/conf/apache*. The filename is *httpd.conf*.

The Apache and MySQL servers stay running as long as the MAMP application is open. When you quit MAMP, the servers stop. If you use MAMP frequently, you can add it as a login item so that it automatically starts. For more information about login items, see Chapter 2.

Enabling Remote Login

One feature common to all web servers is the ability to upload and change files. If you need to remotely add, edit, or delete files stored on your Mac, enable the Remote Login feature built into OS X. This service allows you to use SSH and SFTP applications—like the Terminal application and Panic's Transmit FTP client (*http://www.panic.com/transmit/*, $$$)—to securely modify documents and keep an eye on your Mac while you're away from home.

Here's how to enable your Mac's built-in SSH server:

1. From the **Apple** menu, select **System Preferences**.
2. Select **Sharing**. The dialog shown in Figure 24-2 appears.

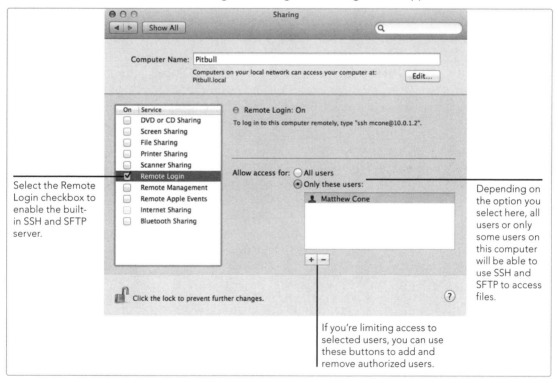

Select the Remote Login checkbox to enable the built-in SSH and SFTP server.

Depending on the option you select here, all users or only some users on this computer will be able to use SSH and SFTP to access files.

If you're limiting access to selected users, you can use these buttons to add and remove authorized users.

FIGURE 24-2: Enabling the built-in SSH server

3. Select the **Remote Login** checkbox.
4. (Optional) To restrict SSH and SFTP access to certain users on your computer, select **Only these users** and then click the **+** button to add authorized users.

It can take a couple of seconds for the SSH server to start. Once it does, you'll see the status indicator turn green. Now you can remotely access your Mac via SSH and SFTP.

Making Your Website Accessible to the World

If you're like most Mac users with home Internet access, your IP address provided by your ISP isn't static, so your website won't immediately be available outside of your local area network. Of course, hosting a website on your Mac doesn't do you much good if your friends, extended family, and virtual co-workers can't access it. You'll need to enable port forwarding and use dynamic DNS to make your website accessible to the world.

Enabling Port Forwarding

If you have a broadband Internet connection, you'll probably need to configure port forwarding on your router or use a port-forwarding utility like Lighthouse (*http://codelaide.com/blog/products/lighthouse/*, $$). Most modern routers allow multiple computers to connect to the Internet through one connection and one IP address. This creates problems when people outside your local area network try to access your Mac—the router doesn't know how to process these external access requests. Port forwarding allows external requests for your website to reach your Mac.

Manually configuring port forwarding on your router can be tricky, but it's the safest bet. Since the instructions for every router are different, check *http://portforward.com/* for instructions for your brand. If you'd rather try to enable port forwarding with software, you can install Lighthouse. Since Lighthouse works with most routers, this is a better option for users with MacBooks—Lighthouse can automatically configure port forwarding wherever you go with a handy feature called UPnP (Universal Plug and Play).

Here's how to use Lighthouse:

1. Double-click the Lighthouse application. Lighthouse automatically detects your router and places an icon in the menu bar, as shown in Figure 24-3.
2. From the **Lighthouse** menu, select **Start Profile** and then select **Http & Https**.

If Lighthouse has associated itself with your router, you'll see that information here.

Select this option to edit the profiles and associate them with applications.

You can create profiles for services and protocols. Select a profile to make that service available to the outside world.

FIGURE 24-3: *The Lighthouse menu*

3. From the **Lighthouse** menu, select **Start Profile** and then select **Ssh**.
4. To automate this process in the future, select **Edit Port Mapping Profiles** from the **Lighthouse** menu. The window shown in Figure 24-4 appears.
5. In the top pane, select **Http & Https** and then click **Change** to add the MAMP application as a trigger for this profile.
6. In the top pane, select **Ssh** and then click **Change** to add the MAMP application as a trigger for this profile.
7. Click **Save & Close**.

Now launching the MAMP application automatically starts the **Http & Https** and **Ssh** port-mapping profiles. This is a practical way to daisy-chain all of the web server startup tasks together—if you set MAMP as a login item, it will trigger port-mapping profiles for the Apache and SSH servers when you turn on your Mac.

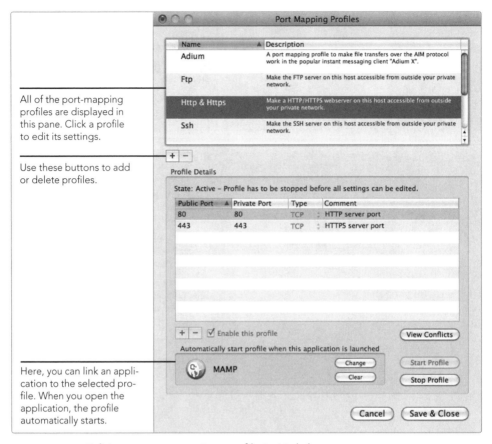

All of the port-mapping profiles are displayed in this pane. Click a profile to edit its settings.

Use these buttons to add or delete profiles.

Here, you can link an application to the selected profile. When you open the application, the profile automatically starts.

FIGURE 24-4: *Editing a port-mapping profile in Lighthouse*

Using Dynamic DNS

With port forwarding enabled, people can access your website by typing your router's IP address in their browser's address bar. But IP addresses can be difficult to remember, and if your router has a dynamic IP address, it might be different the next time someone tries to access your website. That's where dynamic DNS can help.

Dynamic DNS continuously monitors your Mac's DNS settings. When your IP address changes, a utility application on your Mac uploads the new DNS settings to a centralized server, which attaches the information to a static hostname. The result is that your website is available from the same domain name at all times, just like a regular website.

Here's how to use dynamic DNS:

1. Register for a Dyn account (*http://www.dyn.com/*, $$). You'll create a domain name for your website when you register.

✳ **NOTE:** To use your own top-level domain name (i.e., *http://www.yoursite.com/*), purchase one of the custom DynDNS products.

2. Download, install, and launch the DynDNS Update Client application (*http://dyn.com/support/clients/mac/*, free).
3. Log in to your DynDNS account. The window shown in Figure 24-5 appears.

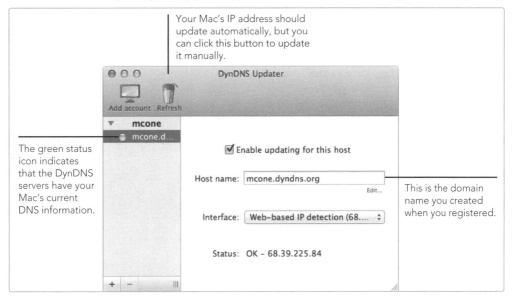

FIGURE 24-5: *The DynDNS Updater interface*

4. Click **Refresh** to send your Mac's current IP address to the DynDNS servers.
5. Quit the DynDNS Updater application. The service continues to run in the background, notifying the DynDNS servers when your IP address changes.

Congratulations! Your Mac is now a real web server, and your website is available to anyone with an Internet connection. Note that it can take a couple of minutes for the DNS servers to update. To test it yourself, pick up your iPhone and try loading your website while connected to your cellular provider's network, or head over to a friend's house and try accessing it from there.

Additional Ideas for Turning Your Mac into a Web Server

If you have a database-driven website, be aware that other solution stacks are available. XAMPP (*http://www.apachefriends.org/*, free) is an open source stack that provides the same functionality as MAMP, but in a different way. You might prefer it. There is also a professional version of MAMP that offers additional features and functionality. MAMP Pro (*http://www.mamp.info/en/mamp-pro/*, $$$) allows you to set up a mail server, configure virtual hosts, and use a custom dynamic DNS solution. And if you need to host more than one website on your Mac, check out VirtualHostX (*http://clickontyler.com/virtualhostx/*, $$$)—an application that takes the guesswork out of setting up multiple websites using virtual hosts.

And finally, remember that the advice provided in this chapter is not really suited for major websites. For one thing, your Internet service provider can tell if you're running a busy server, and it won't be happy if you are. If you need to host a high-traffic website on your Mac, consider getting a business broadband connection and installing OS X Server, a version of OS X that is specially designed for turning Macs into servers. To learn how to secure a Mac running a web or FTP server, see Chapter 30.

25

Wirelessly Sharing a Printer and Hard Drive

Wirelessly sharing a printer and USB hard drive is a revelation. Unplug the cables, move the devices off of your desk, and start moving freely around your home or office—still with easy access to the devices. The AirPort Express and AirPort Extreme Base Station make this simple. (You can use the AirPort Express to share a printer but not a hard drive.) You'll wonder how you ever lived without this functionality.

Project goal: Wirelessly share a printer and USB hard drive on your home or office network.

What You'll Be Using

To untether yourself from your devices, you'll use the following:

 AirPort Express or AirPort Extreme Base Station (*http://www.apple.com/airportexpress/, http://www.apple.com/airportextreme/*, $$$)

 AirPort Utility

Sharing a Printer

Many new printers are already capable of connecting to wireless networks. But using a printer's interface to connect it to the wireless network can be confusing, and once you get it hooked up, how to access the printer from your Mac isn't always clear. That's why using an AirPort Express or AirPort Extreme Base Station to wirelessly share printers is a good idea—getting connected is dirt simple, and printers are easy to access from any Mac in your home or office.

Connecting the Printer to the Base Station

The first step is to connect the printer's USB cable to the AirPort Express or AirPort Extreme Base Station. If you have multiple printers in your home or office, you can connect them all by using a USB hub. (Both base stations have only one USB port.)

Here's how to connect a printer to the AirPort Express or AirPort Extreme Base Station:

1. If necessary, move the printer closer to the base station so that the USB cable will reach from one to the other.
2. Turn the printer and the base station on.
3. Connect the printer's USB cable to the base station's USB port.

That's all you have to do. The AirPort Express or AirPort Extreme Base Station recognizes the printer, and any user connected to the wireless network can access it.

Printing Wirelessly from Your Mac

There's no special configuration necessary to print from the network printer. Just select **Print** from the **File** menu and look for the printer in the **Printer** menu, as shown in Figure 25-1. It should be listed in the Nearby Printers section.

Remember, any user on your wireless network can access this printer. If you work in an office, try to place the base station and the printer in a central location so users can easily pick up their printouts.

FIGURE 25-1: *Verify that the printer is displayed in the list.*

Sharing a Hard Drive

You might be wondering why anyone would want to share a hard drive wirelessly. After all, external hard drives are pretty small these days, and it's not that difficult to tote one around the house. But even if mobility is not a concern, there are other reasons why you might want to connect a hard drive to your wireless network.

A *network drive* can be used to share photos, movies, and music with other people in your home or office. And if you live alone, you can use a network drive to automatically perform Time Machine backups from anywhere in the house. Just make sure to connect the hard drive to your Mac for the initial backup—it can take a while. (See Chapter 36 for more information on Time Machine.)

Connecting the Hard Drive to the AirPort Extreme

The first step in creating a network drive is to connect a USB hard drive to the AirPort Extreme. If you don't already have a dedicated USB hard drive for this purpose, you'll need to purchase one. In fact, you could purchase two or three—the AirPort Extreme allows you to connect multiple drives with a USB hub.

Here's how to connect a USB hard drive to an AirPort Extreme Base Station:

1. Verify that the AirPort Extreme Base Station is turned on.
2. Connect the USB hard drive to the AirPort's USB port. If you already have another device connected to that port, you will need to use a USB hub to connect all of the devices.
3. Open the AirPort Utility application. (It's in the Utilities folder.)
4. Select the AirPort Extreme Base Station. The pop-up window appears, as shown in Figure 25-2.

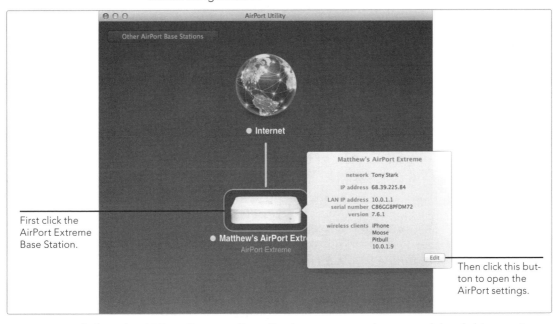

First click the AirPort Extreme Base Station.

Then click this button to open the AirPort settings.

FIGURE 25-2: *Select the AirPort Extreme Base Station to access the network hard drive settings.*

5. Click **Edit**.
6. Click **Disks**. The window shown in Figure 25-3 appears. Verify that your hard disk is listed in the pane.

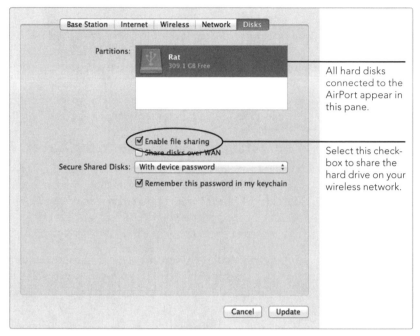

FIGURE 25-3: *Verify that your hard disk is listed.*

7. Select the **Enable file sharing** checkbox.
8. Click **Update**. The AirPort Extreme Base Station will restart.

Now your hard drive is connected to your AirPort Extreme Base Station and shared on your wireless network. But leave the AirPort Utility application open—you're about to learn how to control access to the drive so that only authorized users can access it.

Controlling Access to the Network Drive

The AirPort Extreme provides several options for controlling access to a network drive. You can create a single password that everyone can use, create separate accounts for every user who accesses the drive, or just use the password you set for the AirPort Extreme Base Station.

Creating a Single Shared Password

Creating a shared password for the network drive offers the best balance between security and accessibility. With this option, you can create a single password to share with all of the users who need to access the drive.

Here's how to create a single shared password:

1.   From the **Secure Shared Disks** menu, select **With a disk password**, as shown in Figure 25-4.

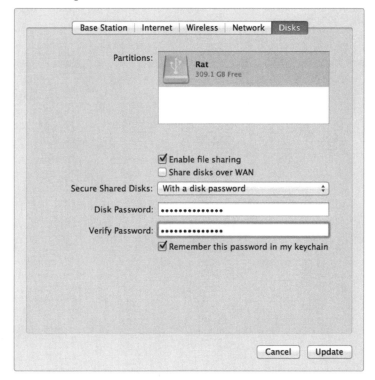

FIGURE 25-4: *Securing the network drive with a single password*

2.   Enter a password in the **Disk Password** and **Verify Password** fields.
3.   (Optional) Select the **Remember this password in my keychain** checkbox to save the disk password in the Keychain Access application.
4.   Click **Update**. Wait for the AirPort Extreme to restart.

Now the network drive is protected by a single password, and any user you share it with can access the devices on your network.

Creating a Separate Account for Each User

If you need to control access on a user-by-user basis, creating separate accounts is the way to go. Each user will have a unique username and password. You can even grant users one of three types of access: read and write, read only, or no access.

Here's how to create separate accounts for users:

1.   From the **Secure Shared Disks** menu, select **With accounts**, as shown in Figure 25-5.

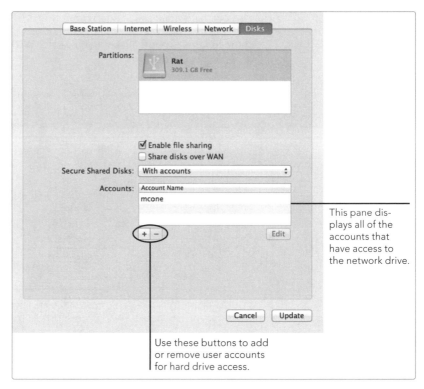

This pane displays all of the accounts that have access to the network drive.

Use these buttons to add or remove user accounts for hard drive access.

FIGURE 25-5: *Adding individual accounts to control access to the network drive*

2. Click the **+** button to add an account. The dialog shown in Figure 25-6 appears.

FIGURE 25-6: *Creating an account for a user*

3. Enter a username for the user in the **Account Name** field.
4. Enter a password for the user's account in the **Account Password** and **Verify Password** fields.
5. Select an access level from the **File Sharing Access** menu.

6. Click **Save**.
7. Repeat this process for other users on your network who need access to the network drive.
8. Click **Update**. Wait for the AirPort Extreme to restart.

Users will be able to log in with their usernames and passwords after the AirPort Extreme restarts.

Using the AirPort Extreme's Password

If you're the only person using the wireless network, or if you trust the other people using the network, you can use the AirPort Extreme's password to protect the network drive. This option is not recommended, however, because anyone who has the password will be able to change your AirPort Extreme's configuration.

Here's how to protect the network drive with the AirPort Extreme's password:

1. From the **Secure Shared Disks** menu, select **With device password**.
2. (Optional) Select the **Remember this password in my keychain** checkbox to save the disk password in the Keychain Access application.
3. Click **Update**. Wait for the AirPort Extreme to restart.

Users will be able to log in with the AirPort Extreme password after the base station restarts.

Accessing the Hard Drive Wirelessly

Now that you've protected your network drive with a password, any user connected to the wireless network can access it from his Mac. All he has to do is open a new Finder window—the AirPort Extreme is listed under the Shared section in the sidebar, as shown in Figure 25-7.

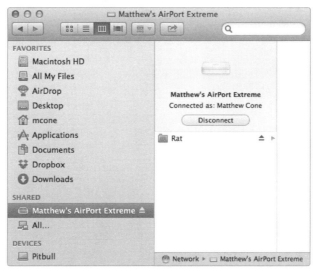

FIGURE 25-7: *A network user opens a Finder window to access the network drive.*

If the AirPort Extreme is not displayed in a user's Finder window, you might have to adjust the Finder Preferences on his computer. To do so, select **Preferences** from the **Finder** menu and then select the **Connected servers** checkbox. The AirPort Extreme should now be displayed in the user's Finder window.

Additional Ideas for Wirelessly Sharing a Printer and Network Hard Drive

As mentioned earlier in the chapter, you can connect a USB hub to the AirPort Extreme to share multiple printers and hard drives with the users on your wireless network. You can also share other devices, such as scanners.

If you want to take this whole sharing thing to the next level, you can use the AirPort Extreme to share the network drive over the Internet. To do so, select the **Share disk over WAN** checkbox in the Disks pane in the AirPort Utility application. Then enable port forwarding for ports 445 and 548 and, for easier access, set up dynamic DNS. (For more information about port forwarding and dynamic DNS, see Chapter 24.) When you're away from home, switch to the Finder, select **Connect to Server** from the **Go** menu, and then enter your router's IP address or your dynamic DNS URL.

26 Synchronizing Files Between Computers

You haven't experienced true frustration until you've tried using more than one computer on a daily basis. Keeping your files organized and current on multiple computers is a nightmare! Some people store all of their files on an external drive and carry it around with them. Other people use Dropbox or iCloud to access their files remotely. But those options were never designed for full *synchronization*—the process of establishing data consistency on multiple devices—and they aren't capable of synchronizing *all* of the files between your computers.

For bulletproof file synchronization, you'll need to use a third-party application called ChronoSync. It compares the files on your computers and then automatically updates the files to keep the data on all of your computers current. The best part is that the application is flexible enough to be used in a variety of situations. You can use ChronoSync to synchronize the data on multiple computers, backup files, or even mirror drives.

This chapter walks you through the process of setting up ChronoSync on your computers and choosing the right synchronization option for your particular situation. You'll also learn about advanced settings like scheduling, rule-based triggering, and email notifications. By the end of this chapter, the nightmare of storing files on multiple computers will be over!

Project goal: Synchronize all of your files between the computers you use.

What You'll Be Using

To synchronize files between computers, you'll use the following:

 ChronoSync (*http://econtechnologies.com/pages/cs/chrono_overview.html*, $$$)

 ChronoAgent (*http://econtechnologies.com/pages/ca/agent_overview.html*, $)

Getting Started with ChronoSync

Setting up ChronoSync correctly is an important step to getting synchronization to work right. First you'll install ChronoSync on your primary Mac and ChronoAgent on the other computers you use. Then you'll connect all of the computers together in the ChronoSync application.

Installing ChronoSync and ChronoAgent

The first step is to install the ChronoSync application on your primary Mac. This application is the brains behind the entire operation—it controls how and when all of the computers are synchronized. You'll also need to install a preference pane called ChronoAgent on the other computers you use. ChronoAgent is just a service. You can't do anything with it on the client computers, so that's why it's important to install the ChronoSync application on the Mac you use the most.

Connecting All of the Computers

After you've installed the ChronoSync and ChronoAgent applications, it's time to connect the computers. Ideally, you'll be able to connect all of the computers to the same local area network (LAN) for this initial connection process. Otherwise you'll need to follow the instructions in Chapter 23 to enable Back to My Mac on all of the computers.

Here's how to connect all of the computers to ChronoSync:

1. On the client computer with ChronoAgent installed, select **System Preferences** from the **Apple** menu.
2. Click **ChronoAgent**. The window shown in Figure 26-1 appears.

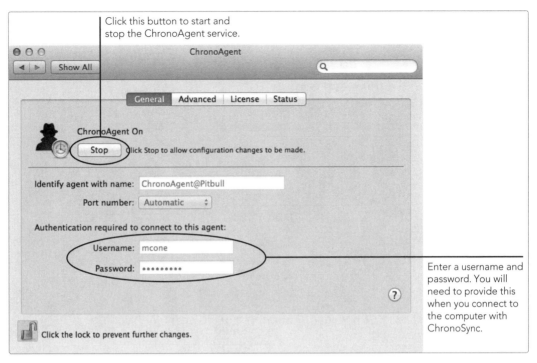

Click this button to start and stop the ChronoAgent service.

ChronoAgent

Show All

General | Advanced | License | Status

ChronoAgent On

Stop Click Stop to allow configuration changes to be made.

Identify agent with name: ChronoAgent@Pitbull

Port number: Automatic

Authentication required to connect to this agent:

Username: mcone

Password: •••••••••

Enter a username and password. You will need to provide this when you connect to the computer with ChronoSync.

Click the lock to prevent further changes.

FIGURE 26-1: *Manually starting ChronoAgent on every client computer*

3. Enter a username and password in the **Username** and **Password** fields.
4. Click **Start**. The ChronoAgent service starts.
5. Repeat this process on all of your client computers.
6. On the Mac with ChronoSync, open the ChronoSync application.
7. From the **ChronoSync** menu, select **Preferences**.
8. Click **Connections**.
9. Click the **+** button. The window shown in Figure 26-2 appears.
10. Enter a name for the connection in the **Profile Name** field.
11. From the **Connect to** menu, select a computer running ChronoAgent.
12. Enter the username and password—the ones you specified in the Chrono-Agent preference pane—in the **Username** and **Password** fields.
13. (Optional) Click **Test** to test the connection between the two computers.
14. Click the **Mappings** tab. The window shown in Figure 26-3 appears.
15. From the **Mapping Mode** menu, select **Basic**. This feature automatically attempts to match the user and group accounts on the two Macs.
16. From the **Remote User Account** menu, verify that your local user account is mapped to an account on the remote computer. If it's not, select an account from the menu.
17. Click **Save**.
18. Repeat this process for every computer you want to synchronize.

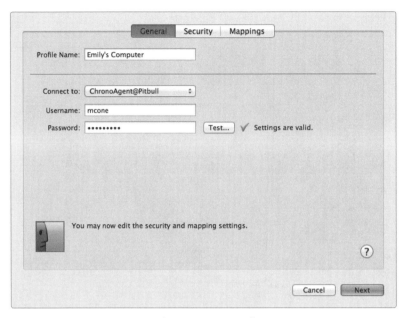

FIGURE 26-2: *Connecting ChronoSync to all computers running ChronoAgent*

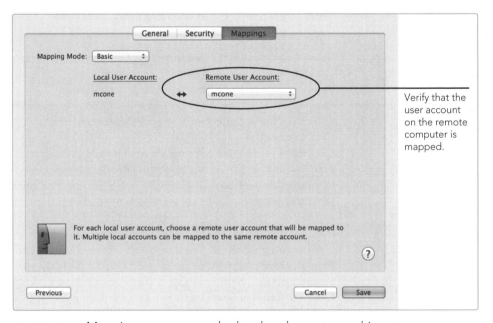

Verify that the user account on the remote computer is mapped.

FIGURE 26-3: *Mapping accounts on the local and remote machines to ensure proper syncing*

All of your computers are connected to ChronoSync. You're ready for the next step—setting up synchronizations.

Setting Up Synchronizations

This is the fun part. You get to decide what you want to synchronize, select a synchronization option, test everything to make sure it works, and then schedule ChronoSync to automatically compare and move files at selected times. By the time you reach the end of this section, you'll have created an automated synchronization system.

Selecting Folders and Volumes to Synchronize

What do you want to keep synchronized? You can select a folder like your user folder or documents folder, or an entire volume like your hard drive. It all depends on how much data you want to keep mirrored. Remember, it can take a lot of time to transfer all of these files over the Internet, or even a LAN.

Here's how to select a folder or volume to synchronize:

1. Open the ChronoSync application.
2. From the sidebar, click **Setup**. The window shown in Figure 26-4 appears.

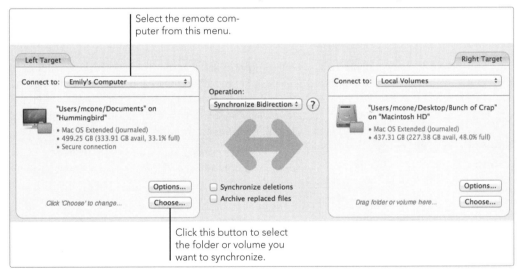

FIGURE 26-4: *Connecting computers and selecting a folder or volume for synchronization*

3. From the Left Target pane, select the remote computer from the **Connect to** menu.
4. From the Left Target pane, click **Choose**.
5. Select the folder or volume on the remote computer that you want to synchronize, and then click **Select**.

6. From the Right Target pane, select **Local Volumes** from the **Connect to** menu.
7. From the Right Target pane, click **Choose**.
8. Select the folder or volume on the local computer that you want to synchronize, and then click **Select**.

Now the Readiness State pane should indicate that ChronoSync is configured and ready to synchronize the two computers. You're ready to synchronize files between the two computers!

Selecting a Synchronization Option

This next step is important: How do you want ChronoSync to synchronize your files? There are options for virtually every type of setup. Before you make a decision, carefully review the available settings and think about how you want your files to be transferred.

Here are the available synchronization options in ChronoSync:

▶   Backup Left-to-right: The left target is monitored for changes and compared to the right target. If changes are detected, the modified files will be copied to the right target. (Backup Right-to-left does the same thing, but switches the targets.)

▶   Synchronize Bidirectional: Both targets are monitored for changes. If there are changes detected on a target, the modified files will be copied to the other target.

▶   Blind Backup Left-to-right: The left target is monitored for changes. If there are changes detected, the modified files will be copied to the right target. If you modify a file on the right target, the file on the left target will not replace it unless you later modify the file on the left target. (Blind Backup Right-to-left does the same thing, but switches the targets.)

▶   Mirror Left-to-right: Files are copied only left to right. If a file is modified, the left file will overwrite the right file. (Mirror Right-to-left does the same thing, but switches the targets.)

▶   Bootable Left-to-right: A bootable copy of the left target is copied to the right target. You must specify a volume to use this option. (Bootable Right-to-left does the same thing, but switches the targets.)

For most people, Synchronize Bidirectional is the ideal option. This will keep the files on both of your computers synchronized, no matter which computer you use to modify a file. You'll never have to wonder whether your files are up to date. Those who work primarily on one computer will want to investigate the other options, which heavily favor one computer.

Here's how to select a synchronization option:

1. Open the ChronoSync application.
2. From the sidebar, click **Setup**. The window shown in Figure 26-5 appears.

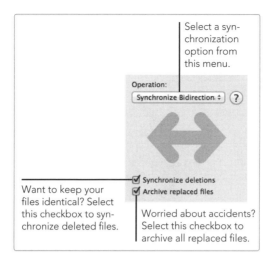

Select a syn-
chronization
option from
this menu.

Operation:

Synchronize Bidirection. ⬍ (?)

Synchronize deletions
Archive replaced files

Want to keep your
files identical? Select
this checkbox to syn-
chronize deleted files.

Worried about accidents?
Select this checkbox to
archive all replaced files.

FIGURE 26-5: *Selecting a synchronization option*

3. From the **Operation** menu, select a synchronization option.
4. (Optional) Select the **Synchronize deletions** checkbox to synchronize deletions on both computers. This means that if you delete a file on one computer, it will also be deleted on the other computer, if you selected a synchronization option that supports this feature.
5. (Optional) Select the **Archive replaced files** checkbox to save files that are replaced during the synchronization process.

Everything is set up—now you're ready to try a test synchronization.

Synchronizing Your Files

This is the moment of truth: Does your setup work the way you've configured it? First, *back up the hard drives on both computers*. For instructions on backing up your computer, see Chapter 36. This is very important! If anything goes wrong during the synchronization, you'll be able to restore your files.

Here's how to synchronize your files:

1. Open the ChronoSync application.
2. Verify that all of the synchronization options are set up the way you want them.
3. (Optional) Click **Trial Sync** to perform a trial synchronization. (No files will be copied during the trial run.) The window shown in Figure 26-6 appears.
4. (Optional) Verify that the files will be moved to the correct places.
5. (Optional) Click **Synchronize** to run the trial. If there are no errors, you're ready to synchronize your files.
6. In the main ChronoSync window, click **Synchronize**. ChronoSync transfers files to make the data consistent on both computers.

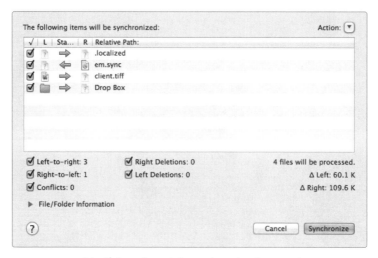

FIGURE 26-6: *Verifying the trial synchronization options*

The synchronization is complete. Check both computers to make sure that the files were transferred correctly. If it worked, save the synchronization configuration by selecting **Save As** from the **File** menu. You'll need to open this configuration to perform this synchronization again in the future.

Scheduling Synchronizations

ChronoSync allows you to schedule synchronizations so that they occur automatically on certain days of the week, or at certain times of the day. For example, you could schedule a transfer at the end of the day, before you leave the office, so that all of the files on your work computer are transferred to your home computer by the time you leave. Then you could schedule another transfer in the morning, before you leave home, so that all of the files are waiting for you at the office.

Here's how to schedule synchronizations:

1. Open the ChronoSync application.
2. Click **Add to Schedule**. The window shown in Figure 26-7 appears.
3. Select the **Active** checkbox.
4. Select an interval from the **Run Sync** menu.
5. Set the hours and minutes. You can select multiple hours and minutes.
6. Click **OK**.

That's it! ChronoSync will automatically synchronize your computers at the intervals you've selected, as long as all of the computers are turned on and ChronoSync is running.

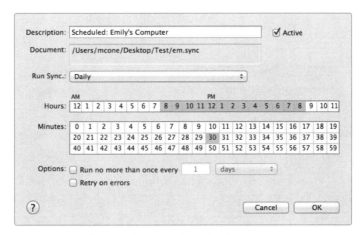

FIGURE 26-7: *Scheduling synchronizations*

Monitoring ChronoSync

You've set up ChronoSync to synchronize files on multiple computers, but don't stop there. There are a couple of other features you should know about before you kick back and let ChronoSync work its magic. In this section, you'll learn how to monitor previous and current synchronizations to make sure everything is working correctly and get email notifications when a sync has been completed.

Monitoring Synchronizations

It's important to periodically check on ChronoSync to make sure it's moving all of your files to the right places. Fortunately, this is one application that keeps good logs. It's easy to tell what's happened—if you suspect a problem, or just want to see which files were transferred, follow these instructions.

Here's how to monitor synchronizations:

1. Open the ChronoSync application.
2. From the sidebar, select **Analyze**. The window shown in Figure 26-8 appears.
3. Verify that there are no errors, and that synchronizations are occurring the way you expect them to.

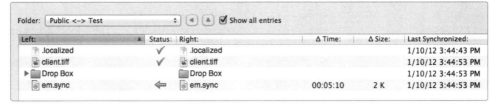

FIGURE 26-8: *Monitoring synchronizations*

To find more information about errors that have occurred, click the **Log** button to see the raw, unfiltered ChronoSync event log.

Getting Notifications

Want to know when a synchronization has been completed? Use ChronoSync's email notification feature. Just enter your email address and the application will notify you via email.

Here's how to get notifications:

1. Open the ChronoSync application.
2. From the sidebar, select **Options**. The window shown in Figure 26-9 appears.

FIGURE 26-9: *Setting up notifications*

3. Select the **Send email** checkbox.
4. Enter your email address in the **to** field.
5. From the **File** menu, select **Save** to save the configuration.

That's it. Now ChronoSync will send you an email message every time a synchronization has been completed.

Additional Ideas for Synchronizing Files

Synchronizing files is a great solution for those who use two or more computers every day, but it might be overkill for some people. If you're on the fence about whether to purchase ChronoSync, try using iCloud and Dropbox first. Those cloud-based storage and synchronization options aren't nearly as comprehensive as ChronoSync, but that can be an advantage for people who need less. To get started with iCloud and Dropbox, see Chapter 22.

ChronoSync can also be used to create a bootable backup on an external hard drive—something that could come in handy when performing troubleshooting tasks or restoring files after upgrading your hard drive. For other backup options, see Chapter 36.

PART 6

Serious
Security

27

Creating Strong Passwords and Storing Them Securely

Most of the personal information you store on computers is kept private until you enter a username and password combination to access your corner of the digital world. Every time you use an ATM, access your email account, or log in to a computer, you are using password authentication—one of the most effective security controls available.

But anyone who has ever used passwords is also familiar with the problems that accompany them. How do you create different passwords for different accounts and manage to remember them all? If you create simple or memorable passwords, a criminal might guess them. But if you create strong passwords—with long strings of random characters, numbers, and punctuation marks—you might forget them.

With your Mac and two applications called Keychain Access and 1Password, there's now a better way to create strong passwords and manage them all.

Project goal: Create strong passwords and store them in an encrypted database.

What You'll Be Using

To develop passwords no one else can crack and keep them somewhere safe, you'll use the following:

 Keychain Access

 1Password (*https://agilebits.com/onepassword/mac*, $$$)

Understanding Password Management Applications

Password management applications like Keychain Access and 1Password are secure digital notebooks for your passwords. These applications help you create strong passwords that are difficult to crack, and then they store the passwords in encrypted repositories that are off-limits to everyone except you. The result is a complete list of all of your passwords that is protected by a single master password, as shown in Figure 27-1.

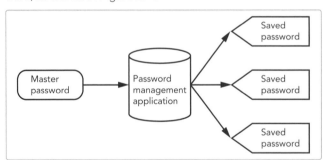

FIGURE 27-1: *With a password management application, you have to remember only one password to access all of your other passwords.*

Consider what this means: If you use a password management application, you have to remember only the one master password. All of the other saved passwords can be copied out of the password management application once you authenticate with your master password.

Rejoice, information-overloaded individual! The days of having to remember dozens of passwords are over. Now you can use 30-character passwords without having to memorize them.

Tips for Creating Strong Passwords

As you read this, criminals are running password-cracking applications against databases to brute-force their way into accounts like yours. How do you create strong passwords to protect yourself?

Here are some guidelines you can follow to minimize your risk:

▶ Do not use dictionary words in your passwords.

▶ Make sure that your passwords contain at least eight characters.

▶ Use numbers and punctuation marks in your passwords.

▶ Change your passwords every three months.

The strength of the password should correspond to the level of risk, as shown in Figure 27-2. You don't need to create a 30-character password for a free game website that does not store your personal information. In fact, you could use the same simple password for all of your low-risk accounts—memberships in online forums, news websites, and so on. The damage would be limited if one of those accounts were compromised.

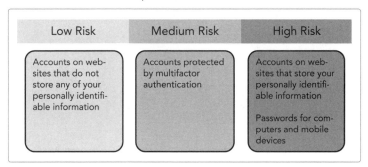

FIGURE 27-2: Modify the strength of your password according to the sensitivity of the account.

Medium-risk accounts are those that are protected by multifactor authentication—that is, both something you have and something you know. An example is your ATM card and PIN. In theory, a criminal would not be able to access one of these accounts with just your password.

High-risk accounts protect devices or sensitive personal information. These are the accounts that you should take great care to protect. For example, you wouldn't want a criminal to guess the password to your online stock-trading account.

Using Keychain Access

OS X provides a built-in method for securely storing passwords, notes, keys, and other access information. You can access these encrypted repositories, called *keychains*, by using a password management application called Keychain Access. The Keychain Access interface is shown in Figure 27-3.

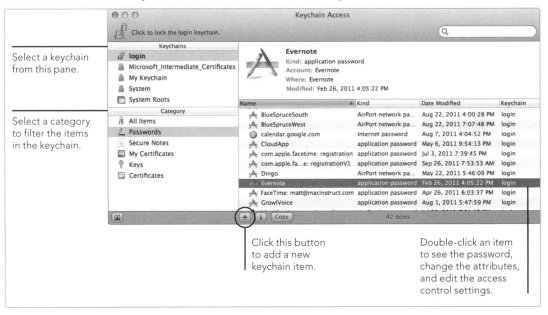

Select a keychain from this pane.

Select a category to filter the items in the keychain.

Click this button to add a new keychain item.

Double-click an item to see the password, change the attributes, and edit the access control settings.

FIGURE 27-3: *The Keychain Access window provides easy access to all of your saved passwords, notes, keys, and certificates.*

When you save any kind of password on your Mac, like a password for a wireless router or a website login, it's stored in your keychain. (Passwords saved in applications like Safari are also stored in your keychain.) So when you open Keychain Access, you'll probably see a lot of saved passwords.

＊ **NOTE: You need to unlock the keychain to access your passwords. Click the lock icon to authenticate with your username and password. For more information, see "Locking and Unlocking the Keychain" on page 281.**

There are already several keychains on your Mac, each of which has several categories of items, such as passwords, secure notes, keys, and certificates. You can use the Keychain Access application to create as many keychains as you want, but the existing keychains will probably work for most users.

Creating and Saving Passwords to the Keychain

You can manually create and save passwords to a keychain using the Keychain Access application. This is useful for storing username and password combinations for bank accounts, websites, and other computers.

Here's how to use Keychain Access to create and save passwords manually:

1. Open the Keychain Access application. (It's located in the Utilities folder.)
2. Select a keychain from the Keychains pane.
3. Select **Passwords** from the Category pane.
4. Click the **+** button to add a new keychain item. The dialog shown in Figure 27-4 appears.

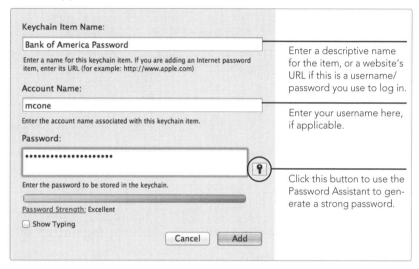

FIGURE 27-4: *Adding a new keychain item*

5. Enter a name for the keychain item in the **Keychain Item Name** field. This should be a descriptive name that will enable you to identify the item in a list. If the password is for a website account, enter the website's URL as the name.
6. If a username is associated with this password, enter it in the **Account Name** field.
7. Enter a password in the **Password** field or click the key button to randomly generate a strong password. The Password Assistant dialog shown in Figure 27-5 appears when you click the key button.
8. Select a password type from the **Type** menu. If you don't need to memorize the password, select **Letter & Numbers** or **Random** for maximum security.
9. Move the **Length** slider to adjust the length of the password. Longer passwords are more secure, so if you don't need to memorize the password, make it as long as possible.

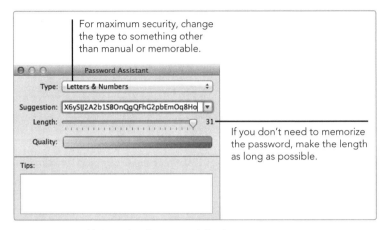

For maximum security, change the type to something other than manual or memorable.

Password Assistant

Type: Letters & Numbers

Suggestion: X6ySIJ2A2b1SBOnQgQFhG2pbEmOq8Ho

Length: 31

Quality:

Tips:

If you don't need to memorize the password, make the length as long as possible.

FIGURE 27-5: *Using the Password Assistant to create a strong password*

10. Close the Password Assistant window.
11. Click **Add**. The password has been saved to the keychain.

Now the password is stored in your Mac's keychain. You can access it with Keychain Access by double-clicking the item you just created.

For menu bar access to the passwords in the keychain, enable the menu bar icon in the Keychain Access preferences.

Protecting Other Sensitive Information with the Keychain

Besides passwords, you can also use the Keychain Access application to store credit card numbers, PINs, phone numbers, secret notes, and any other information you want to keep secure. Everything in the keychain is protected with Triple Data Encryption Standard (DES) encryption.

The *Secure Note* is the best keychain item for storing this kind of information. You can enter short strings or large blocks of text in just about any format you want.

Here's how to use Keychain Access to save a secure note:

1. Open the Keychain Access application (located in the Utilities folder).
2. Select a keychain from the Keychains pane.
3. Select **Secure Notes** from the Category pane.
4. Click the **+** button to add a new keychain item. The window shown in Figure 27-6 appears.
5. Enter a descriptive name for the note in the **Keychain Item Name** field.
6. Enter the note in the **Note** field.
7. Click **Add**. The note has been saved to the keychain.

If a secure note seems like overkill for a code you want to store, remember that shorter passcodes, like PINs, can also be stored as password items.

FIGURE 27-6: Using Keychain Access to encrypt notes

Locking and Unlocking the Keychain

The keychain on your Mac is encrypted and protected from unauthorized access until you authenticate with the password to unlock it. By default, the keychain password is the same as the password for your user account; you can change the password by selecting **Edit ▸ Change Password for Keychain**.

✳ *WARNING:* **Do not forget your keychain password. If you do, you will permanently lose access to all of the passwords and information stored in the keychain.**

When you first open the Keychain Access application, you'll need to click the lock button to unlock the keychains, as shown in Figure 27-7.

Before closing the Keychain Access application, you should click the lock button again to lock the keychains. (The keychain locks automatically if your computer is idle for a while.)

FIGURE 27-7: Click the lock icon to lock and unlock the keychains.

Repairing and Backing Up the Keychain

Clearly, losing the information stored in your keychain would be disastrous. You'd have to reset all of your passwords! To head off any potential password nightmares, you should back up your keychains on a regular basis.

Keychains are automatically backed up when you perform a system-wide backup, like a Time Machine backup. But a separate procedure allows you to perform individual backups of your keychains by repairing them and copying them to a different location. (*Repairing* is a precaution that can fix problems with keychains before the backup. You wouldn't want to back up a corrupt keychain!)

Here's how to back up your keychains:

1. Open the Keychain Access application. (It's located in the Utilities folder.)
2. Select **Keychain Access ▸ Keychain First Aid**.
3. Enter your username and password and then click **Start**.
4. If problems are found, select **Repair** and then click **Start**.
5. Close the Keychain First Aid window.
6. In the Finder, copy the files in the */Users/<username>/Library/Keychains/* folder—where *<username>* is your account on the computer—to the backup destination (preferably on a different hard drive).

To restore your keychains, move the backup files to the */Users/<username>/Library/Keychains/* folder.

✳ *NOTE:* OS X hides your user Library folder by default. To show the Library folder, open the Finder, hold down OPTION, and select *Library* from the *Go* menu.

Using 1Password

Keychain Access is pretty good at what it does, but it may not exactly suit your needs. It's difficult, for example, to save a website's password in a web browser and then automatically fill it in the next time you visit the website. A third-party application called 1Password (*https://agilebits.com/onepassword/mac*, $$$) is an alternative to Keychain Access that fixes many of its annoyances. It's so expensive that it's hard to recommend to casual users, but anyone who cares deeply about strong passwords won't be caught without this program.

The 1Password application resembles Keychain Access, as shown in Figure 27-8. One difference is that 1Password calls its keychain a "vault." A more significant difference is that you can have only one. The categories in 1Password are a bit more intuitive than the ones found in Keychain Access. Instead of the password and secure note items—the only two modifiable items in Keychain Access—1Password separates logins, accounts, identities, secure notes, software licenses, and wallet items into different categories.

Adding new items is easy. Just select a category from the left pane and then click the **+** button under the center pane. The password-generation features are similar to the ones in Keychain Access.

If you're not fond of the window layout, you can change it by clicking the three buttons at the top of the window.

Using the 1Password Browser Extension

The 1Password application itself is fairly unremarkable—it alone would not provide you with much of an incentive to switch from Keychain Access. What really differentiates 1Password from Keychain Access is 1Password's seamless integration with web browsers.

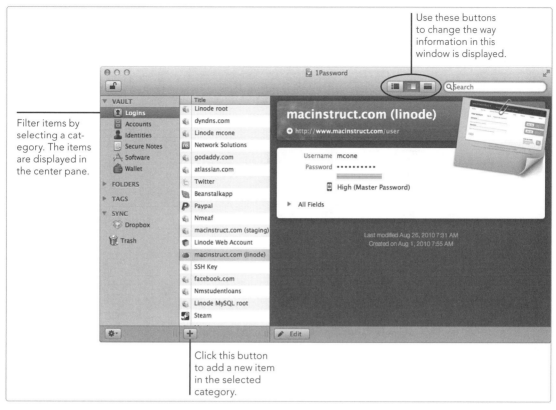

Use these buttons to change the way information in this window is displayed.

Filter items by selecting a category. The items are displayed in the center pane.

Click this button to add a new item in the selected category.

FIGURE 27-8: *The 1Password interface resembles Keychain Access but is cleaner and easier to use.*

In fact, once you install the 1Password browser extensions, you might never use the actual application again. You can create, save, and retrieve passwords directly from the browser extension—it can even autocomplete the login information on websites. Extensions are available for Safari, Chrome, and Firefox.

Here's how to install the 1Password browser extensions:

1. Open the 1Password application.
2. Select **1Password ▸ Preferences**.
3. Click **Browsers**.
4. Click **Install Extensions**. Quit and reopen your web browsers after the extensions have been installed.

When you reopen your web browsers, you'll see the 1Password extension next to the address bar, as shown in Figure 27-9.

Click the extension button and then click the buttons on the sidebar of the window to access the different features. When you visit a website that 1Password has saved a login for, click the extension button to autocomplete the username and password fields.

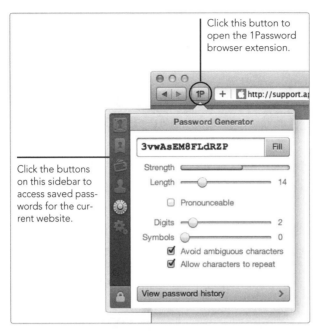

Click this button to open the 1Password browser extension.

Click the buttons on this sidebar to access saved passwords for the current website.

FIGURE 27-9: *The 1Password browser extension makes it easy to create and access passwords from within your web browser.*

Integrating 1Password with Dropbox

Another advantage of 1Password is its ability to store your encrypted repository of passwords in the cloud. Dropbox integration is built in, and once you enable it, your passwords will be available on other Mac, iOS, Windows, and Android devices. This feature is becoming increasingly important as we find ourselves using multiple devices—including computers, smartphones, and tablets—to access online services.

Here's how to enable 1Password's integration with Dropbox:

1. If you haven't already signed up for a Dropbox account (*http://www.dropbox .com/*) and installed the Dropbox client application on your Mac, do that now. It's free! (See Chapter 22 for more information about Dropbox.)
2. Open the 1Password application.
3. Select **1Password ▸ Preferences**.
4. Click **General**. The window shown in Figure 27-10 appears.
5. Click **Move to Dropbox**. 1Password transfers the encrypted repository of passwords to your Dropbox.

Now you can access your passwords from other devices running the 1Password application—a useful feature when you're out of the office with nothing but your iPhone!

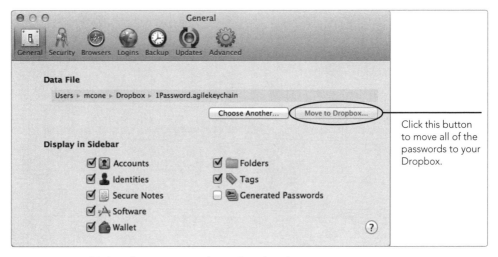

FIGURE 27-10: *Uploading passwords to the cloud*

✽ **NOTE:** You might be wondering whether it's safe to store your passwords in the cloud. The short answer is "probably." Nothing is ever totally secure, but this setup is pretty safe. The 1Password data file is encrypted, and everything you store in Dropbox is encrypted, too. Even if someone managed to gain access to your Dropbox account, she still wouldn't be able to access your passwords without cracking the encryption or guessing your master password.

Additional Ideas for Creating Strong Passwords and Storing Them Securely

For those who don't want to use the Keychain Access or 1Password applications, plenty of other options are available. Some websites let you generate strong passwords for free. (See, for example, *http://strongpasswordgenerator.com/*.)

There are also lots of third-party password management applications out there. KeePass (*http://keepass.info/*, free) is an open source application that requires the Mono development framework (*http://mono-project.com/*, free) to run on Macs. LastPass (*https://lastpass.com/*, free) is another option.

You can also store your passwords in a text file on an encrypted disk image. (Use the Disk Utility application to create the encrypted disk image. Select **File ▸ New Blank Disk**, and when the New Blank Image window appears, select an option from the Encryption menu.) You'll have to enter a password every time you want to access the passwords on the disk image. The disadvantage of this option is that you won't be able to access the passwords from any iOS, Windows, or Android devices. However, the money you save may make jumping through the extra hoops worthwhile.

28

Enabling Firmware Password Protection

Firmware password protection is another layer of security that can help safeguard your Mac and the data stored on it. With it enabled, users are prevented from booting from another startup disk or entering single-user mode—a command-line interface that can be accessed at startup. This feature is especially effective in enterprise or educational environments where administrators can secure the physical hardware but cannot be present to prevent tampering by employees or students. For example, unauthorized users can't start the computer from a USB emergency drive—like the one described in Chapter 38—when firmware password protection is enabled.

Firmware password protection isn't a substitute for encryption or physical controls. If your Mac is stolen, a criminal could replace the RAM to reset the firmware password or remove the hard drive to extract your data. But when firmware password protection is used in conjunction with physical controls and account passwords, it can be an effective deterrent to would-be criminals.

Project goal: Enable firmware password protection on your Mac.

What You'll Be Using

To add another layer of security to your Mac, you'll use the following:

▸ Firmware Password Utility

▸ Mac OS X Install DVD (if running Mac OS 10.6 or earlier)

Understanding Firmware Password Protection

To understand how firmware password protection works, you need to know a little about your Mac's hardware. Older Apple computers with PowerPC processors used *Open Firmware* as an interface between the operating system and the firmware; newer Macs with Intel processors use an *Extensible Firmware Interface (EFI)*, as shown in Figure 28-1. Setting a password in Open Firmware or EFI provides low-level protection at the hardware level.

The firmware password is disabled by default. When you enable it, your Mac's firmware is protected from unauthorized changes. Your Mac will continue to function as before, with no need to enter the firmware password during normal operation. Users are prompted for a password only when they try to change the firmware's state by entering single-user mode or booting from a different startup disk.

If you forget your firmware password, you'll need to remove the RAM modules to reset it. (Some MacBook owners will need to schedule an appointment at their local Apple Store.) You should use the same precaution with the firmware password as you would with any password—commit it to memory.

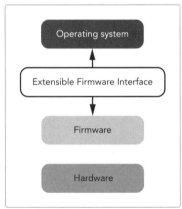

FIGURE 28-1: *The Extensible Firmware Interface connects firmware to the operating systems in Macs with Intel processors.*

Enabling the Firmware Password

To enable the firmware password, you'll need to boot from a different startup disk. Users running Mac OS 10.7 or later can boot from the Recovery HD partition. Users with Mac OS 10.6 or earlier will need to boot from the OS X Install DVD.

Here's how to enable the firmware password:

1. If your Mac is running OS 10.7 or later, restart your computer, hold down the OPTION key, and then select the **Recovery HD**. If your Mac is running OS 10.6 or earlier, insert your Install DVD, hold down the OPTION key, and then select the **Install DVD**.
2. Wait for the operating system to load and then select **Utilities ▸ Firmware Password Utility**.
3. Click **Turn On Firmware Password**.
4. Enter a password and then verify it. This is the firmware password for your Mac.
5. Click **Set Password**.
6. Restart your computer and hold down the OPTION key. A password prompt appears.
7. Enter the firmware password and then click the **right arrow** button. You can now select a startup disk.

To disable your Mac's firmware password, follow these instructions and deselect the **Require password to start this computer from another source** checkbox in the Firmware Password Utility.

Additional Ideas for Protecting Your Mac at the Hardware Level

For greater protection, use physical controls in conjunction with firmware password protection and encryption. (See Chapter 32 for more information about encryption.) Mobile users can invest in cable locks to secure their portable computers to immovable surfaces while working in public. Enterprise administrators should invest in case locks to prevent users from gaining access to internal computer components, like the hard drive and RAM. Ultra paranoid? You could even go all out and bolt your Mac Pro to the floor!

29 Encrypting Your Mac's Internet Connection

Public wireless networks provide a free and convenient way to access the Internet with your Mac. At least that's the public's perception of the thousands of Wi-Fi hotspots available at cafés, libraries, and universities around the world. From a criminal's perspective, however, these open networks present a ripe opportunity to collect a wealth of personally identifiable information. Easy-to-use software tools allow practically anyone in a café—including the person sitting right next to you—to capture the unencrypted usernames, passwords, email messages, and credit card numbers you enter on websites while using the public wireless network.[1]

1. For more information, see Kate Murphy, "New Hacking Tools Pose Bigger Threats to Wi-Fi Users," *New York Times*, February 16, 2011, *http://www.nytimes.com/2011/02/17/technology/personaltech/17basics.html*.

You can protect your personal information on public wireless networks by *encrypting* your Mac's connection to the Internet. Encryption prevents the information you transfer across the Internet from being read by anyone except the intended recipient. In this chapter, you'll learn about three ways to encrypt the data transferred to and from your Mac:

▶ HTTPS encrypts information sent to and from websites that support the protocol.

▶ Virtual private network (VPN) connections create encrypted tunnels between your Mac and third-party servers.

▶ SOCKS proxy servers create encrypted tunnels between your mobile Mac and your home desktop computer.

By the end of the chapter, you should feel comfortable using at least one of these methods to transfer your private information over public wireless networks.

Project goal: Encrypt your Mac's Internet connection with HTTPS, a VPN connection, or a SOCKS proxy server.

What You'll Be Using

To keep your information safe over a public wireless network, you'll use the following:

 Firefox (*http://www.mozilla.com/*, free)

 HTTPS Everywhere Extension for Firefox (*http://www.eff.org/ https-everywhere/*, free)

 WiTopia's personalVPN service (*http://www.witopia.net/*, $)

 Viscosity (*http://www.thesparklabs.com/viscosity/*, $ or free with WiTopia subscription)

 SSH Tunnel Manager (*http://projects.tynsoe.org/en/stm/*, free)

Understanding How Attackers Capture Data on Public Wireless Networks

It's hard to protect yourself when you don't know what to protect against. That's why you need to know how criminals capture data on public wireless networks. The methods presented in this chapter protect you against the most common types of attacks: session hijacking and man-in-the-middle attacks.

It's a good idea to assume that criminals could be capturing your packets, no matter what wireless network you're using. Once you stop trusting wireless networks, you can start implementing security controls on your Mac to protect your data in any environment.

Session Hijacking

The immediate danger presented by a public wireless network is that anyone connected to the network can "hijack" one of your unencrypted sessions and gain access to your email account, social networking profile, or ecommerce order information. All a criminal has to do is use a tool like the Firesheep extension for Firefox.[2] It's a little like watching a stock ticker, except the criminal is seeing all of your website sessions fly by on his screen. When he selects one of your sessions, he'll be able to use a website with your hijacked credentials and see nearly everything you can see—email messages, social networking preferences, and so on.

Man-in-the-Middle Attacks

When using your Mac in a new public place, you also connect to its public wireless network for the first time. If you're like most people, you do this by clicking the AirPort icon in the menu bar and selecting a wireless network that is open and looks legitimate. But how do you know that the network is legitimate? What if you're actually connecting to someone else's computer? That's a man-in-the-middle attack. The computer that you're connected to can capture all the information you transmit. Some of the more skilled criminals can even redirect URLs starting with *https* to unencrypted websites, making this the most dangerous type of attack.

Forcing HTTPS Encryption

HTTPS, or *hypertext transfer protocol secure*, is a protocol that protects against data-sniffing and packet-analysis attacks by encrypting the information transferred between your Mac and the website to which you're connected. You already use HTTPS when you log in to your bank's website or make purchases online with your credit card—all web pages with URLs starting with *https* are protected. Depending on your web browser, a lock icon appears or the address bar turns green to indicate that you're accessing a website encrypted by HTTPS.

The main problem with HTTPS is that organizations are responsible for implementing it on their websites and HTTPS isn't used as often as it should be. Many websites still don't use HTTPS to protect things like login web pages, job applications, and account registration forms. This is the type of information that can be exposed on public wireless networks.

Ideally, you would use HTTPS to connect to every website. Unfortunately, that's not always possible for various reasons,[3] but you can still force some websites to use HTTPS by installing Firefox (*http://www.mozilla.com/*, free) and the HTTPS Everywhere extension (*http://www.eff.org/https-everywhere/*, free).

---

2. This tool is easy enough for a 10-year-old to install and use. Seriously. Check it out at Eric Butler's site: "Firesheep," *{codebutler}* [blog], October 24, 2010, *http://codebutler.com/firesheep/*.

3. For an explanation of why using HTTPS isn't always possible, see Scott Gilbertson, "HTTPS Is More Secure, So Why Isn't the Web Using It?" *Ars Technica*, March 2011, *http://arstechnica.com/business/2011/03/https-is-more-secure-so-why-isnt-the-web-using-it/*.

Using the HTTPS Everywhere Extension

The Electronic Frontier Foundation (EFF), one of the few nonprofit organizations dedicated to protecting the public's digital rights, maintains HTTPS Everywhere. The extension works for the handful of websites it supports, but it cannot force HTTPS on every website. The project is currently more of a proof of concept than a practical way to ensure security, but the extension is worth a look since it protects many popular websites and is regularly expanded and updated.

Here's how to install and use the HTTPS Everywhere extension for Firefox:

1. Open the Firefox application. If Firefox is not installed on your Mac, you can download it for free from *http://www.mozilla.com/.*
2. Download and install the HTTPS Everywhere extension from *http://www.eff .org/https-everywhere/.*
3. Restart Firefox after you install the HTTPS Everywhere extension.
4. Select **Tools ▸ Add-ons**.
5. Select **Extensions**. The window shown in Figure 29-1 appears.

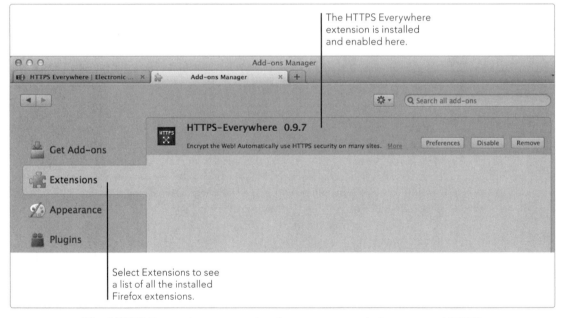

FIGURE 29-1: The HTTPS Everywhere extension forces some websites to use HTTPS.

6. Click **Preferences**. The dialog shown in Figure 29-2 appears.
7. Select the websites you want to protect with the HTTPS Everywhere extension.
8. Click **OK**.

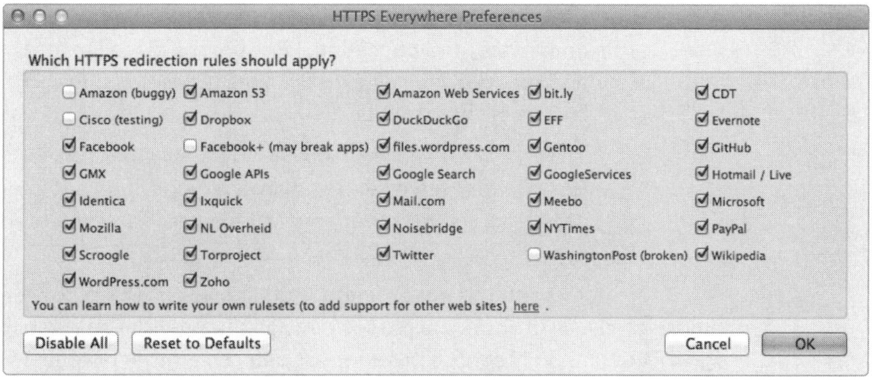

FIGURE 29-2: *The list websites you can protect with the HTTPS Everywhere extension.*

The extension is now enabled. One thing to keep in mind is that HTTPS Everywhere only encrypts data sent to or from the websites shown in Figure 29-2. You'll need to use a VPN or SOCKS proxy server to protect data transferred to other websites or with different protocols, like Telnet, FTP, or SMTP.

Using Other Options to Force HTTPS

Safari users can download their own HTTPS extension called SSL Everywhere (*https://github.com/nearinfinity/ssl-everywhere.safariextension*, free). It's not quite as convenient as the Firefox extension (you have to compile it yourself), but it is another option.

And in a pinch, you can try forcing HTTPS yourself. The next time you're staring at an unencrypted form, try adding an s to the *http* in address bar and reloading the page. It just might work.

Using a VPN Connection

VPNs are secure virtual networks that provide encrypted connectivity regardless of your geographic location. When you connect to a VPN server, you create a secure tunnel between your Mac and the VPN server. No one can see or access any of the encrypted data being transferred through the tunnel, HTTPS or otherwise.

Of the three solutions provided in this chapter, VPN offers the best balance of security and convenience. As long as you use it correctly, it's nearly always reliable.

There are also several other advantages to using a VPN connection:

▶ *Conceal your IP address.* Depending on the wireless network, your Mac might be assigned a unique numerical address that can be logged and tracked. Using a VPN allows you to hide this IP address to remain anonymous.

- ▸ *Circumvent restrictions placed on Internet surfing.* Some governments, employers, and educational institutions place limitations on the websites and services you can access. In many cases, using a VPN allows you to bypass such restrictions.

- ▸ *Thwart packet analysis.* You already know that criminals using the same wireless network can collect and analyze your data, but Internet service providers can also track your every move. Using a VPN protects your data from prying eyes, no matter where you're working.

This setup is not entirely secure, however. The biggest risk is the VPN service itself—all of your data passes through the provider's servers, so make sure you trust the VPN service provider you select. Another potential problem is that the data transferred between the VPN server and the web servers is not encrypted. If the traffic from the VPN server is being monitored, your information could be captured. Of course, these risks are relatively trivial when compared to the risks inherent in using public wireless networks.

Selecting a VPN Service Provider

Before you can connect your Mac to a VPN, you'll have to find a service provider. This is the company that provides the VPN software, generates the digital certificates for authentication, and maintains the server on the other end of the connection. There is a lot of variation among VPN service providers, and not all of them are "Mac-friendly," so you should do a bit of research before signing up. Some of the most popular Mac-friendly companies providing VPN service are WiTopia, HotSpotVPN, and VyprVPN.

VPN service is not typically free. Expect to pay a subscription fee—usually $5–$20 per month—for reliable and secure VPN service. Some organizations claim to provide free VPN service, but be careful! Many of the websites offering free VPN service are scams.

WiTopia's personalVPN service (*http://www.witopia.net/*, $) is used as an example in this section. This product is inexpensive and provides the right balance of security and convenience for most users. Mac users can download a preconfigured version of the Viscosity application (*http://www.thesparklabs.com/viscosity/*, $ or free with WiTopia subscription) for VPN access.

Manually Connecting Your Mac to a VPN

As part of the process of registering for VPN service, your provider generates a unique digital certificate and creates a client application bundle for your Mac. Of course, the process and the VPN client applications vary from provider to provider. This example picks up after you register for WiTopia's personalVPN service and install the Viscosity application.

Here's how to connect your Mac to a VPN:

1. Open the Viscosity application. The icon shown in Figure 29-3 appears in the menu bar.

2. From the **Viscosity** menu, select a VPN server.
3. To verify that the VPN connection is working, visit an IP address location lookup website, such as *http://whatismyip.com/*. Your "location" should now appear to be different than your actual physical location.

FIGURE 29-3: *The Viscosity menu bar icon*

That's it—your Mac's connection to the Internet is now encrypted. And as an added bonus, your Mac is also anonymous on the Internet, or as anonymous as you can make it without using an anonymity network, such as Tor. Unfortunately, there's no free lunch. What you gain in anonymity, you can lose in convenience and accessibility.

Here's one example of how your newfound anonymity can create some serious headaches: If your VPN server's IP address location doesn't match the city in your credit card billing address, you may not be able to make purchases on some websites. Your homegrown VPN security setup can trigger companies' protective mechanisms, invoking security safeguards and effectively preventing you from accessing web services legitimately. In other words, using a VPN to protect your information from criminals can make you look like a criminal yourself!

Configuring Your Mac to Automatically Connect to a VPN

True road warriors—the ones who live in airports and subsist on coffee and the occasional biscotti—are constantly connecting to public wireless networks and are therefore most at risk. If you fit into this category, consider configuring Viscosity to automatically start and connect to one or more VPN servers when you log in to your Mac. It's a simple way to encrypt your Mac's Internet connection all the time, no matter where you're working.

Here's how to configure your Mac to automatically connect to a VPN:

1. From the **Viscosity** menu, select **Preferences**. The window shown in Figure 29-4 appears.
2. Select the VPN server you want to connect to on a regular basis and then click **Edit**. The dialog shown in Figure 29-5 appears.
3. Select the **Connect when Viscosity opens** checkbox.
4. Click **Save**. Repeat this process for every VPN server you want Viscosity to automatically connect to when you log in.

* *NOTE:* **You only need to connect to one VPN server. However, using multiple VPN connections can provide redundancy and greater bandwidth.**

5. Click **General**. The dialog shown in Figure 29-6 appears.
6. Select the **Start Viscosity at Login** checkbox.
7. Select the **Reconnect active connections on wake** checkbox.

Click Connections to see a list of available VPN servers.

FIGURE 29-4: *The Viscosity preferences window*

Select a server and click Edit to modify the connection settings.

Select the checkbox to automatically connect to this server when you open Viscosity.

FIGURE 29-5: *The VPN server preferences window*

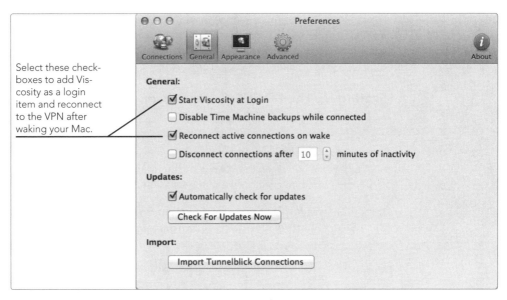

Select these check-boxes to add Viscosity as a login item and reconnect to the VPN after waking your Mac.

FIGURE 29-6: *Configuring Viscosity to start at login*

Now Viscosity is a login item, so the application automatically starts and connects to the specified VPN servers when you log in to your Mac. It's also configured to reconnect to the VPN servers when you wake your Mac from sleep.

Using a SOCKS Proxy Server

A SOCKS proxy server is another encryption option that, well, just *sounds* nerdy. It works a little differently than a VPN connection, but the end result is essentially the same—all of the data transferred between your Mac and a server is encrypted. The main difference here is that you'll implement the entire solution yourself by using another Mac—one at your home or office—as the SOCKS proxy server. When you're on the road, you'll create an encrypted SSH tunnel between your laptop and the proxy server.

There are several advantages to using a SOCKS proxy server. For one thing, it's probably more secure than any VPN service. Since you own the server, you can rest assured that your information is not being captured by a third party—something VPN users always worry will happen on third-party VPN servers. The lack of subscription fees is another benefit. As long as you have a home Internet connection and a spare Mac to use as the server, you can do this for free. And, for what it's worth, you'll have the satisfaction of knowing that you implemented an encryption solution by yourself.

There are some drawbacks. You need to have another Mac available to use as the server, and it needs to be left on when you're away from home, which could result in higher electric bills. Another drawback is the bandwidth utilization. When you transmit data through the SOCKS proxy, it has to pass through your home

Internet connection twice—once from the website to your server and then again from the server to your MacBook. That's something to keep in mind if your Internet provider has bandwidth restrictions. Finally, a SOCKS proxy server solution is more difficult to set up and use than HTTPS encryption or a VPN connection.

Setting Up the SOCKS Proxy Server

Ready to take the plunge? Then it's time to set up the SOCKS proxy server. This is the easy part—all you have to do is turn on the built-in SSH server and enable port forwarding. Remember, you're doing this on the Mac at home so that you can connect to it while you're on the road with your MacBook.

Here's how to configure a Mac as a SOCKS proxy server:

1. From the **Apple** menu, select **System Preferences**.
2. Select **Sharing**. The dialog shown in Figure 29-7 appears.

Select the Remote Login checkbox to turn this Mac into a SOCKS proxy server.

Depending on the option you select here, all users or only some users will be able to use this computer as a SOCKS proxy server.

If you're limiting access to selected users, you can click these buttons to add and remove authorized users.

FIGURE 29-7: Enable Remote Login and the built-in SSH server to turn a Mac into a SOCKS proxy server.

3. Select the **Remote Login** checkbox.
4. If necessary, enable port forwarding for SSH port 22. Follow the instructions in Chapter 24 to install and configure the Lighthouse port-forwarding application, if you haven't done so already.

That's it—this Mac is configured as a server that you can connect to when you're away from home. Now all you have to do is make sure it stays turned on, logged in, and connected to the Internet.

✳ **NOTE:** **If your server is connected to a home network, your router's IP address could change at any time, without notice. Obviously, this can be a problem when you're away from home and have no way to determine your router's new IP address. To create a domain name for your server that stays consistent, regardless of the router's IP address, follow the instructions in Chapter 24 to set up dynamic DNS on the server.**

Manually Connecting Your Mac to a SOCKS Proxy Server

Now comes the tricky part. You'll need to configure your MacBook to connect to the server you just set up. You're going to learn two methods, one in this section and one in the next. No matter which method you use, you'll follow the same two-step process: Connect to the SOCKS proxy server via SSH and then configure the system or specific applications to use the secure tunnel.

In this section, you'll learn how to manually connect to the server with the Terminal application and use Firefox to surf the Internet through the proxy. This is an ideal solution for people who have only an occasional need for a secure Internet connection. Those who frequently use public wireless networks should consider using the method presented in the next section.

Here's how to manually connect your Mac to a SOCKS proxy server:

1. Open the Terminal application.
2. Now you need to initiate the secure connection to your home computer. Type **ssh** *username@xxx.xxx.xx.xx* **-D 2001**, where *username* is your account name on the server and *xxx.xxx.xx.xx* is the IP address of the server.
3. Press RETURN. The Terminal application warns you about the authenticity of the host, as shown in Figure 29-8.

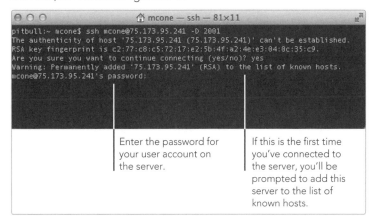

FIGURE 29-8: *The Terminal application allows you to connect to the SOCKS proxy server.*

* NOTE: If your server is connected to a home network, it's probably behind a firewall, in which case you'll need to use the IP address of your router. You can find that IP address by visiting *http://www.whatismyip.com/* while connected to your home network.

4. Type **yes** and press RETURN. The Terminal application prompts you for the password of your user account on the server.
5. Type your password and press RETURN. Your Mac is now connected to the SOCKS proxy server.
6. Open the Firefox application.
7. From the **Firefox** menu, select **Preferences**.
8. Select **Advanced**.
9. Click **Network**. The window shown in Figure 29-9 appears.

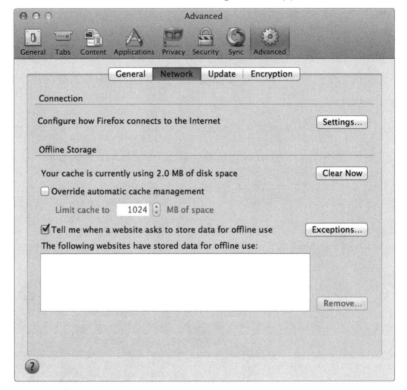

FIGURE 29-9: *The Firefox application allows you to route websites through your SOCKS proxy server.*

10. Click **Settings**. The dialog shown in Figure 29-10 appears.
11. Select the **Manual proxy configuration** radio button.
12. In the **SOCKS Host** field, type **127.0.0.1**.
13. In the **Port** field next to the SOCKS Host field, type **2001**.
14. Click **OK**.

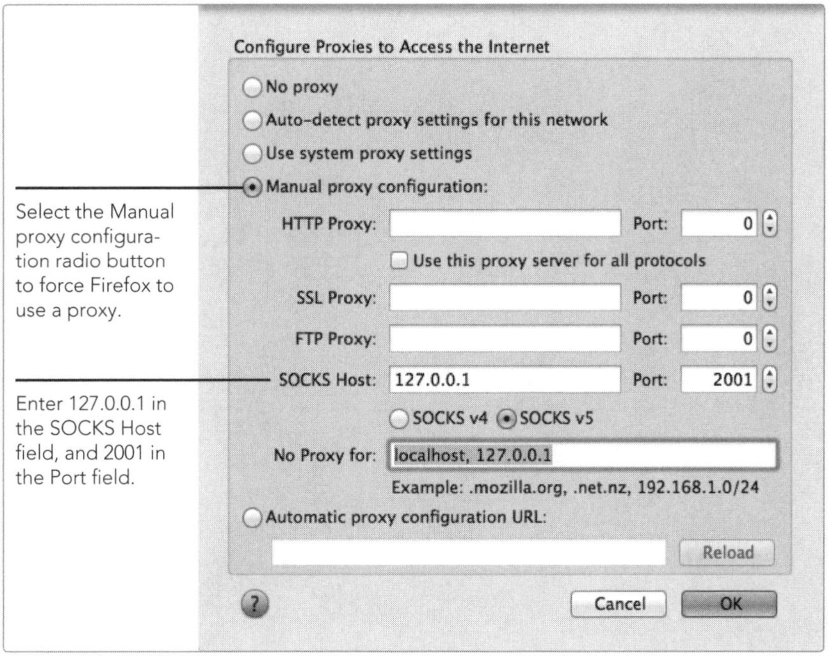

Select the Manual proxy configuration radio button to force Firefox to use a proxy.

Enter 127.0.0.1 in the SOCKS Host field, and 2001 in the Port field.

FIGURE 29-10: *Setting SOCKS proxy server settings in Firefox*

Now you can use the Firefox application to surf the Web through the SOCKS proxy server. To verify that you're connected to the SOCKS proxy server, visit *http://www.whatismyip.com/*—the IP address displayed on the web page should match the IP address of the SOCKS proxy server or your home router.

The connection to the SOCKS proxy server stays active as long as you leave the Terminal application open. You could, of course, create an AppleScript and add it as a login item to automatically connect to the proxy server when you log in. To learn more about AppleScript, see Chapter 12.

Configuring Your Mac to Automatically Connect to a SOCKS Proxy Server

There are a couple of problems with the previous method. One is that it only allows you to transmit data through a single protocol (HTTP) with one application (Firefox). If you want to surf the Internet with a different web browser, like Safari, or protect the data transmitted through a different protocol, like POP or SMTP for sending or receiving email, you'll need to create a secure, system-wide tunnel to the SOCKS proxy server. Second, you have to remember to manually connect to the proxy server every time you log in to your Mac.

To eliminate these issues, we'll connect to the server with the SSH Tunnel Manager application (*http://projects.tynsoe.org/en/stm/*, free) and configure system preferences to redirect all data through the proxy. The entire process is automated, so you won't have to manually connect to the server when you're out on the town.

Here's how to configure your Mac to automatically connect to a SOCKS proxy server:

1. Open the SSH Tunnel Manager application. The window shown in Figure 29-11 appears.

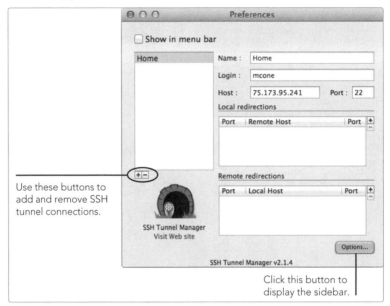

Use these buttons to add and remove SSH tunnel connections.

Click this button to display the sidebar.

FIGURE 29-11: *Enter information about the SOCKS proxy server in the SSH Tunnel Manager application.*

2. Click the **+** button.
3. Type a name for the connection in the **Name** field.
4. Type the username for your account on the server in the **Login** field.
5. Type the IP address of the SOCKS proxy server in the **Host** field.
6. Type **22** in the **Port** field.
7. Click the **Options** button.
8. Select the **Auto Connect** checkbox.
9. Select the **Enable SOCKS4 proxy** checkbox, and type **8080** in the **Port** field.
10. Quit the SSH Tunnel Manager application and reopen it.
11. Add the SSH Tunnel Manager application as a login item. (See the instructions in Chapter 2.)
12. From the **Apple** menu, select **System Preferences**.
13. Select **Network**. The dialog shown in Figure 29-12 appears.
14. From the sidebar, select the active network interface.

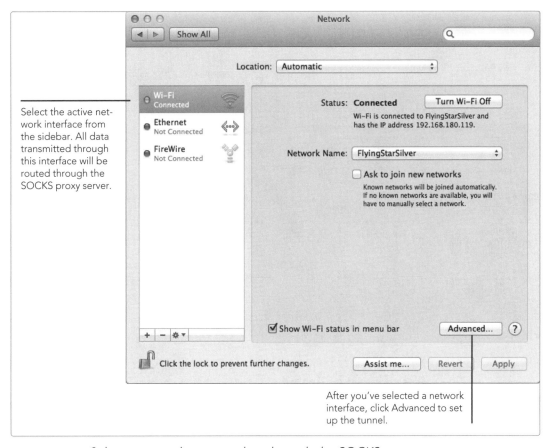

Select the active network interface from the sidebar. All data transmitted through this interface will be routed through the SOCKS proxy server.

After you've selected a network interface, click Advanced to set up the tunnel.

FIGURE 29-12: *Select a network to route data through the SOCKS proxy server.*

15. Click **Advanced**.
16. Click **Proxies**. The dialog shown in Figure 29-13 appears.
17. Select the **SOCKS Proxy** checkbox.
18. Type `localhost` and `8080` in the **SOCKS Proxy Server** fields.
19. Click **OK**.

Your Mac now automatically connects to the SOCKS proxy server when you log in. To verify that you're connected to the SOCKS proxy server, visit *http://www .whatismyip.com/*—the IP address displayed on the web page should match the IP address of the SOCKS proxy server or your home router.

The whole process is completely automated—you don't need to worry about connecting to the proxy server every time you connect to a public wireless network. That should provide some peace of mind if you're a mobile Mac user.

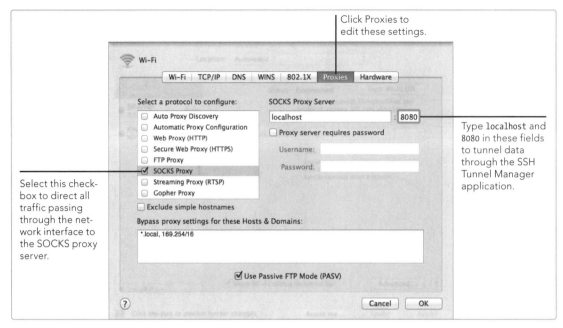

Click Proxies to edit these settings.

Select this check-box to direct all traffic passing through the network interface to the SOCKS proxy server.

Type localhost and 8080 in these fields to tunnel data through the SSH Tunnel Manager application.

FIGURE 29-13: *Set your network preferences to direct data through the proxy server.*

Additional Ideas for Encrypting Your Mac's Internet Connection

You just learned three methods for encrypting your Mac's Internet connection and protecting your data, but there are other ways of doing the same thing. Real geeks, for example, might go all out and create their own virtual server by using a product like Amazon's EC2.[4] And the super paranoid might refuse to use public wireless networks at all, instead tethering the laptop to a mobile MiFi access point or cellular connection while on the road.

DNS encryption is another service you might want to consider using. Why? Every time you access a website with your computer, a DNS server logs the request, which can be traced back to you and your computer. You can protect that personally identifiable information by encrypting your DNS traffic. To do so, download and install the free DNSCrypt software (*http://www.opendns.com/technology/dnscrypt/*).

The lengths you go to, and the security controls you implement, should depend entirely on the data you transmit over public wireless networks. Are you transmitting sensitive financial or personal data while working in airports? Are you using old and insecure protocols, like telnet and FTP, on your Mac in a coffee shop? If the answer to either of these questions is yes, your data is at high risk, and you should take precautions to protect it.

....

4. See, for example, the instructions from Peter Dikant, "Setting Up a VPN-Server on Amazon EC2," *No pain no gain* [blog], October 8, 2010, *http://www.dikant.de/2010/10/08/setting-up-a-vpn-server-on-amazon-ec2/*.

30 Enabling Firewalls

In a perfect world, you could connect your computer to the Internet and never have to worry about it being attacked. But this isn't a perfect world. Chances are that criminals are scanning your computer for vulnerabilities right now. To protect your Mac, you need to monitor and control its network connections.

Your Mac's network connection is a two-way street. When you use an application on your computer to find information on the Internet, it creates an outgoing connection to retrieve the data you've requested. Once the data is located, a server creates an incoming connection to deliver the information to your Mac. This ask-for-and-receive delivery method is the basis of all network connectivity.

The problem is that your Mac sometimes receives unwelcome network connections. Criminals can use network-scanning tools to knock on your Mac's door, see if it's home, and find out what kind of security defenses are in place. Worse yet, you might have unknowingly installed a malware application on your computer that silently initiates connections to a server on the Internet.

Fortify your Mac's defenses by blocking incoming applications' connections with the firewall built into OS X, creating custom rules to block incoming connections at the network level, and using a third-party application called Little Snitch to monitor and block outgoing connections.

Project goal: Turn on your Mac's firewall and control outgoing and incoming connections to the Internet.

What You'll Be Using

To protect your Mac from potentially damaging Internet connections, you'll use the following:

 System Preferences

 NoobProof (*http://www.hanynet.com/noobproof/*, free)

 Little Snitch (*http://www.obdev.at/products/littlesnitch/*, $$$)

Understanding How Firewalls Work

A *firewall* is a set of rules that permits or denies incoming network connections. The goal is to block malicious and irrelevant connections while allowing legitimate connections to pass.

The firewall built into OS X is an *application firewall* that permits or denies incoming network connections to specific applications. A *network firewall* called ipfw permits or denies incoming connections to specific ports and protocols. (You'll use the NoobProof application to create ipfw rules later in this chapter.) Application and network firewalls are software based and can be used together in conjunction with one another.

There are also hardware-based firewalls, some of which are built into routers. One may be built into the one in your home. This is another layer of protection against the outside world, but you can't rely solely on hardware firewalls. If you left your software-based firewall turned off and used your MacBook in an Internet café that did not have a hardware-based firewall, you'd be completely exposed to malicious incoming traffic from the Internet.

While firewalls handle incoming connections, Little Snitch addresses potential problems with outgoing connections. The applications installed on your Mac can communicate with servers without your knowledge, but Little Snitch prevents this by allowing you to specify rules that control how applications communicate with the outside world.

✳ *NOTE:* Firewalls like ipfw and NoobProof are capable of blocking outgoing connections, but they allow all outgoing connections by default. Therefore, you have to block outgoing connections on an application-by-application basis—a process known as *blacklisting*. Little Snitch blocks all outgoing connections by default, so you have to allow connections on an application-by-application basis—a process known as *whitelisting*. Whitelisting is generally considered to be safer than blacklisting.

The OS X Application Firewall

The software-based application firewall in OS X should be turned on at all times, unless it's interfering with your Mac's connections to the Internet. It's easy to enable, and it provides the absolute minimum level of protection you need at any given time.

This is primarily an application firewall, which means that it can allow or block incoming connections to applications on your Mac. It also provides some general preventative options, like stealth mode, that reduce the overall number of irrelevant connections your Mac accepts.

Turning On the OS X Firewall

Here's how to turn on the firewall built into OS X:

1. From the **Apple** menu, select **System Preferences**.
2. Click **Security & Privacy**.
3. Click **Firewall**. The window shown in Figure 30-1 appears.
4. Click the lock icon to authenticate with your username and password.
5. If the firewall is not currently on, click **Turn On Firewall**. The firewall starts, and the default set of rules is applied.
6. Click **Firewall Options**. The window shown in Figure 30-2 appears.
7. Deselect the **Block all incoming connections** checkbox. This is your firewall's panic button and should be used only in emergencies when you want to block practically every incoming connection.
8. (Optional) Click **+** to add an application. This allows you to modify whether the application can receive incoming connections or not. Most applications need to accept incoming connections, but there may be exceptions. For example, if you don't want Microsoft Word to receive any incoming connections from the Internet, you could add Microsoft Word to the list and set it to **Block all incoming connections**. Select an application and click **−** to remove it from the list.
9. Select the **Automatically allow signed software to receive incoming connections** checkbox. This allows all of the applications vetted and verified by Apple to receive incoming network connections.
10. (Optional) Select the **Enable stealth mode** checkbox. This prevents other individuals from scanning your computer for open ports.
11. Click **OK**. Your firewall preferences are saved.

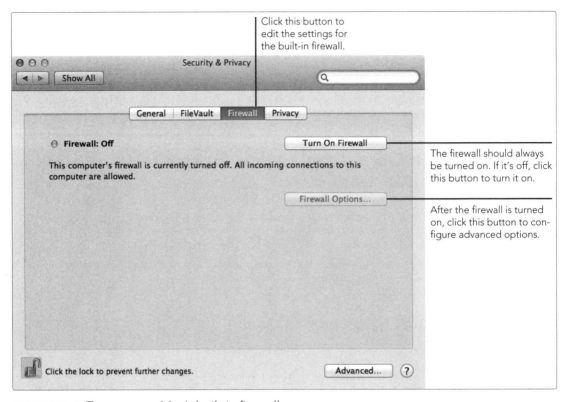

Click this button to edit the settings for the built-in firewall.

The firewall should always be turned on. If it's off, click this button to turn it on.

After the firewall is turned on, click this button to configure advanced options.

FIGURE 30-1: *Turn on your Mac's built-in firewall.*

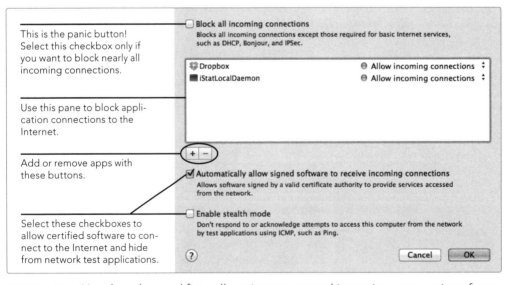

This is the panic button! Select this checkbox only if you want to block nearly all incoming connections.

Use this pane to block application connections to the Internet.

Add or remove apps with these buttons.

Select these checkboxes to allow certified software to connect to the Internet and hide from network test applications.

FIGURE 30-2: *Use the advanced firewall settings to control incoming connections from the Internet.*

Now your Mac's firewall is on and blocking incoming connections according to the settings you configured.

Monitoring the OS X Firewall Logs

Turning on the built-in firewall is important, but don't just take our word for it. The next time you're surfing the Internet at a café, open the Console application (it's in the Utilities folder) and take a peek at the firewall log, as shown in Figure 30-3. These are all of the connections that have been blocked, including the port scans and connection attempts to blocked applications.

FIGURE 30-3: *Use the Console application to view the* appfirewall.log *file.*

In this example, the Mac was being scanned for open ports with a utility like nmap. We know because each line entry is for a different port—a telltale sign of a port-scanning utility.

If the Internet café you're patronizing is typical, your firewall will block several hundred connections over a couple of hours—proof you need a good firewall!

Creating ipfw Rules with NoobProof

Turning on OS X's application firewall is a good start. But application firewalls aren't capable of blocking connections to any of the 65,535 different software ports that computers can use to communicate with each other. So you should also have a network firewall capable of blocking port-level connections.

Fortunately, a network firewall—called ipfw, or the FreeBSD IP packet filter—is included with every Mac. The problem with ipfw is that it's an advanced command-line utility and can be difficult to configure using only the Terminal application. To work with it easily, you can use a graphical frontend application called NoobProof (*http://www.hanynet.com/noobproof/*, free). Don't laugh at the name—this is a sophisticated application!

Here's how to use NoobProof to create ipfw rules and start the network firewall:

1. Open NoobProof.
2. Click **Wizard Configuration**. The dialog shown in Figure 30-4 appears.

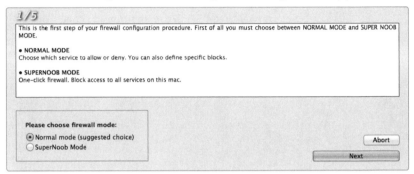

FIGURE 30-4: *Choose to allow or deny all connections by default.*

3. Select **Normal mode** to allow all connections by default or **SuperNoob Mode** to deny all connections by default. Don't let the names of the options throw you off—these are both legitimate choices that reflect different philosophies. Allowing all connections means that your Mac will accept incoming connections on any port except those you explicitly deny. Denying all connections means that your Mac will reject incoming connections on any port except those you explicitly allow. (In SuperNoob mode, NoobProof uses a stateful operation firewall, which initiates dynamic connections as needed with applications like Safari or Mail.) Normal mode is usually the easier option, but SuperNoob Mode provides greater security for those who don't use OS X sharing services like Remote Access or Internet Sharing.
4. Click **Next**. If you selected **Normal mode**, the dialog in Figure 30-5 appears. (If you selected SuperNoob Mode, you skip to the last screen of the wizard. See Figure 30-8)

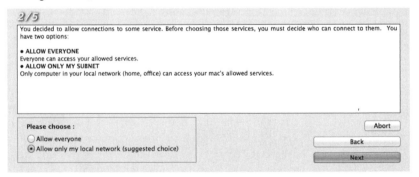

FIGURE 30-5: *Choose to allow connections from all users or only users on your local network.*

5. Select **Allow everyone** to allow incoming connections from all users or **Allow only my local network** to allow incoming connections only from users on your local network. Allowing only local network users is recommended, but you'll want to allow everyone if you're making services accessible to the outside world—for instance, if you're hosting your own website with the instructions provided in Chapter 24.

6. Click **Next**. The dialog in Figure 30-6 appears.

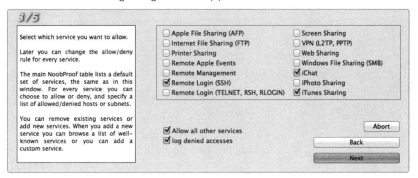

FIGURE 30-6: *Select services to make available for incoming connections.*

7. Select the services you want to make available for incoming connections. You won't need to select many services, unless you're using your Mac as a server.

8. Click **Next**. The dialog shown in Figure 30-7 appears.

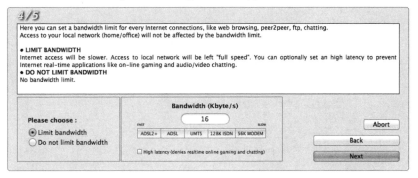

FIGURE 30-7: *Enterprise administrators may want to limit bandwidth with an ipfw rule.*

9. Home users should select **Do not limit bandwidth**. Enterprise administrators might want to select **Limit bandwidth** to control how much bandwidth this Mac can consume—a feature that could be useful in school computer labs!

10. Click **Next**. The dialog shown in Figure 30-8 appears.

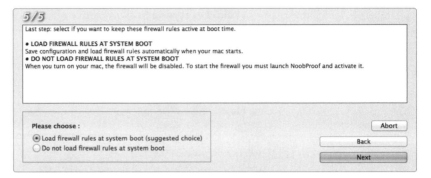

FIGURE 30-8: *Choose whether to load these firewall rules when your Mac starts up.*

11. You should set the firewall rules to load automatically when your Mac starts up by selecting **Load firewall rules at system boot**. If you don't want to start the firewall automatically, select **Do not load firewall rules at system boot**—just remember that you'll have to start the firewall manually.

12. Click **Next**. The window shown in Figure 30-9 appears.

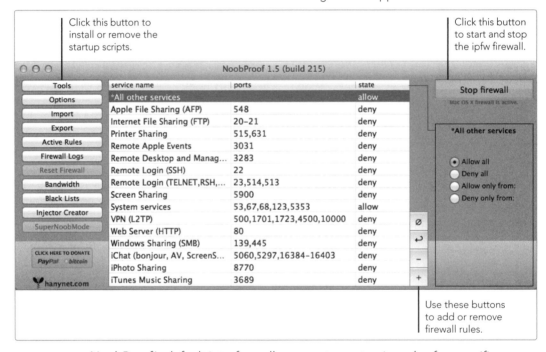

FIGURE 30-9: *NoobProof's default interface allows you to customize rules for specific services and ports.*

That's it. Now you have two firewalls protecting your computer—double the protection! Use NoobProof's default interface to edit any of the settings you just configured.

Administrators might be interested in the fact that they can build and deploy enterprise-wide firewall rules with NoobProof's Injector Creator tool. Just follow the process outlined in this chapter to create the rule set and then click the **Injector Creator** button to create an executable application that can be run on other Macs on the network.

Monitoring and Controlling Outgoing Connections

You've learned how to block incoming connections—the requests originating from other computers trying to access your Mac—but what outgoing connections? The applications on your Mac communicate with various servers to do things like check for updates, upload information, and verify license information. An application called Little Snitch (*http://www.obdev.at/products/littlesnitch/*, $$$) allows you to monitor and control these outgoing connections. Little Snitch has three components that help you monitor and control outgoing connections: real-time alerts, the Little Snitch Configuration application, and the menu bar icon.

Real-time alerts appear when an application is attempting to initiate an outbound connection for which there is no saved rule, as shown in Figure 30-10. If you decide to allow a connection, you can select options in the alert window to allow the application to make the connection once, until the application quits, or forever. You can also choose to let the application make connections to any port or server, connections to any server on the port requested, connections to any port to the server requested, or only connections to the server and port requested.

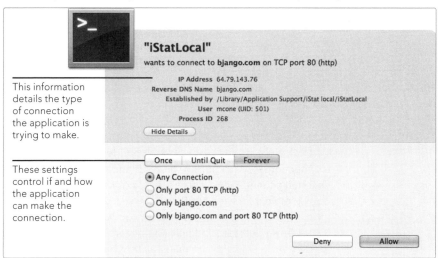

FIGURE 30-10: *A real-time alert notifies you that an application is trying to initiate a connection to a server on a specific port.*

The alerts can seem overwhelming at first. Don't worry—fewer alerts are displayed as time goes on. By accepting outgoing connections from trusted applications forever, you will build a database of trusted applications and outgoing connections.

Little Snitch is not very effective at monitoring applications like Safari that constantly connect to different network resources. You'd receive an alert every time you tried to visit a website! So pick your battles wisely. Consider accepting any connection from Safari forever, but leave alerts displayed for new third-party applications set to **Once** or **Until Quit**. Watch the alerts carefully and don't trust the application until you understand what type of outbound connections it's regularly making.

When you process a real-time alert, Little Snitch creates a rule in another one of its components: the Little Snitch Configuration application (it's in the Applications folder). You can use this interface to manually create new rules or modify any existing rules that have already been created, as shown in Figure 30-11.

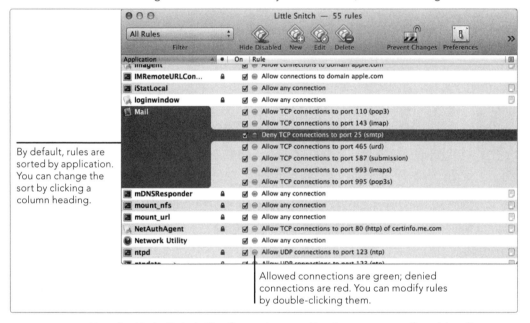

By default, rules are sorted by application. You can change the sort by clicking a column heading.

Allowed connections are green; denied connections are red. You can modify rules by double-clicking them.

FIGURE 30-11: *Use the Little Snitch Configuration application to manually add, edit, or delete rules for outbound connections.*

As you can see, Little Snitch provides fine-grained control over outgoing connections—much better control than the OS X application firewall provides for incoming connections. There are lots of ways to use this application. You could, for example, block the Mail application from using port 25—a notoriously insecure port—to send unencrypted email. You could still allow Mail to connect to port 465, which is the port for sending email securely with SMTP. Use your imagination to deploy Little Snitch to the fullest extent possible.[1]

---

1. For a list of all available TCP and UPD port numbers and the applications that use them, see *http://en.wikipedia.org/wiki/List_of_TCP_and_UDP_port_numbers*.

The other component of Little Snitch is its menu bar icon, which consists of two bars that show incoming and outgoing network traffic. Move the pointer over the menu bar icon, and a window displays all active connections and the transfer rates, as shown in Figure 30-12.

The Little Snitch menu bar icon shows real-time network data transfer.

Move the pointer over the menu bar icon to display this window, which shows active connections.

FIGURE 30-12: *The Little Snitch menu bar icon provides real-time network connectivity information.*

Use the menu bar icon and the network monitor window to keep tabs on connections and find out which application is transferring what. It's not unusual these days to see a large amount of data being transferred in the background without your knowledge. For example, OS X downloads malware definition updates in the background, and some applications like Google Chrome now download updates in the background.

Additional Ideas for Using Firewalls

If the applications in this chapter don't float your boat, there are other firewall applications that you can use. The creator of NoobProof also offers a more advanced ipfw graphical frontend called WaterRoof (*http://www.hanynet.com/waterroof/*, free). Another option, albeit an expensive one, is Internet security company Symantec's Norton (*http://us.norton.com/macintosh/internet-security/*, $$$).

31

Preserving Your Anonymity Online

Practically everything you do online is logged and traceable back to your computer. Law enforcement officials, Internet service providers, and even website administrators can find out what Internet services and resources you accessed, when you accessed them, and what computer you used to access them with.

If this lack of privacy sends shivers down your spine, you'll be happy to hear that there is a way to preserve your anonymity on the Internet. The nonprofit Tor project (short for The Onion Router) is a distributed network of volunteers who use their computers to route Internet traffic anonymously. Install the free Tor client application on your computer to encrypt information transmitted to or from your computer, bypass proxies, keep your physical location confidential, and conceal the identity of the sender and recipient.

This chapter will help you get Tor up and running on your computer to protect your privacy and safeguard the information you transmit on the Internet. It's a small step that can provide big peace of mind.

Project goal: Surf the Internet anonymously, protect data transmitted and received by applications on your computer, and use your Mac as a relay to help others around the world do the same.

What You'll Be Using

To keep your Internet activity private, you'll use the following:

 Tor Browser Bundle and Vidalia Bundle (*https://www.torproject.org/download/*, free)

 System Preferences

Understanding How Tor Works

Tor uses a technique known as *onion routing* to conceal a user's location and pass encrypted messages through a volunteer network of servers around the world. The US Navy created onion routing in 1998 for anonymous communication over a computer network. Today, Tor is used for a variety of purposes by the military, activists, journalists, and people like you.

Onion routing got its name from the data structure, which resembles an onion, as shown in Figure 31-1. A data packet is first "wrapped" in layers of encryption. As the packet traverses the Tor network, each relay in the network decrypts (unwraps) a layer of encryption surrounding the packet. This prevents the operators of the relays from reading the contents of the packets.

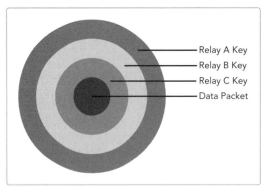

FIGURE 31-1: *The onion data structure protects messages with multiple layers of encryption to prevent the operators of the relays from reading the contents of the message.*

The Tor routing process is illustrated in Figure 31-2. When you send an email, for example, the client application on your computer selects random relays in the network to create an untraceable path to the recipient. (New paths are created every time you create a message.) Since each relay transporting your message is aware of only two other nodes, your identity is protected. No one observing the traffic on the network can tell where the message came from or where it's going.

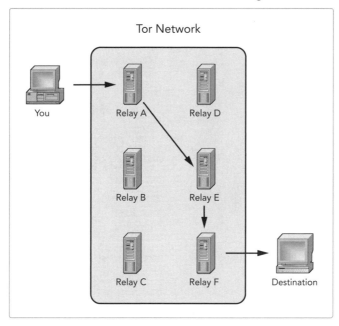

FIGURE 31-2: *Tor protects against traffic analysis by creating a random path from your computer to the recipient.*

As you might imagine, all of this relaying means that Tor can be slow—sometimes painfully slow. Loading a website can take two to four times longer than it would without Tor. For this reason, it's a good idea to save Tor for those occasions when you absolutely have to remain anonymous and keep your message confidential.

Surfing the Internet Anonymously with Tor

Most people just want to use Tor to browse the Web anonymously, without fear of being monitored or tracked. For this reason, the Tor project has created a self-contained package called the Tor Browser Bundle for Mac, which includes everything you need to browse the Internet safely on your Mac. (There are also bundles for computers running Windows and Linux.)

This is the best option for home users who want to get started with Tor fast. And because the browser bundle can be copied to a USB drive, you can use it at school or work to protect online activities there, too.

After you extract the browser bundle and double-click the Tor icon, the Vidalia Control Panel appears, as shown in Figure 31-3. Vidalia automatically attempts to initiate a client connection to the Tor network. Once it connects, the control panel displays a message in the status pane indicating that Tor is ready to use. You can use the control panel to configure Tor's preferences, but it's not necessary at this point—the settings in this bundle have been preconfigured for safe Internet browsing.

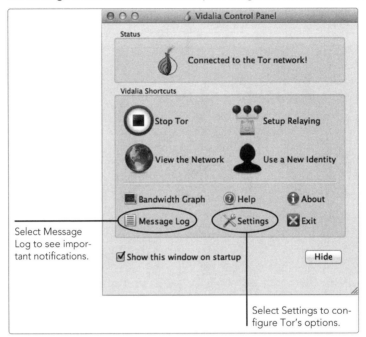

FIGURE 31-3: *The Vidalia Control Panel*

The browser bundle also comes with a web browser that is preconfigured to use Tor. After Vidalia connects to the Tor network, the web browser automatically opens and verifies that it is connected to Tor, as shown in Figure 31-4.

✳ *WARNING:* **Be sure to use the Firefox web browser that comes with the bundle. In this configuration, Tor won't be able to protect data sent or received by any other applications. See "Routing Application Data Through Tor" on page 323 if you'd like to use Tor with other web browsers and applications installed on your computer.**

The bundled version of Firefox comes with a couple of plug-ins for blocking cookies and scripts and forcing HTTPS encryption on websites that support it. Some websites have embedded scripts that can force your computer to reveal its location, completely blowing the cover provided by Tor. For the best privacy protection, block scripts and cookies by enabling the NoScript plug-in—the Tor and HTTPS Everywhere plug-ins are enabled by default.

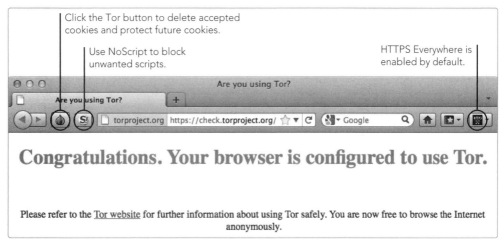

FIGURE 31-4: *Firefox is part of the Tor browser bundle.*

Now you're ready to browse the Internet. Those of you who are old enough to remember phone lines and modems might feel like you're using a 56k modem again. This is one of Tor's main drawbacks—its network is just not as efficient as the unencumbered switched network that is the Internet.

Routing Application Data Through Tor

The Tor Browser Bundle is great for private Internet browsing in a pinch, but there's one problem: By default, it doesn't work with the other applications installed on your Mac. This will be an issue if you want to protect your privacy while using something other than the bundled Firefox browser. For example, if you use the Mail application to send and receive email, those messages won't be routed through Tor when just the browser bundle is in use.

You can solve this problem by downloading the Vidalia Bundle (*https://www.torproject.org/download/*, free)—which includes Tor, Vidalia, Polipo, and Torbutton—and then configuring OS X to use Polipo as the system-wide web proxy. That funnels all of the traffic from your computer through the Tor network. This is similar to creating a SOCKS proxy (see Chapter 29).

Here's how to route application data through Tor:

1. Download and run Tor's Vidalia Bundle. Once you complete this process, Vidalia will need to be running for you to access the Internet—consider adding it as a startup item (see Chapter 2).
2. From the **Apple** menu, select **System Preferences**.
3. Click **Network**.
4. Select a network interface, like **Wi-Fi** or **Ethernet**. (You'll need to repeat these instructions for other network interfaces you use on a regular basis.)
5. Click **Advanced**.

6. Click **Proxies**. The window shown in Figure 31-5 appears.

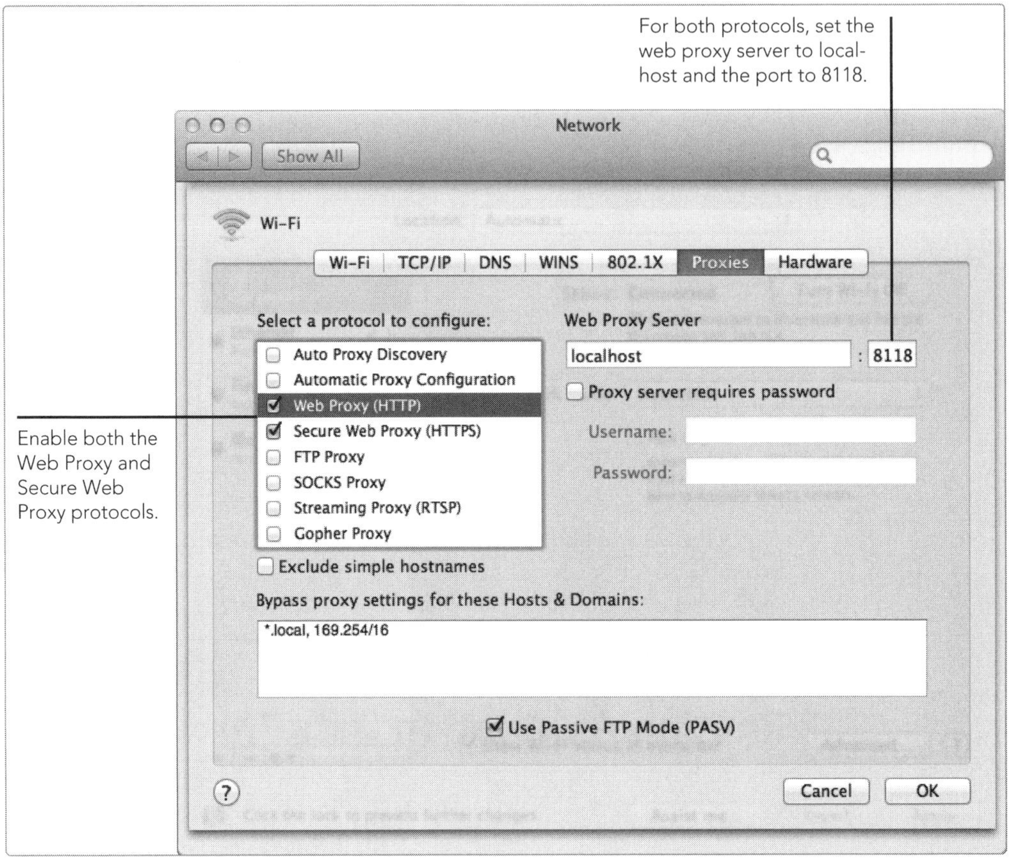

For both protocols, set the web proxy server to local-host and the port to 8118.

Enable both the Web Proxy and Secure Web Proxy protocols.

FIGURE 31-5: *Modify system network settings to route application data through Tor.*

7. Select the **Web Proxy (HTTP)** checkbox. In the **Web Proxy Server** fields, enter **localhost** and **8118**.
8. Repeat step 7 for **Secure Web Proxy (HTTPS)**.
9. Click **OK**.

Now all data sent and received by the applications on your computer will travel through the Tor network. Just remember that from now on the Vidalia application needs to be running for you to access the Internet.

Configuring Your Mac as a Tor Relay

The Tor project is made possible by thousands of volunteers around the world who run relays on their computers. You can contribute to the project by running a relay on your own Mac. This turns your computer into a server that other people can use to anonymize their Internet activities.

Running a relay is free, and it doesn't place you at risk personally. You cannot access any of the data transferred through your computer. Furthermore, the Electronic Frontier Foundation (EFF) believes that running a Tor relay is lawful under US law.

Ideally, you'll run a relay on a computer that you can leave turned on all of the time. This is a server, after all, and the other nodes in the Tor network will rely on it to provide a service.

Here's how to configure your Mac as a Tor relay:

1. Open the Vidalia application. The Vidalia Control Panel appears, and the application connects to the Tor network.
2. Click **Settings**.
3. Click **Sharing**.
4. Select **Relay traffic inside the Tor network (non-exit relay)** to turn on relaying. The window shown in Figure 31-6 appears.

✳ *WARNING:* **Do not run an exit relay from your home. Exit relays are special front-facing computers for all traffic from the Tor network—any data that passes through them can be traced back to the relay's IP address. If you run an exit relay from a personal computer, it can attract the attention of law enforcement personnel, resulting in the possible seizure of your computer.**

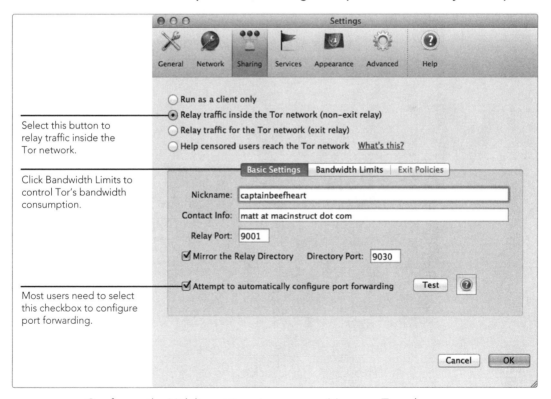

FIGURE 31-6: Configure the Vidalia settings to use your Mac as a Tor relay.

5. Enter a name for your server in the **Nickname** field. This uniquely identifies your Mac on the Tor network.

6. (Optional) Enter your email address in the **Contact Info** field.

7. Select the **Attempt to automatically configure port forwarding** checkbox. This allows traffic from the Tor network to pass through your router. You can click **Test** to make sure it's working.

✳ *NOTE:* **If Tor's built-in port-forwarding test fails, you'll need to manually configure your router to forward the ports 80, 443, 9001, and 9030. You can find instructions for your router at** *http://www.portforward.com/.*

8. Click **Bandwidth Limits**.

9. Select an upload speed from the menu. This can be used to limit the bandwidth transferred by the Tor application.

10. Click **OK**. Your computer is now set up as a Tor relay.

You can monitor the Tor traffic passing through your computer in real time by clicking the **Bandwidth Graph** button in the Vidalia Control Panel. Nothing will happen at first. It takes a couple of hours for your computer's IP address to propagate through the Tor network, but once it does, your bandwidth graph will look similar to the one shown in Figure 31-7.

Monitor the graph over the next couple of hours to determine whether you need to adjust Tor's bandwidth settings. You might not want Tor consuming a massive amount of bandwidth every month—that might be expensive and attract the attention of your Internet service provider.

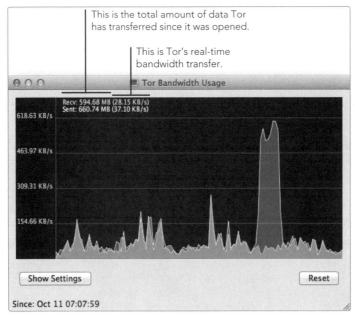

FIGURE 31-7: Monitor Tor's bandwidth consumption with the Bandwidth Usage graph.

Additional Ideas for Preserving Your Anonymity Online

Like any application or protocol, Tor is vulnerable to attacks—even some that could compromise your anonymity. For this reason, it's a good idea to watch out for some common pitfalls:

▶ Do not use Tor to engage in illegal activity.

▶ Be careful when using applications and browser plug-ins with Tor. Some applications, like BitTorrent clients, will still record and transmit your IP address. (Speaking of BitTorrent, it's considered bad etiquette to use the Tor network for file sharing in general.)

▶ Tor encrypts your data only to the exit relay—it is your responsibility to ensure that sensitive data is encrypted the rest of the way. Use HTTPS whenever possible.

Advanced users can use Amazon's EC2 cloud computing platform to run a Tor relay. It even has a free tier (*http://aws.amazon.com/free/*) that works perfectly with Tor—see the Tor Cloud website (*https://cloud.torproject.org/*) for installation instructions.

32

Encrypting Your Hard Disks and Backups

Consider, briefly, the unthinkable: Your Mac is stolen. What happens next?

You'll lament losing the machine. If you didn't back up your files, you'll shed tears for the years of lost data. And then you might wonder whether the criminal might have stolen your computer not for the computer itself but for your data on the hard disk. Yikes!

Whole disk encryption is insurance against the last part of this nightmare scenario. When it's enabled on your computer, all of the data stored on your hard disk is encrypted with XTS-AES 128 encryption. Not even the NSA or CIA could access the encrypted files on your hard disk without your account password.

This free data protection is baked into OS X with a feature called FileVault 2. Turn this on, and your data is protected automatically—you won't even notice the difference.

Project goal: Turn on FileVault whole disk encryption to protect your data.

What You'll Be Using

To encrypt your hard disks, you'll use the following:

 System Preferences

 FileVault 2

Checking Partitions and Backing Up Your Hard Disk

Stop. Before you do anything else in this chapter, back up your hard disk (see Chapter 36). The process of turning FileVault on is practically foolproof, but whole disk encryption is serious stuff. Things can go wrong. In a worst-case scenario, you could be completely locked out of your hard disk, losing all of your files in the process. You absolutely, positively need to have current backups before you enable FileVault.

You also need to verify that your hard disk has a partition called *Recovery HD*. (This is where the keys for FileVault will be stored.) To check, open the Terminal application and type **diskutil list**. The current partitions are displayed, like so:

```
pitbull:~ mcone$ diskutil list
/dev/disk0
   #:                      TYPE NAME              SIZE       IDENTIFIER
   0:      GUID_partition_scheme               *500.1 GB    disk0
   1:                       EFI                  209.7 MB    disk0s1
   2:          Apple_CoreStorage                437.3 GB    disk0s2
   3:            Apple_Boot Recovery HD         650.0 MB    disk0s3
```

If you don't see a partition called Recovery HD in the list, you'll need to reinstall OS X on your computer before you turn on FileVault. (If you don't have a Recovery HD, FileVault won't be able to create the cryptographic keys necessary for encrypting and decrypting your hard disk.) You can use a bootable USB drive to reinstall OS X—see Chapter 38 for more information.

✳ *NOTE:* **It's important to back up hard disks that have FileVault enabled. If your hard drive fails, the Recovery HD partition—and the cryptographic keys stored on it—will be lost, making your data inaccessible.**

Turning On FileVault Whole Disk Encryption

The previous version of FileVault debuted in Mac OS 10.3, but it allowed users to encrypt only their home directories. FileVault 2 uses whole disk encryption to protect *all* of the files on your hard disk.

Here's how to turn on FileVault whole disk encryption for the startup disk:

1. From the **Apple** menu, select **System Preferences**.
2. Click **Security & Privacy**.
3. Click **FileVault**. The window shown in Figure 32-1 appears.

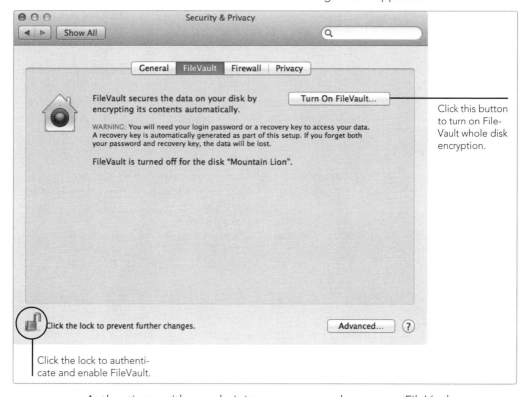

Click this button to turn on File-Vault whole disk encryption.

Click the lock to authenticate and enable FileVault.

FIGURE 32-1: Authenticate with an administrator password to turn on FileVault.

4. Click the lock icon to authenticate with your username and password.
5. Click **Turn On FileVault**. The window shown in Figure 32-2 appears.
6. Other users on your computer need to type in their passwords to be able to unlock the disk after the encryption process is completed. If the users are near the computer, click **Enable User** and ask them to type in their passwords. But don't worry if the users can't type in their passwords right now—you can perform this step later.

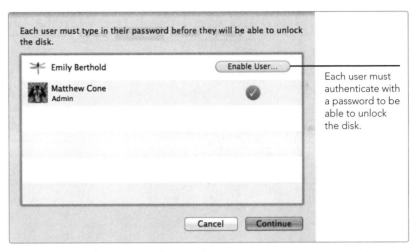

Each user must type in their password before they will be able to unlock the disk.

Emily Berthold   Enable User...

Matthew Cone
Admin

Each user must authenticate with a password to be able to unlock the disk.

Cancel   Continue

FIGURE 32-2: *All users need to authenticate to continue using the computer after you enable FileVault. You can perform this step at any time.*

7.   Click **Continue**. The window shown in Figure 32-3 appears.

The recovery key is a "safety net" which can be used to unlock the disk if you forget your password.

Make a copy and store it in a safe place. If you forget your password and lose the recovery key, all the data on your disk will be lost.

PKM9-WQZ3-BKDL-CFCP-H2ZO-ZNKK

(?)   Cancel   Back   Continue

FIGURE 32-3: *Write down your recovery key and store it in a secure location.*

8.   Write down the recovery key displayed on the screen. This key is your safety net—it can be used to decrypt the hard disk if you ever forget your account password.

✳ *WARNING:* **Do not lose the recovery key. If you forget your account password and do not have your recovery key, you won't be able to decrypt your hard drive, and all of the information on your hard drive will be lost. Store the recovery key in a safe place, like a lock box or safety deposit box.**

9.   Click **Continue**. The window shown in Figure 32-4 appears.

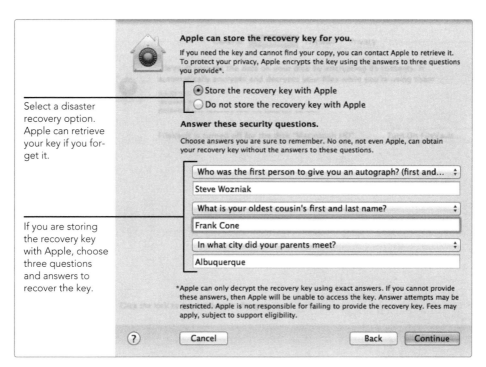

Select a disaster recovery option. Apple can retrieve your key if you forget it.

If you are storing the recovery key with Apple, choose three questions and answers to recover the key.

FIGURE 32-4: Provide answers to security questions in case you ever need to contact Apple and get the recovery key.

10. Here's another safety net—Apple can store your recovery key in an encrypted database and return it to you if ever lose it. Select **Store the recovery key with Apple** to send the recovery key to Apple. You'll need to select three questions and answer them. The answers to these questions will need to be provided to Apple in the event you lose the recovery key, so make sure you pick memorable questions and answers. If you're uncomfortable with Apple storing your recovery key, select **Do not store the recovery key with Apple**.

11. Click **Continue**. The window shown in Figure 32-5 appears.

12. FileVault is now ready to encrypt your computer's hard disk. Click **Restart** to start the encryption process.

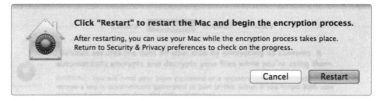

FIGURE 32-5: Restart your computer to start encrypting your hard drive.

You'll notice one change right away—FileVault requires you to authenticate immediately after the computer turns on. (If you had automatic login disabled, you'll notice that this screen replaces the account login window.) This is a requirement of whole disk encryption. The entire hard disk is protected until you provide your password. Only after you authenticate can your Mac access the files necessary to start up.

The encryption process starts when your computer turns back on. This can take quite a bit of time depending on the size of your hard disk (a good rule of thumb is four hours for every 250GB). You can use your computer while the hard disk is being encrypted. Of course, heavy computer usage slows down the encryption process.

You can monitor FileVault's progress in System Preferences, as shown in Figure 32-6.

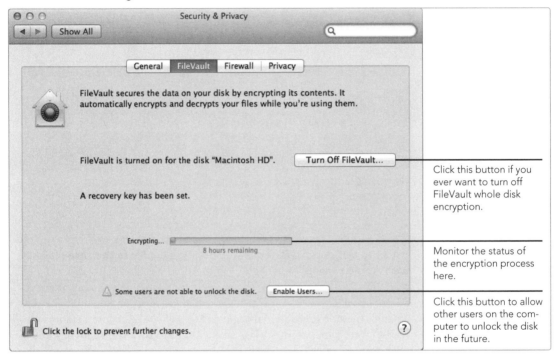

FIGURE 32-6: *Use the FileVault tab in System Preferences to monitor the encryption process, enable users, and turn off FileVault full disk encryption.*

You can also use System Preferences to enable users who are not yet able to unlock the disk. Remember, users need to authenticate with their passwords, so they'll need to be in front of the computer to enable their accounts.

And if you ever want to turn off FileVault whole disk encryption, you can do that in System Preferences too.

✳ *WARNING:* **You cannot create a recovery disk while FileVault is enabled on your computer. Disable FileVault before proceeding with the instructions in Chapter 38—you can enable it again after you have created the recovery disk.**

Encrypting Secondary Volumes

When you turn on FileVault whole disk encryption, it encrypts only the startup disk. There's no way you can use the interface in System Preferences to encrypt *secondary volumes*, or hard disks other than the startup disk. This is a serious limitation for those who rely on external hard drives. If you have any other hard disks connected to your Mac—an external USB hard drive, for example—those hard disks are still unencrypted, putting you back at square one.

Fortunately, the diskutil command-line utility provides a workaround that allows you to encrypt hard disks other than the startup disk. This method has a couple of limitations: Other startup disks cannot be encrypted, and your user home directory must be on the startup disk, not one of the secondary volumes.

Here's how to encrypt secondary volumes with FileVault whole disk encryption:

1. Open the Terminal application and type the following command:

   ```
   diskutil cs convert /Volumes/diskname -passphrase [password]
   ```

2. Replace *diskname* with the name of the volume you want to encrypt and *password* with the secret code you want to use to encrypt the hard drive. When you press RETURN, your Mac starts encrypting the volume. The process can take a while, just as it did for the startup disk.
3. To check the status of the conversion process, type the following command in Terminal:

   ```
   diskutil cs list
   ```

   Check under the volume's name for a line that starts with Size (Converted). This indicates the status of the encryption process.

   Repeat the steps in this section to encrypt other secondary volumes.

* *WARNING:* **As with the startup disk, the cryptographic keys for secondary drives are also stored on the Recovery HD partition. Do not encrypt a secondary drive if you plan to use it with more than one computer.**

Encrypting Time Machine Backup Disks

Encrypting your computer's hard disk addresses the immediate threat of a criminal stealing your computer and accessing the files, but what about your backup drives? By default, when Time Machine performs a backup, it copies data from the encrypted disk to an unencrypted disk—one that anyone can access. If someone broke into your house and stole your Time Machine backup disks, he could access all of your files.

You can solve this problem by encrypting your Time Machine backup disks with FileVault. The result is the same as encrypting your startup disk—your backup disks will be encrypted with XTS-AES 128 whole disk encryption and protected with users' account passwords.

Here's how to encrypt a Time Machine backup disk:

1. From the **Apple** menu, select **System Preferences**.
2. Click **Time Machine**.
3. Click **Select Disk**. The window shown in Figure 32-7 appears.

FIGURE 32-7: *Turn on encryption for your Time Machine backup disks.*

4. Select the Time Machine backup disk.
5. Select the **Encrypt backups** checkbox.
6. Click **Use Disk**. The window shown in Figure 32-8 appears.

FIGURE 32-8: *Set a password for the encrypted Time Machine backup disk.*

7. Type a password and then verify it.
8. Type a password hint to help you remember the password.
9. Click **Encrypt Disk**. FileVault starts encrypting the Time Machine backup disk.

As when you encrypt your startup disk, you should expect the backup disk encryption process to take approximately four hours for every 250GB. Once the process completes, your backup files will be encrypted.

Additional Ideas for Using Full Disk Encryption

There's no real reason to use anything but FileVault for your whole disk encryption needs. It's a great built-in solution that does not degrade your Mac's performance. But if for some reason you don't want to use FileVault, you should know about some other options.

TrueCrypt (*http://www.truecrypt.org/*, free) is an open source solution that provides more features than FileVault. Symantec's PGP Whole Disk Encryption (*http://www.symantec.com/business/whole-disk-encryption/*, $$$) and Sophos SafeGuard (*http://www.sophos.com/en-us/products/encryption/safeguard-disk-encryption-for-mac.aspx*, $$$) are two commercial solutions.

Use these third-party solutions at your own risk. After Apple released an OS X software update in 2010, users who had installed Symantec's PGP Whole Disk Encryption product discovered that their computers were unbootable. Such problems are rare but are always a possibility.

PART 7

Monitoring, Troubleshooting, and Maintenance

33

System and Process Monitoring

OS X is designed to make computing easy. Everything from the icons to the applications is user friendly. But behind the slick graphical user interface is a powerful Unix-based operating system full of processes, threads, and load averages.

System monitoring helps you head off potential problems and find the root cause of full-blown issues. If your computer is running slowly, you can use the tricks presented in this chapter to investigate the problem. You might find that one application is using all of the memory or that the processor is being hogged by an application that isn't responding. System monitoring also helps build your overall understanding of the system by letting you see what's going on "under the hood."

Most of the tools you need are already installed on your Mac. Activity Monitor lets you see how hard the processor and its cores are working, how much memory is being used, and which processes are active. A command-line utility called *top* presents most of this information in the Terminal application. And if you're a real geek who wants to see all this information all the time, you can use a third-party application called iStat Menus to place gauges with real-time system information in the menu bar.

Project goal: Monitor your Mac's processor, memory, and hard drive activity.

What You'll Be Using

To keep track of how your Mac is running, you'll use the following:

 Activity Monitor

▶ top

 iStat Menus (*http://bjango.com/mac/istatmenus/*, $$)

Why You Need to Monitor Your Mac

Computers are complex systems with lots of components—processors, hard drives, memory modules, and so on—working harmoniously together. Figuratively, these components are a pool of resources that can be tapped by the operating system and applications.

The operating system itself handles the process of resource allocation. Under normal conditions, the user doesn't even know that resources are being allocated and shared. You open two applications on your Mac, for example, and memory is automatically shared between them as you go about your day. But if all of the resources have already been allocated to one application, the user's computing experience will be negatively affected. This is when you'll notice something wrong—maybe a slight sluggishness that wasn't there before or the dreaded "spinning pinwheel."

The threefold goal of system monitoring is prevention, troubleshooting, and resolution. Ideally, you can preemptively monitor your computer in real time for warning signs indicating that the system is starting to operate outside of normal conditions. Like the gauges on a car's dashboard that warn you of low oil pressure or an overheating engine, the monitoring tools on your Mac indicate how resources are currently being allocated and used. The monitoring tools can also be used to diagnose and fix problems that are already affecting your Mac's performance.

Learning the Lingo

To monitor your Mac like a pro, you need to learn certain terminology. Many of these terms are exclusive to the world of system monitoring—you won't hear them anywhere else. Get started by familiarizing yourself with the terms in Table 33-1.

Table 33-1: System Monitoring Terms

Term	What it means
Process	A process (called a *command* when you're running top) is essentially a container for an open application, its environment variables, the state of the application's input and output, and the application's accumulated resource usage. Every open application has one or more processes associated with it.
PID	Stands for *process identifier*. These unique, temporary numbers are given to processes for tracking purposes. You can use the PID to "kill" or terminate a process (and its corresponding application) in the Terminal application—just type `kill` *pid*.
Thread	A thread is the smallest unit of execution that the operating system can schedule. A process can contain multiple threads.
CPU	Stands for *central processing unit*. Refers to a computer's processor and its utilization. Note that multicore processors (e.g., "dual core" or "quad core" processors) are essentially multiple processors on one chip—they can be displayed as one processor or multiple processors.
Disk Activity	The amount of data read from, or written to, a particular hard disk.
Disk Usage	The amount of space that is utilized or available on a particular hard disk.
Network	The amount of data transferred over your network interface—typically the AirPort card or Ethernet port.
Real Memory	The amount of physical *random access memory (RAM)* an application is currently using. This number fluctuates in real time depending on how many windows are open in the application and which actions it's performing.

There's more jargon related to process monitoring floating around out there, but these terms should get you started. After you start using Activity Monitor in the next section, try experimenting with the options available from the View menu to find other helpful statistics and information.

Using Activity Monitor

One of the best tools for real-time system monitoring is an application installed on every Mac. Activity Monitor, shown in Figure 33-1, provides at-a-glance information that can help you diagnose problems quickly.

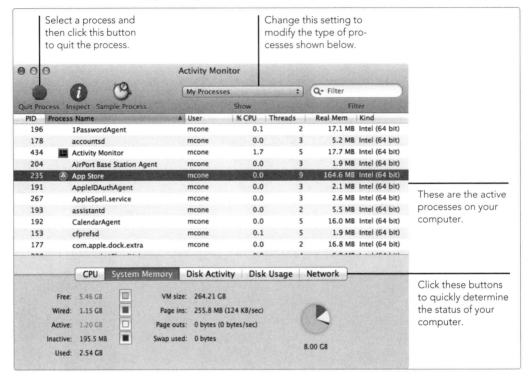

FIGURE 33-1: *Activity Monitor provides system information at a glance.*

The top pane displays all of the active processes. You can sort the processes by clicking the column headers. For example, if you wanted to see which processes were consuming the greatest percentage of the CPU, you would click the **% CPU** column header.

To see the nitty-gritty details of a specific process, select it and then click **Inspect** (or just double-click the process). A window appears with all of the available information about the process.

You can use Activity Monitor to quit a process consuming an excessive amount of memory or percentage of the CPU. (Remember that quitting a process also quits the associated application.) Select the problem process in the list and then click **Quit Process**.

Use the bottom part of the window to access general information about the system. You can click the buttons to see specific system information summarized, as shown in Figure 33-2.

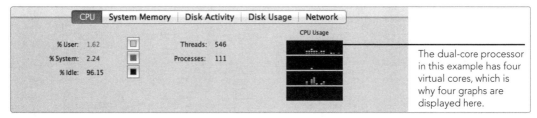

FIGURE 33-2: *The bottom portion of the Activity Monitor window summarizes system information.*

If you're experiencing trouble, your first stop should be the CPU and System Memory tabs. If either the CPU or memory is overallocated (close to 100 percent utilization), your computer has a problem that can probably be traced to a rogue process. Most Macs have powerful processors that should never be fully utilized, unless you're playing a brand-new video game or doing other graphic-intensive work like transcoding video.

System memory is a different story. The total amount of memory available to applications is the free memory plus the inactive memory. If your computer's memory is maxed out, OS X will automatically quit open applications that don't have any windows open. If there's still no memory available, your Mac will start using *virtual memory*—that is, it will use hard drive space instead of physical memory (RAM).

Using virtual memory will significantly slow your computer. Watch the number of *page outs*: Any number of page outs indicates that your computer is using virtual memory. Try quitting open applications to free up some memory. If quitting applications doesn't help, consider installing larger memory modules, if possible. (The memory modules in some Macs can't be changed.)

Using top

top is one of those age-old command-line utilities that geeks swear by (and sometimes at). It doesn't provide any real advantage over Activity Monitor—most of the information provided is exactly the same—but it sure does look cool! To try it out, open the Terminal application, type **top**, and then press RETURN. (To exit top, you can press Q.) The result is shown in Figure 33-3.

By default, top sorts the processes by their PID, which is not very useful—you probably won't be able to tell which processes are consuming the greatest share of the CPU, for example. You can sort processes by using the order modifier. For example, if you want top to sort all processes by percentage CPU consumption, you could type **top -o cpu**. And if you'd like to see a cumulative display of allocated resources over time, you could type **top -S**.

To see the other available modifiers, type **man top**.

```
● ○ ○                          ⌂ mcone — top — 110×27
Processes: 134 total, 2 running, 132 sleeping, 717 threads                    19:30:16
Load Avg: 1.77, 1.81, 1.61❶CPU usage: 2.80% user, 3.3% sys, 94.15% idle
SharedLibs: 17M resident, 9684K data, 0B linkedit.
MemRegions: 36615 total, 1876M resident, 99M private, 1058M shared.
PhysMem: 1470M wired, 3368M active, 392M inactive, 5230M used, 2959M free.
VM: 274G vsize, 1124M framework vsize, 1096239(0) pageins, 0(0) pageouts.
Networks: packets: 1210052/1010M in, 886122/110M out. Disks: 204360/3578M read, 154837/3221M written.

PID   COMMAND      %CPU  TIME     #TH  #WQ  #POR #MREG RPRVT  RSHRD RSIZE  VPRVT VSIZE PGRP PPID STATE
2313  automountd   0.0   00:00.02 10   4    61   71    940K   216K  2260K  46M   2415M 2313 1    sleeping
2312  taskgated    0.0   00:00.00 2    0    31   45    548K   340K  1888K  37M   2398M 2312 1    sleeping
2302  top          6.4   00:03.75 1/1  0    30   30    1524K  216K  2224K  17M   2378M 2302 2297 running
2297  bash         0.0   00:00.00 1    0    20   24    368K   216K  1124K  17M   2378M 2297 2296 sleeping
2296  login        0.0   00:00.01 2    1    33   64    816K   216K  2112K  42M   2411M 2296 1231 sleeping
2291  xpchelper    0.0   00:00.01 2    2    37   49    932K   288K  4452K  51M   2411M 2291 1    sleeping
2290  distnoted    0.0   00:00.00 2    1    40   52    492K   240K  1188K  40M   2409M 2290 2287 sleeping
2289  mdworker     0.0   00:00.08 3    1    53   78    1672K  15M   6088K  35M   2434M 2289 2287 sleeping
2287  launchd      0.0   00:00.00 2    0    53   48    376K   416K  824K   32M   2401M 2287 1    sleeping
2285  CVMCompiler  0.0   00:00.13 1    0    30   69    6896K  228K  15M    25M   2398M 2285 143  sleeping
2277  cookied      0.0   00:00.01 2    1    45   57    1076K  232K  1788K  50M   2411M 2277 143  sleeping
2276  quicklookd   0.0   00:00.33 6    1    101  239   10M    21M   23M    69M   2995M 2276 143  sleeping
2257  xpchelper    0.0   00:00.03 2    2    38   48    1288K  288K  4824K  50M   2410M 2257 1    sleeping
2236  cupsd        0.0   00:00.04 3    1    48   62    1236K  220K  2868K  60M   2421M 2236 1    sleeping
2233- mdworker32   0.0   00:00.54 1    1    52   93    4044K  18M   8064K  55M   658M  2233 143  sleeping
2049  ocspd        0.0   00:00.35 3    1    48   66    1204K  8728K 3384K  25M   2425M 2049 1    sleeping
1887  mdworker     0.0   00:03.87 4    1    58   115   13M    18M   26M    54M   2447M 1887 143  sleeping
1231  Terminal     0.2   00:02.46 6    2    131  220   9596K  53M   26M    37M   2510M 1231 143  sleeping
```

By default, top orders processes by process ID.

You can sort processes by percent CPU consumption, or any other attribute, by using a modifier when you execute the **top** command.

❶ Monitor CPU usage here. *User* is the percentage allocated to applications running under your account, *sys* is the percentage allocated to OS X, and *idle* is the percentage of unused CPU.

❷ Monitor physical memory usage here. Remember, the amount of available memory is inactive plus free.

❸ Monitor virtual memory usage here. Keep an eye on those page outs!

FIGURE 33-3: *top displays real-time system information in the Terminal application.*

* **NOTE:** To kill a process at the command line by PID, type `kill -9` PID#, where PID# is the process number shown in top. For example, in Figure 33-3, you'd type `kill -9 1231` to kill the Terminal's process.

Using iStat Menus

iStat Menus (*http://bjango.com/mac/istatmenus/*, $$) places indicators in the menu bar to help you keep track of real-time system information and watch for minor issues. It gives you several menus and indicators to choose from, and everything is completely customizable. The iStat Menus interface is shown in Figure 33-4.

There probably isn't enough room on your menu bar for all of the indicators, so you'll need to pick and choose which ones to enable. Which ones should you use? That depends on your needs and your Mac. For example, if you have a MacBook Air with limited memory, you might want to enable the memory indicator so you know when to quit applications before your memory is maxed out.

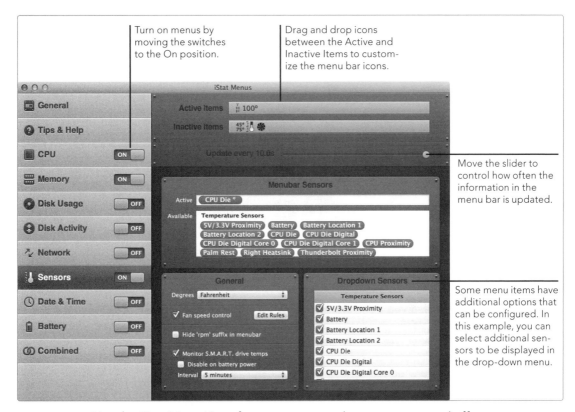

Turn on menus by moving the switches to the On position.

Drag and drop icons between the Active and Inactive Items to customize the menu bar icons.

Move the slider to control how often the information in the menu bar is updated.

Some menu items have additional options that can be configured. In this example, you can select additional sensors to be displayed in the drop-down menu.

FIGURE 33-4: *Use the iStat Menus interface to turn menu bar gauges on and off.*

Other useful indicators are CPU, disk activity, and sensors. CPU usage can be an early indicator of problems. As you learned in the previous section, most Macs have powerful processors that sit idle most of the time. If your CPU usage is continuously at 50 percent, you might have a problem process. Similarly, the disk activity indicator shows how much data is being read from and written to the hard disk—excessive data transfers could also indicate a process gone rogue or processes that just take a lot of time and energy to complete, like whole-disk encryption, Spotlight indexing, and so on.

The sensors indicator collects temperature data from multiple points inside your Mac. High temperatures indicate that some of your computer's components are working overtime. Sometimes this is to be expected. If you're playing a CPU-intensive game, the temperature is going to go up, and your Mac's fans are going to turn on. But if the temperature skyrockets when you're not doing anything out of the ordinary, you might have a bad process.

Enabled indicators are displayed in the menu bar. You can click an indicator for additional information, as shown in Figure 33-5.

Keep an eye on the indicators when you work on your Mac. These are the gauges that indicate how your computer is performing!

The iStat menus are always visible in the menu bar, no matter what application is active.

Click an iStat menu for more real-time system information.

FAN SPEED CONTROL
Active Set: **Default**

TEMPERATURES	
5V/3.3V Proximity	111°
Battery	86°
Battery Location 1	88°
Battery Location 2	86°
CPU Die	140°
CPU Die Digital	135°
CPU Die Digital Core 0	135°
CPU Die Digital Core 1	135°

FIGURE 33-5: *After you turn on the iStat menus, they're available in the menu bar.*

✳ *NOTE:* If you don't want to pony up for iStat Menus, check out MenuMeters, a free alternative (*http://www.ragingmenace.com/software/menumeters/*, free). And if you're not too keen on having system information in your menu bar, check out iStat Pro (*http://www.islayer.com/apps/istatpro/*, free), a free Dashboard widget.

Additional Ideas for Monitoring Your Mac

One thing that wasn't mentioned in this project is gut instinct. System-monitoring tools are extremely useful, but you're the only one who can read and interpret the information. It takes a while to get a feel for your Mac's normal operating conditions—what temperature is normal for your CPU, for example. To start monitoring, turn on the iStat Menus indicators and observe the numbers for a while. Once you get a feel for what's normal, you'll be able to recognize stats that are out of the ordinary.

34 Repairing Disk Permissions

Did you know that the file and folder permissions on your Mac could be changed without you knowing it? Installers, applications, system crashes, and even unscheduled shutdowns can invisibly change the permissions on your Mac.

Don't worry—it's totally harmless most of the time. In fact, some installers need to change permissions before they can move files into your Applications folder. But if incorrect permissions are set for critical system files, applications may not be able to access the information, or users may be able to access too much information. That can translate into big problems down the road.

Fortunately, you can avoid these kinds of pitfalls by repairing disk permissions. This process looks at files and compares the current permissions to the baseline settings that Apple expects and recommends. If discrepancies are discovered, the permissions are automatically restored to their original settings, fixing access problems and closing security loopholes.

Project goal: Repair disk permissions manually and then create an automated process to repair disk permissions on a regular basis (once per month or at an interval of your choosing).

What You'll Be Using

To fix disk permissions and then set up scheduled permissions repairs, you'll use the following:

    Disk Utility

    CronniX (*http://code.google.com/p/cronnix/*, free)

How Repairing Disk Permissions Works

Access to the files and folders on your Mac is controlled by *permissions*—rules that govern which users and applications can read, write, and execute the files and folders. Permissions function as security controls that protect your data from unauthorized access, so when a file's or folder's permissions are out of whack, personal information on your computer can be exposed to attackers. Worse yet, incorrect permissions could make critical files inaccessible to applications or the operating system itself, preventing your computer from operating correctly.

It's not uncommon for permissions to deviate from the original settings. That's why you should plan to repair disk permissions regularly, especially if you frequently install applications. Restoring file permissions to their original values maintains Apple's intended operating environment on your Mac and protects your system from unauthorized access.

Every time you install software from Apple, a *receipt* is placed in */var/db/receipts*. These receipts hold information about every file installed, including the original file permissions. When you repair disk permissions, Disk Utility compares the actual permissions of files stored on your hard drive with the original permissions kept in */var/db/receipts*. If a discrepancy is discovered, the file's original permissions are restored from the appropriate receipt.

* *NOTE:* **The repair disk permissions process checks and restores permissions only on files installed by Apple installers. The process does not affect files installed by third parties.**

Verifying and Repairing Disk Permissions Manually

If you're experiencing problems with your Mac, verifying and repairing the disk permissions is a good place to start troubleshooting.

You can manually verify and repair disk permissions with an application called Disk Utility, which is preinstalled on every Mac. Even if your Mac is working perfectly, you'll want to repair permissions with Disk Utility a couple of times a year to prevent problems.

Here's how to manually verify and repair disk permissions with Disk Utility:

1. Open the Disk Utility application—it's in the Utilities folder in the Applications folder.
2. From the sidebar, select a hard disk or partition.
3. Click **First Aid**. The window shown in Figure 34-1 appears.

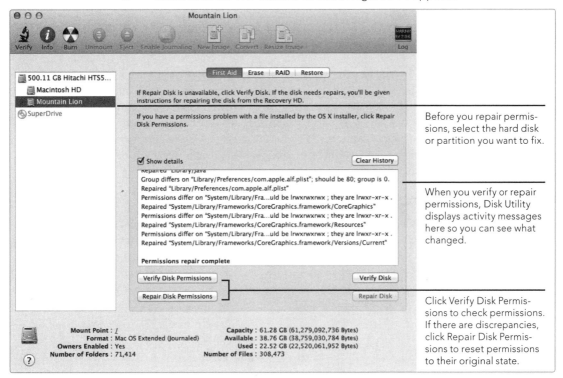

FIGURE 34-1: *Use Disk Utility to manually repair permissions.*

✳ ***NOTE:*** **To watch Disk Utility restore permissions in real time, select the *Show details* checkbox. You'll start seeing text fly by after you click *Verify Disk Permissions* or *Repair Disk Permissions*—those are the permissions being restored!**

4. Click **Verify Disk Permissions** to check whether or not you need to repair permissions.
5. Click **Repair Disk Permissions** to correct discrepancies and put permissions back to their original state.

It takes a couple of minutes for Disk Utility to repair permissions. Once it's finished, you'll see a message indicating that the permissions repair is complete.

Repairing Disk Permissions Automatically

Using Disk Utility to repair permissions is fine, as long as you actually remember to do it once in a while. But ideally you won't use Disk Utility at all. Instead, you'll create an automated process to repair permissions in the background, so you'll never have to run the process manually again.

The following shell command for invoking Disk Utility makes automation possible:

```
sudo diskutil repairPermissions /
```

Of course, you need to do more than just open the Terminal application and execute the command—that would only repair permissions once, just as when you use Disk Utility. You could stick this command (sans **sudo**) in an AppleScript or an Automator action and add it as a login item to repair permissions every time you log in to your Mac, but you shouldn't need to repair permissions that frequently. Instead, you can use an age-old Unix utility called *cron* for greater control over scheduling.

cron Crash Course

cron is a time-based job scheduler that runs in the background and allows your Mac to execute commands at a specified interval. You interact with cron by adding scheduled jobs to a cron table, called a *crontab*. cron's format consists of five time variables and a command, as shown in Figure 34-2. For example, 5 0 * * * *command* would execute *command* five minutes after midnight every day of the week, every week of every month.

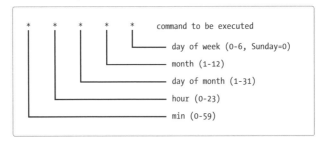

FIGURE 34-2: *cron scheduling definitions*

cron can be used to schedule any command, shell script, or AppleScript. You can use the Terminal application to edit your Mac's crontab, but it's easier to add and remove cron jobs with an open source application called CronniX (*http://code.google.com/p/cronnix/*, free).

Using CronniX to Schedule Repairs

Here's how to use CronniX and create a cron job to automatically execute the Disk Utility command at midnight of the first day of every month:

1. Open the CronniX application.
2. Click **New**. The window shown in Figure 34-3 appears.

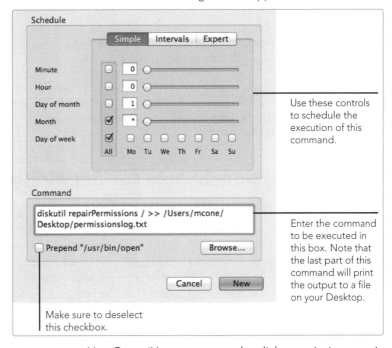

Use these controls to schedule the execution of this command.

Enter the command to be executed in this box. Note that the last part of this command will print the output to a file on your Desktop.

Make sure to deselect this checkbox.

FIGURE 34-3: *Use CronniX to automate the disk permission repair process.*

3. Type **0** in the **Minute** field. This sets the command to execute at the top of the hour.
4. Type **0** in the **Hour** field. This sets the command to execute at midnight.
5. Type **1** in the **Day of month** field. This sets the command to execute on the first day of the month.
6. Select the **Month** checkbox. This sets the command to execute every month of the year.
7. In the **Day of week** row, select the **All** checkbox.

8. Type the following command in the **Command** box, where *username* is your username in OS X:

```
diskutil repairPermissions / >> /Users/username/Desktop/permissionslog.txt
```

✳ *NOTE:* **You might have noticed that we modified the command displayed in "Automating Disk Permission Repairs" on page 352. The second part of this command prints Disk Utility's output to a file on your Desktop so you can verify that the cron job executed successfully. If you don't need the log, just delete the** *>> /Users/username/Desktop/permissionslog.txt* **portion of the command.**

9. Deselect the **Prepend "/user/bin/open"** checkbox.
10. Click the **New** button to save the job.

That's it—you've successfully added the job to your Mac's crontab. Now your Mac will automatically repair disk permissions at midnight of the first day of every month. If you ever want to delete the job, open CronniX, select the job, and then click **Delete**.

Additional Ideas for Repairing Disk Permissions

If you haven't figured it out already, my recommendation is to repair disk permissions on a regular basis. But you should know that not everyone is convinced. In fact, some experts say that disk permissions repairs should be performed for troubleshooting but not necessarily as part of your scheduled maintenance activities.[1] If you have doubts about the effectiveness of repairing disk permissions, do some research and draw your own conclusions.

---

1. For example, see this article by John Gruber, *http://daringfireball.net/2006/04/repair_permissions_voodoo/*.

35

Verifying and Repairing the Hard Disk

If you had to rank components in order of importance, your Mac's hard disk would be pretty high on the list. After all, the hard disk is your Mac's long-term memory that keeps track of files and folders. Unfortunately, there can be discrepancies between what is actually stored on your hard disk and what OS X *thinks* is stored there. This can lead to all sorts of nasty problems, including missing files, random crashes, and interruption of the boot sequence—something that can prevent you from even starting your Mac!

Fortunately, you can fix most of these issues with Disk Utility, the same application you learned about in Chapter 34. If that doesn't work, you can try *fsck*, a command-line utility that's usually the option of last resort. The goal is to resolve directory discrepancies and restore your Mac's hard disk to its former glory.

Project goal: Verify and repair your hard disk.

What You'll Be Using

To verify and repair your hard disk, you'll use the following:

 Disk Utility

► fsck

Should You Verify and Repair Your Hard Disk?

In Chapter 34, you learned how to repair disk permissions on a regular basis, as part of a routine maintenance schedule. However, unlike repairing disk permissions, verifying and repairing the hard disk is *not* something you should do every month. In fact, you should perform these procedures only *after* you've experienced a problem.

What kinds of problems indicate that you should verify the hard disk? Depending on which file, directory, or sector of the hard disk is affected, applications could crash, files could go missing, or your system could start crashing randomly. If any of these problems strike your computer, verifying and repairing the hard disk is the first step you should perform. But it's only one troubleshooting task, and it's not guaranteed to work in every situation.

And finally, remember that just because you can repair the hard disk doesn't mean that you should rely on doing so exclusively. If there's one certainty in life, it's that every electronic component in your Mac—including your hard disk—will fail eventually. In Chapter 36, you'll learn how to make backups of all the data stored on your Mac's hard disk, just in case the unthinkable happens. (Don't forget, all Macs have a limited one-year warranty.)

Verifying the Hard Disk

If your Mac's hard disk is behaving strangely and you suspect a problem, *verify disk* is the first procedure you should perform. This step will check your hard disk's directory information and notify you of problems that need to be repaired.

Here's how to verify a hard disk with Disk Utility:

1. Open the Disk Utility application. The window shown in Figure 35-1 appears.
2. From the sidebar, select a hard disk or partition.
3. Click **First Aid**.
4. Click **Verify Disk** to check whether or not you need to repair your hard disk.

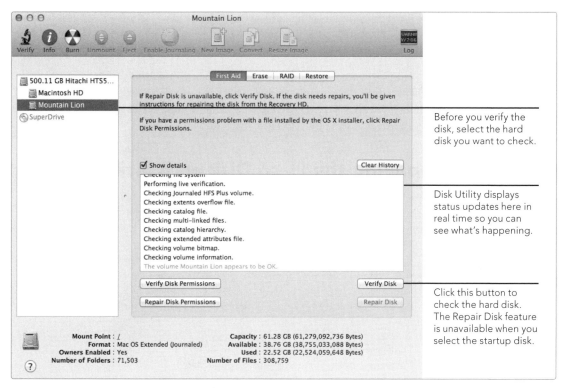

FIGURE 35-1: *Use Disk Utility to verify a hard disk.*

After Disk Utility completes the verification, it displays a message in the status window indicating whether or not you need to repair the hard disk. If you need to perform repairs, follow the instructions in the next section.

Repairing the Hard Disk with Disk Utility

So you used Disk Utility to verify the hard disk, and you got bad news—you have to repair your Mac's hard disk. Now what? Disk Utility can be used to repair the startup disk but only if you start up from a different disk. After you've booted from a different disk, you can open the Disk Utility application again and repair the hard disk. Here's how to repair your Mac's hard disk with Disk Utility:

1. Start from a different disk. If your Mac is running OS 10.7 or later, restart your computer, hold down the OPTION key, and then select the **Recovery HD**. (Or if necessary, boot from your emergency USB drive. See Chapter 38.) If your Mac is running OS 10.6 or earlier, insert your Install DVD, hold down the OPTION key, and then select the **Install DVD**.

2. Wait for the operating system to load and then select **Disk Utility** from the OS X Utilities window.

3. Click **Continue**. The Disk Utility window appears.

4. From the sidebar, select a hard disk or partition.
5. Click **First Aid**.
6. Click **Repair Disk**.

This is the moment of truth. Can Disk Utility repair the problems with your Mac's hard disk? If so, your hard disk is back in business—no further action is necessary. But if Disk Utility can't do the job and your hard disk still needs to be repaired, you'll have to try using a different tool.

Repairing the Hard Disk with fsck

If you tried using Disk Utility to repair the hard disk and it didn't work, things aren't looking good. In fact, there's a real possibility that you'll need to replace your Mac's hard drive. But there's at least one other tool you can use before you throw in the towel.

A powerful Unix utility called fsck (shorthand for "filesystem check") might be able to help—it runs a comprehensive test and repair process that consists of five phases. To use fsck effectively, you'll have to boot your Mac in single-user mode.

Here's how to boot in single-user mode and repair your Mac's hard disk with fsck:

1. Shut down your Mac if it's turned on.
2. Press the power button to turn on your Mac.
3. Immediately press and hold the ⌘ and S keys. When you see white text appear on the screen, your Mac has entered single-user mode—you can release the keys.
4. Type **/sbin/fsck -fy** at the prompt.
5. Press RETURN.

fsck starts testing and repairing your hard disk. Eventually, you'll see one of the following messages:

`** The volume` *name of hard disk* `appears to be OK`

---

or

`***** FILE SYSTEM WAS MODIFIED *****`

The first message indicates that your hard disk was examined and no problems were discovered. The second message indicates that fsck discovered problems and tried to fix them. If the second message appears, run fsck again by typing **/sbin/fsck -fy** at the prompt and repeat until you get the first message, indicating that fsck has found and fixed all the problems with your hard disk.

To restart your Mac, type **reboot** at the prompt and then press RETURN. If fsck fixed your hard drive, your Mac should start and operate normally.

Additional Ideas for Repairing the Hard Disk

Disk Utility and fsck should fix most problems with your Mac's hard disk. If those tools don't do the trick, you have two options: Try using a third-party disk repair utility, or give up and purchase a new hard drive.

I recommend that you try using a third-party disk repair utility first. Here are some of the best utilities out there:

▸ DiskWarrior (*http://www.alsoft.com/diskwarrior/*, $$$) is one of the very best tools for repairing disk problems.

▸ DiskTools Pro (*http://www.macwareinc.com/products/DiskToolsPro/overview .html*, $$$) is another good choice for picking up where Disk Utility leaves off.

▸ TechTool Pro (*http://www.micromat.com/*, $$$) is actually a collection of troubleshooting and maintenance tools—you can use it exclusively for hard disk repairs.

▸ AppleJack (*http://applejack.sourceforge.net/*, free) makes single-user mode friendly. After you install this utility and boot in single-user mode, you'll have several powerful disk utilities at your disposal.

Some of these applications are expensive, but the investment might be worth it. Many of these tools can fix problems that Disk Utility and fsck just can't repair. If you can't fix your hard disk with any utility and you absolutely *need* the data on the disk, you could send it to a company like DriveSavers Data Recovery (*http://www.drivesaversdatarecovery.com/*) for help that is costly, but nearly always effective.

36 Making Better File Backups

The data stored on your computer might not seem like it's worth very much. But think about all of the time you've spent creating documents, making movies, editing photos. . . . All of that work represents a lot of effort—and money. If you're an author, musician, or web designer, the files stored on your computer could be worth thousands of dollars. Backing up the data on your Mac is cheap insurance against a cata-strophic hard drive failure.

Of course, if like you're like many Mac users, you're already backing up your computer. But have you tested your backups to make sure they're working? Would you know how to restore from a backup if disaster did strike? And do you have multiple backups to protect against the ultimate disaster—losing both your primary hard drive and your backup? If not, you need to learn how to make *better* file backups.

In this project, you'll create a backup plan for your data. Then you'll learn how to perform backups with one of three solutions: Time Machine, SuperDuper, or CrashPlan. Finally, you'll test your backups and learn how to restore from them. You might not be able to prevent hard drive failures, but you'll always be able to guarantee the safety and security of your data.

Project goal: Make better file backups to protect the data stored on your Mac.

What You'll Be Using

To protect your files no matter what happens, you'll use the following:

 Time Machine

 TimeMachineEditor (*http://timesoftware.free.fr/timemachineeditor/*, free)

 SuperDuper (*http://www.shirt-pocket.com/SuperDuper/*, $$$)

 CrashPlan (*https://www.crashplan.com/*, subscriptions start at $1.50/month)

Creating a Backup Plan

A backup plan is simply the steps you take personally to protect the data on your Mac. No two individuals need to have the same backup plan, but when creating your own backup plan, be sure to consider the following points:

▶ Everyone should have at least one backup. Creating a backup is important, even if you use your computer only occasionally. Nobody wants to lose his or her data!

▶ Keep your backups current. It's not enough to back up your hard drive and forget about it—you need current backups to fall back on if your primary hard drive fails. It's best to create an *automated backup process* to automatically perform backups in the background.

▶ Test your backups. If you don't know if they work, you can't rely on them. On this point, SuperDuper is the ideal backup solution—all you have to do to test is boot from your SuperDuper backup drive.

▶ Keep redundant backups in different locations. Always think about the worst-case scenario. If your house burned down, would you lose your computer and all of your backups?

▶ Don't be lulled into complacency. It's easy to start making backups and then forget to update or test them. Or worse yet, you might start thinking that you really don't need backups at all. Remember, just because nothing has gone wrong doesn't mean that it won't.

With this information, and by taking into consideration the importance of your data, you should be able to create a backup by using Time Machine, Super-Duper, CrashPlan, or some combination of these three solutions.

Backing Up with Time Machine

Time Machine is the free backup service baked into OS X. Once you connect an external hard drive and turn on Time Machine, it performs incremental and auto-mated backups of your Mac every hour. You can even configure Time Machine to back up to multiple external drives. If you accidently delete a file or if something happens to your primary hard drive, you can use Time Machine's browser to "go back in time" to a previous backup of your computer and restore the missing files.

There are disadvantages to Time Machine. For example, you can't boot from a Time Machine backup, which makes it difficult to test. But overall it's a great backup solution, especially for beginners. If you've never backed up your hard drive before, Time Machine is a great place to start.

Making Your First Time Machine Backup

To get started with Time Machine, you'll need a dedicated external hard drive—preferably one with a storage capacity that at least matches your Mac's internal hard drive. This is important, because the more storage capacity the external hard drive has, the more backups Time Machine can make and the better your backups will be.

Here's how to make your first Time Machine backup:

1. Connect the backup drive to your computer.
2. From the **Apple** menu, select **System Preferences**.
3. Select **Time Machine**. The dialog shown in Figure 36-1 appears.

FIGURE 36-1: *Enabling Time Machine is as easy as sliding the on/off switch.*

4. Slide the on/off switch to *ON*.
5. Select the backup drive and then click **Use Backup Disk**.

✳ *NOTE:* **To encrypt the backup disk, select the** *Encrypt backup disk* **checkbox. You should probably only encrypt the backup disk if you have enabled File-Vault. For more information, see Chapter 32.**

Time Machine will start backing up your hard drive in a couple of minutes. Once it starts, you can monitor the progress in System Preferences, as shown in Figure 36-2, or by using the Time Machine menu bar icon.

The initial backup can take a couple of hours, depending on the size of your hard disk and the speed of your external hard drive.

FIGURE 36-2: Use System Preferences to monitor Time Machine's progress.

Scheduling Backups

The first time you create a Time Machine backup, all of the files on your computer are copied to the backup drive. After the initial backup is complete, Time Machine will update your backup every hour whenever your Mac is turned on and the backup drive is connected. All files that have been modified are copied to the backup drive, including databases that store a lot of smaller files. For example, if you use Microsoft Entourage for email, its entire database is flagged for backup every time you receive an email message. All of this writing can significantly reduce the life of your backup drive!

If this seems excessive, you can use a third-party application called Time-MachineEditor (*http://timesoftware.free.fr/timemachineeditor/*, free) to change the automated backup schedule. (Apple does not provide a way to modify the schedule in OS X.)

Here's how to schedule Time Machine backups with TimeMachineEditor:

1. Open the TimeMachineEditor application. The dialog shown in Figure 36-3 appears.
2. Select one of two options: **Interval** or **Calendar Intervals**. The interval option provides hourly backups, and the calendar interval allows you to schedule backups at daily, weekly, or monthly intervals.
3. Create the schedule and then click **Apply**.
4. Move the on/off switch to *ON*.

FIGURE 36-3: *Control the timing of Time Machine backups with TimeMachineEditor.*

✳ *NOTE:* **This next part is counterintuitive—you'll turn Time Machine *off*. You just need to do this so TimeMachineEditor can override the default schedule set by Time Machine.**

5. From the **Apple** menu, select **System Preferences**.
6. Select **Time Machine**.
7. Slide the on/off switch to *OFF*. You've just turned Time Machine "off" so that TimeMachineEditor can schedule the backups.

Keep an eye on the Time Machine application for the next few days. Are the backups being performed according to the schedule you specified? If not, use the TimeMachineEditor application to edit the schedule.

Excluding Files from Backups

By default, Time Machine backs up all of the files on your hard drive, but you may not want it to do that. For example, if you have a folder full of large temporary files that don't need to be backed up, you could tell Time Machine to *exclude* those files from its backups—saving space on your backup drive and improving the quality of your backup. You can also exclude the OS System folder if you want to back up only your documents and important files.

Here's how to exclude files from your Time Machine backup:

1. From the **Apple** menu, select **System Preferences**.
2. Select **Time Machine**.
3. Click **Options**. The dialog shown in Figure 36-4 appears.
4. Click the **+** button.
5. Select the files and folders you want to exclude from the Time Machine backup and then click **OK**.
6. Click **Save**.

Time Machine will exclude the selected files and folders from the backup. Use this feature carefully!

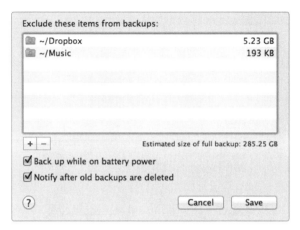

FIGURE 36-4: *Exclude files and folders so Time Machine doesn't back them up.*

Using a Network-Attached Storage Device

Time Machine works only when the backup drive is connected to your computer. But what if you have a laptop and you work in different places around the house or office? In that case, you can configure Time Machine to use a network-attached storage device, which is just a fancy name for a hard drive connected to your wireless network.

You may have heard of Time Capsule (*http://www.apple.com/timecapsule/*, starting at $299), an Apple product that combines an AirPort Extreme wireless base station and a dedicated hard drive for Time Machine backups. Time Capsule is easy to use—you just plug it in and select it in the Time Machine preferences—but it's also expensive.

A cheaper option is to connect a USB drive to an AirPort Extreme base station. The setup process is the same—just select the wireless hard drive in the Time Machine preferences. If you have connected a hard drive to a router other than an AirPort Extreme, enter the following command in the Terminal application to make the hard drive visible:

```
defaults write com.apple.systempreferences TMShowUnsupportedNetworkVolumes 1
```

Whether you purchase Time Capsule or connect a USB drive to a wireless router, you'll want to perform the initial backup with the drive connected to your Mac. Otherwise that first backup could take weeks!

Making an Exact Copy of Your Hard Disk

Time Machine is a wonderful automated backup application. The only problem is that a Time Machine backup cannot be used as a startup disk—you have to boot from the OS X Recovery Disc and then restore the backup to your Mac's hard drive.

That's annoying, especially if you need an exact copy of your hard disk that you can boot from at the drop of a hat.

A third-party application called SuperDuper (*http://www.shirt-pocket.com/SuperDuper/*, free for cloning, $$$ for all features) takes the guesswork out of cloning your hard drive. After you use SuperDuper to make a backup, you'll have a bootable copy of your Mac's hard drive. It's nice knowing that you can immediately use the backup as a startup disc if your primary hard drive bites the dust.

Making Your First SuperDuper Backup

You'll want to purchase a dedicated external hard drive for SuperDuper, just as with Time Machine. (Of course, you can use an existing external hard drive if you happen to have one lying around.) SuperDuper will erase this backup hard drive the first time you create a backup, so if you have any important files stored on it, make sure you make copies.

Here's how to make your first SuperDuper backup:

1. Connect the backup drive to your computer.
2. Open the SuperDuper application. The dialog shown in Figure 36-5 appears.

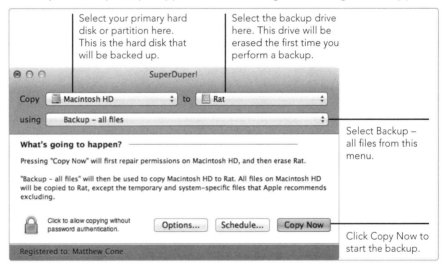

FIGURE 36-5: *Use SuperDuper to create an exact copy of your hard disk.*

3. From the **Copy** menu, select the hard disk or partition that you want to back up. SuperDuper will create an exact copy of this hard disk or partition.
4. From the **To** menu, select the backup hard disk. SuperDuper will create the copy on this hard disk.
5. From the **Using** menu, select **Backup – all files**. This is a backup script that will copy all of the files on the primary hard drive to the backup disk.
6. Click **Copy Now**. SuperDuper creates the backup.

Creating the first backup can take a while—you are copying *all* of your files to the backup drive, after all. You can use your computer while SuperDuper is backing up the hard drive, but realistically, you'll want to initiate the first backup right before you go to sleep or leave the office for the day. Once it's finished, you should test it to make sure it's working.

Testing Your SuperDuper Backup

Backups that don't work or are only partially complete are worse than worthless—they provide a false sense of security and can leave you up a creek if something does happen to your primary hard drive. You should always test SuperDuper backups immediately after creating them.

Here's how to test a SuperDuper backup:

1. Connect the backup drive to your computer.
2. From the **Apple** menu, select **System Preferences**.
3. Select **Startup Disk**.
4. Select the backup drive.
5. Click **Restart**. Your computer restarts and boots from the SuperDuper backup drive.
6. Verify that your Mac starts normally and that all of your files are accessible. (Try opening a couple of applications just to make sure that everything works.)

If it seems like it works, it probably does. Bad SuperDuper backups usually don't even boot, so you're in good shape if you can start up your computer from the backup drive. To stop testing, set your primary hard drive as your startup disk and restart your computer.

Scheduling and Updating SuperDuper Backups

Now you have a clone of your hard drive that you can use as a startup disk, but how do you update it? Use SuperDuper's *Smart Update* feature to perform automatic, intelligent backups according to a custom schedule. It compares your backup drive to the primary hard disk or partition and copies any modified files—and only those modified files—to the backup drive. Making a smart update takes a fraction of the time of the initial backup.

You can use SuperDuper's scheduling options to automatically update your backup according to a schedule or when you connect the backup drive to your Mac. The scheduling options work best for desktop Mac users—the people who always leave their backup drives connected to their computers. Laptop users should elect to automatically update when the backup drive is connected to the Mac. (The only disadvantage is that you have to remember to manually connect the drive—the process isn't quite as automated as with the scheduling option. See Chapter 18 for more information about creating reminders and alerts.)

Here's how to schedule and update SuperDuper backups:

1. Connect the backup drive to your computer.
2. Open the SuperDuper application.

3.   Click **Options**. The dialog shown in Figure 36-6 appears.

FIGURE 36-6: *Use the Smart Update feature to intelligently update an existing SuperDuper backup.*

4.   Select the **Repair permissions on Macintosh HD** checkbox.
5.   From the **During copy** menu, select **Smart Update *Backup Drive* from Macintosh HD**.
6.   Click **OK**.
7.   Click **Schedule**. The dialog shown in Figure 36-7 appears.
8.   To automatically update your SuperDuper backup according to a schedule, select the **On the following schedule** checkbox. Select one or more weeks of the month and one or more days of the week. Then set a time to start copying.
9.   To automatically update your SuperDuper backup when you connect the backup drive, select the **When you connect *Backup Drive* to your Macintosh** checkbox.
10.   Click **OK**.

Now you've scheduled SuperDuper to automatically update your backup at the specified time or when you connect the backup drive to your computer. The backup will occur automatically, as long as the backup drive is connected to your computer at the scheduled update time.

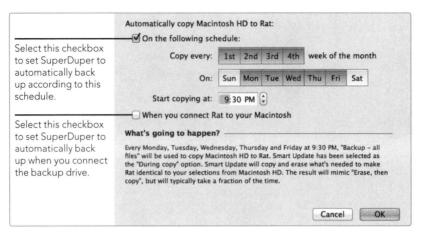

Select this checkbox to set SuperDuper to automatically back up according to this schedule.

Select this checkbox to set SuperDuper to automatically back up when you connect the backup drive.

FIGURE 36-7: *Schedule SuperDuper to automatically clone your hard drive.*

Storing Backups on the Internet

It's critically important that you store at least one of your backups in a safe, secure location. That's why the Internet (or the *cloud*, if you're down with the lingo) could be an ideal location to store backups. Think about it. There's no physical hard drive to steal, and the backup will be there even if your house burns to the ground. If you have a fast Internet connection and your service provider doesn't charge for bandwidth, you should give online backups a whirl.

Internet backup services are a dime a dozen—how do you pick one? Take a look at three factors: subscription pricing, storage space, and application usability. According to a comprehensive *Macworld* review of online backup services,[1] Crash-Plan (*https://www.crashplan.com/*, subscriptions start at $1.50/month) is one of the best available. This is the service discussed in this section.

Making Your First CrashPlan Backup

In many ways, getting started with CrashPlan is the most difficult part. It can take days or even weeks to upload all of the gigabytes of data on your hard drive to CrashPlan's servers. Fortunately, the entire upload takes place in the background, so it won't interfere with your day-to-day computer usage. All you'll need to do while CrashPlan is performing the initial backup is keep your computer turned on and connected to the Internet as much as possible.

Here's how to back up your computer with CrashPlan:

1. Download and install the CrashPlan application for OS X (*https://www .crashplan.com/consumer/download.html?os=Mac*), if you haven't already. It's free to download and try.

2. Open the CrashPlan application. The dialog shown in Figure 36-8 appears.

---

1. You can read the review by Glenn Fleishman, "Online Backup Services," *Macworld*, September 7, 2009, at *http://www.macworld.com/article/142606/2009/09/online_backup.html.*

FIGURE 36-8: *You can create a free CrashPlan account from within the application.*

3. If you don't have a CrashPlan account, select **New Account**. (You'll automatically receive a free 30-day trial.)
4. Complete the account profile information.
5. Click **Create Account**. The dialog shown in Figure 36-9 appears. CrashPlan will scan your hard drive for files—wait until all of the files have been scanned.

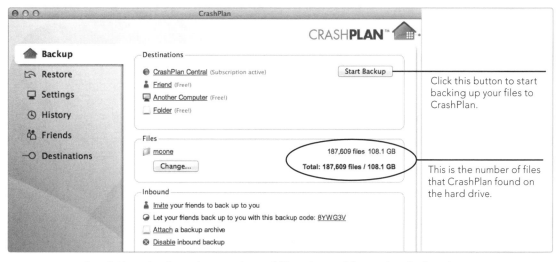

FIGURE 36-9: *CrashPlan displays the number of files that will be uploaded to the servers.*

6. Click **Start Backup**. CrashPlan starts backing up your files to its servers. This can take several days, depending on the size of your hard drive and speed of your Internet connection.

Keep an eye on CrashPlan's interface to monitor its progress. You can also pause the backup if you need more bandwidth or want to put your Mac to sleep.

Or, if you're the impatient type, you can forget the whole "initial upload" thing and send a backup of your hard drive to CrashPlan. For a hefty fee ($124.99), CrashPlan will take all of the files on the hard drive and synchronize them with your account. This is an option for those who want an online backup of their hard drive but don't have the time or inclination to perform the first step.

Configuring CrashPlan's Network Options

After you've uploaded your first backup, CrashPlan will update that backup any-time you create, modify, or delete a file. The process occurs invisibly in the back-ground. You don't need to tinker too much with CrashPlan's options—it's already configured to do everything automatically.

One set of options you might want to take a look at is network settings. These control how much bandwidth CrashPlan consumes when uploading and downloading files—an important consideration for those who pay for bandwidth or have slow Internet connections.

Here's how to configure CrashPlan's network options:

1. Open the CrashPlan application.
2. From the sidebar, select **Settings**.
3. Click **Network**. The dialog shown in Figure 36-10 appears.
4. Edit the limits in the WAN column. Lower numbers will cause CrashPlan to send files more slowly.
5. Click **Save**.

Now CrashPlan will transfer files at the rates you specified.

Restoring from Backups

If you have good, current backups, a hard-drive disaster is no biggie. All you have to do is restore from a backup and—bingo—you're back in business. Follow the following instructions for the solution you've used to back up your hard drive.

Restoring from a Time Machine Backup

There are two ways to restore from a Time Machine backup: using your primary hard disk (if it hasn't crashed and burned) or using an OS X recovery disk. Both options are easy to access.

Here's how to restore from a Time Machine backup if your primary hard disk is working:

1. Open the Time Machine application. (It's in your Applications folder.) The Time Machine interface appears, as shown in Figure 36-11.

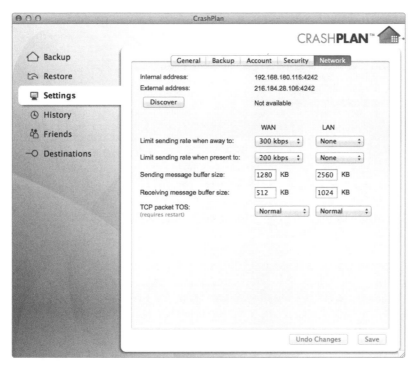

FIGURE 36-10: *Edit CrashPlan's network settings to control how much bandwidth it uses.*

FIGURE 36-11: *Use Time Machine to find a backup from a particular time and then restore it.*

2. Use the arrows to navigate through the backups until you find the one you want to restore. Unless there's a serious problem, you'll probably want to restore from the most recent backup.

3. Click **Restore**. Time Machine restores the selected backup to your hard drive.

If your primary hard disk is not working, you have another option to restore from a Time Machine backup—using an OS X Recovery Disk (see Chapter 38). Here's how to restore from a Time Machine backup if your primary hard disk isn't working:

1. Connect the recovery drive and the backup drive to your computer.

2. Restart your computer and hold down the OPTION key.

* *NOTE:* **If firmware password protection is enabled, you will need to enter your firmware password to proceed.**

3. A list of startup drives appears. Select the emergency drive and then click the arrow directly below the drive. Your Mac starts in recovery mode.

4. Select **Restore From Time Machine Backup**. You will be prompted to select a Time Machine backup drive, a backup snapshot, and a destination drive. The destination drive will be erased, and the backup will be restored to it.

By the way, since there's no way to test a Time Machine backup other than by restoring it, this is the moment of truth—will the backup restore successfully? The answer is probably yes. Time Machine has been around for a couple of years, and Apple has worked out most of the kinks. Still, you should be making at least one other type of backup, such as with SuperDuper or CrashPlan.

Restoring from a SuperDuper Backup

Restoring from a SuperDuper backup is simple. You start up from the backup drive, erase the primary hard drive, and then restore all of the files from backup. It's like backing up, except you're reversing the process by copying all of the files on the backup drive to the primary hard drive.

Here's how to restore from a SuperDuper backup:

1. Connect the backup drive to your computer.

2. Restart your computer and hold the OPTION key.

* *NOTE:* **If firmware password protection is enabled, you will need to enter your firmware password to proceed.**

3. A list of startup drives appears. Select the backup drive and then click the arrow directly below the drive. Your Mac starts up from the backup drive.

4. Open SuperDuper. The dialog shown in Figure 36-12 appears.

5. From the **Copy** menu, select the backup drive.

6. From the **To** menu, select the hard disk or partition you want to restore the backup to.

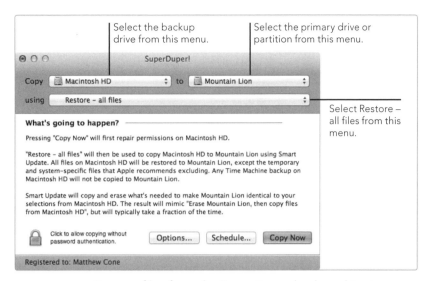

Select the backup drive from this menu.

Select the primary drive or partition from this menu.

Select Restore – all files from this menu.

FIGURE 36-12: *Restore files from the SuperDuper backup drive to your primary hard disk.*

7. From the **Using** menu, select **Restore – all files**. This is a backup script that will restore all of the files from the backup drive to the hard disk or partition you have selected.

8. Click **Options**.

9. Select **During copy ▸ Erase Macintosh HD, then copy files from Backup Drive**. This will erase your primary hard disk or partition before the files are restored from backup.

10. Click **OK**.

11. Click **Copy Now**. SuperDuper starts copying the files on the backup drive to the hard disk or partition you are restoring to.

After all of the files on your backup drive are copied to the primary hard drive, you will be able to use the primary hard drive as your startup disk.

Restoring from a CrashPlan Backup

Depending on how many files and folders you need to restore from CrashPlan, the process can take several days or weeks—just as the initial backup did. This can present a real problem, especially if you need the files from your backup right away. If you can't wait, you could pay CrashPlan a hefty fee ($124.99 and up) to mail you a hard drive with your backup.

Here's how to restore from a CrashPlan backup:

1. If your primary hard disk is not working, you'll need to start up from a different disk. See Chapter 38 for instructions on creating a USB startup drive.

2. Open the CrashPlan application.

3. From the sidebar, click **Restore**. The dialog shown in Figure 36-13 appears.

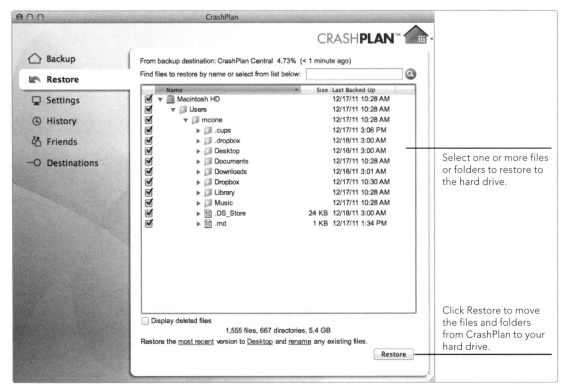

Select one or more files or folders to restore to the hard drive.

Click Restore to move the files and folders from CrashPlan to your hard drive.

FIGURE 36-13: *Restore files from CrashPlan servers to your Mac's hard drive.*

4. Select checkboxes next to the files and folders you want to restore to your Mac's hard drive. Selecting lots of files will increase the download time.

5. Click **Restore**. CrashPlan starts copying the files and folders from the servers to your Mac.

Due to the length of time this takes, restoring from CrashPlan should definitely be the option of last resort—try restoring from another backup first, if you have one. Remember, it's important to keep multiple backups of your data for exactly this reason!

Additional Ideas for Backing Up Your Mac

People are increasingly using cloud solutions to store their documents, music, and other files, and these solutions hold partial backups of your hard disk. Dropbox and iCloud are two examples of this trend—both of those services are discussed in Chapter 22. Cloud solutions like this cannot be considered comprehensive backups, but you could retrieve the stored files in the event of an emergency. In fact, since CrashPlan is so slow, this option could be a reasonable compromise for your most important files—keep them online, in the cloud.

37

Maintaining a MacBook's Battery

Admit it: Working on a laptop at a café or during your morning commute is pretty exhilarating. But that feeling fades fast when you realize you're running out of battery power and are nowhere near a power outlet. That's why it's important to configure a MacBook to conserve power away from home and condition your battery to hold strong charges for years to come.

The lithium-ion battery inside your laptop is one of the best portable power sources available. It holds enough energy to power your machine for hours, and it can be recharged hundreds of times. But there are plenty of ways you can eke out even more time from a single charge. And performing regular maintenance ensures that the battery can continue powering your computer for a long time.

Project goal: Learn how to keep your battery healthy, adjust settings for maximum battery life on the road, and calibrate the battery to maintain its capacity.

What You'll Be Using

To maintain your battery, you'll use the following:

 System Preferences

 coconutBattery (*http://www.coconut-flavour.com/*, free)

 Watts (*http://binarytricks.com/*, $)

Tips for Keeping Your Battery Healthy

Batteries aren't alive, but they're so finicky they might as well be. Like a household pet that needs to be fed in the morning and walked twice a day, your laptop's battery requires constant attention to remain fully operational for as long as possible. Here are some tips that will keep your battery in great shape for the long haul:

▶ **Discharges** Don't keep the battery fully charged all of the time—you did purchase a laptop, so unplug it once in a while, even if you don't leave your desk! On the other hand, don't run the battery down all the way every day. As a general rule, try to use your laptop until a little more than 20 percent of the battery's charge is remaining. *Shallow* discharges, where you run the battery down to 60 to 40 percent, are also good for the battery. You should calibrate the battery by performing at least one full discharge every month (see "Calibrating the Battery" on page 382).

▶ **Temperature** The temperature at which you store and use the battery can have a real impact on its longevity. Ideally, the battery would always be kept at room temperature (between 50°F and 95°F). So don't leave your laptop in the trunk of your car on hot days!

▶ **Long-term storage** If you don't plan on using the laptop for six months or more, you should reduce the battery's charge to 50 percent before storing it in a cool place, like a refrigerator.

All batteries eventually fail, but the batteries in the current generation of Apple portables can hold an 80 percent charge after 1,000 cycles. (A cycle is a full 100 percent discharge, which can span multiple shallow discharges. For example, you would complete a cycle if you discharged the battery to 50 percent on Monday and then recharged and discharged to 50 percent again on Wednesday.) These tips can help you maintain the strength of your battery for up to five years.

Achieving Incredible Battery Life

A portable computer is designed to operate differently when it's connected to a power adapter and when it's not. Performance, not battery life, is the primary concern when you're plugged in. Unlimited energy means you can crank up the volume, make the screen as bright as you want, and perform lots of processor-intensive tasks like watching a movie or playing a game.

Unplug the power adapter, and your Mac switches into power conservation mode. Battery life is the overriding concern. (Of course, you can still make performance a priority while running on battery power, but then you severely limit your battery life.) By default, the screen dims and goes to sleep when the computer is idle for a while.

The main problem for those concerned with extending battery life is that even conservation mode includes several power-draining features—all of which rob your laptop of precious energy. You'll need to manually turn off those features and monitor your battery's status if you're serious about maximizing battery life.

Monitoring the Battery's Status

Monitoring your battery's status can help you see how much time you have left on a single charge, as shown in Figure 37-1.

If the default battery status menu doesn't sate your appetite for battery-related information, try the coconutBattery application (*http://www.coconut-flavour .com/*, free). It provides in-depth information about the battery and your laptop's current energy consumption, as shown in Figure 37-2. You'll be able to see how much energy the battery is currently holding, how much it's capable of holding now compared to its original capacity, and how much it's currently using.

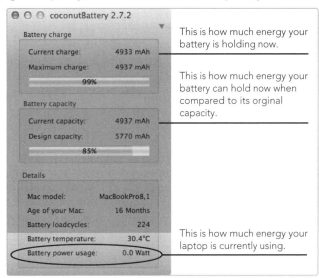

FIGURE 37-1: The battery menu bar icon indicates how much time you have before your laptop conks out.

FIGURE 37-2: The coconutBattery application provides technical information about your battery.

Try to keep the battery power usage number as low as possible to conserve energy. (By the way, don't worry if the battery capacity appears to be low—that can be fixed by calibrating the battery. See "Calibrating the Battery" on page 382)

✳ *NOTE:* **You can also find information about the battery in the System Information application. Select Power from the sidebar for battery health and charge information.**

Configuring Energy Settings

In Chapter 6, you learned how to configure the energy settings when your laptop is using its battery power. Revisit the Energy Saver preferences before a long trip to ensure that the settings are conservative enough. Verify that the **Put the hard disk(s) to sleep when possible** checkbox is selected—this ensures that your hard disk spins down when not in use.

Changing the Display and Keyboard Brightness

Dimming your display and turning off the keyboard backlight is one of the best things you can do to conserve power. Producing all that light is a major drain on your battery! You should turn down the brightness if you're in an environment where you can do so, like an airplane's cabin.

Here's how to change the display and keyboard brightness:

1. From the **Apple** menu, select **System Preferences**.
2. Click **Displays**.
3. Deselect the **Automatically adjust brightness** checkbox. This prevents your laptop from automatically changing the display's brightness to match the room's lighting conditions.
4. Adjust the **Brightness** slider to the lowest possible level. You need to be able to see the screen, of course, but the more you can reduce the brightness, the more power you'll save. The ideal setting is 50 percent. (You can also use the F1 and F2 keys to adjust the brightness.)
5. Click **Show All**.
6. Click **Keyboard**. The window shown in Figure 37-3 appears.
7. To prevent your laptop from automatically changing the keyboard's backlight based on the ambient light levels, deselect the **Adjust keyboard brightness in low light** checkbox.
8. If you want to leave the keyboard backlight turned on, adjust the slider to turn off the backlight when the computer is idle for a certain interval of time. (You can use the F5 or F6 keys to manually adjust the keyboard backlighting level.)

These power saving tips alone can potentially extend your battery life by a couple of hours. The more you turn down the brightness, the more energy you'll save.

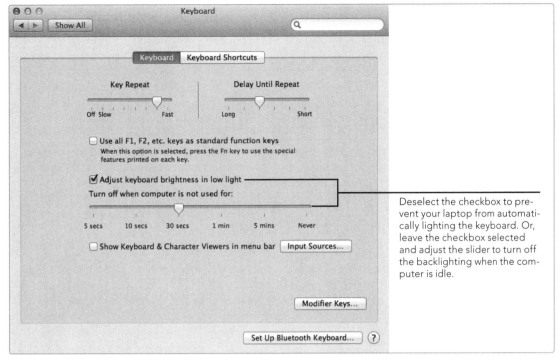

FIGURE 37-3: Use the Keyboard settings to disable automatic keyboard lighting.

Disabling AirPort and Bluetooth

The wireless technologies built into your laptop can consume energy even when they aren't connected to anything. How? They continually search for networks and devices—a feature that's undesirable in locations where there's nothing to connect to, like on an aircraft, for example. If you're working in a remote location where wireless networks aren't available, you should disable AirPort. And if you're not connecting any Bluetooth devices to your Mac while operating on battery power, you should disable Bluetooth.

Here's how to disable AirPort and Bluetooth:

1. From the **AirPort** menu, select **Turn Wi-Fi Off**, as shown in Figure 37-4.
2. From the Apple menu, select **System Preferences**.
3. Click **Bluetooth**.
4. Deselect the **On** checkbox.

You can use the Sidekick application discussed in Chapter 15 to automatically enable and disable AirPort and Bluetooth based on your location or whether or not you're connected to a power adapter.

FIGURE 37-4: Turn AirPort off to reduce unnecessary energy consumption.

Quitting Applications and Disconnecting Peripherals

Open applications are loaded in memory and consume CPU cycles even when you aren't using them. Quit any applications that you don't need open. Pay special attention to *runaway applications* such as web browsers, which can consume a lot of resources if you have many tabs and windows open. Use the instructions in Chapter 33 to keep an eye on processor and memory usage.

Disconnect all peripherals to save energy when operating on battery power. Many peripherals—like external hard drives and the iPhone—draw energy when connected to your Mac. Even those peripherals that aren't powered by your Mac can still drain your battery if they use Bluetooth wireless technology. (You should have already disabled Bluetooth anyway.)

Calibrating the Battery

Whether you leave your portable plugged in most of the time or use it primarily on the road, you'll need to calibrate the battery every month or so to keep it operating at maximum efficiency.

Why is calibration necessary? All batteries in Apple portables have tiny microprocessors that estimate the amount of energy remaining. As you learned in "Monitoring the Battery's Status" on page 379, this is a useful feature when it works correctly—you can use the battery status to see how much juice is left in the battery. Unfortunately, the processor can become confused if you perform too many consecutive shallow discharges. Calibration gets the battery's microprocessor back on track so it can accurately determine how much energy is stored.

Manually Calibrating the Battery

Calibrating the battery is a five-step process. The inconvenient part comes toward the end, when you have to let the laptop sleep for five hours. (It's not a big deal if you can time this to happen when you're sleeping as well.) During the rest of the process, you can use the computer normally.

Here's how to manually calibrate the laptop's battery:

1. Connect your computer to the power adapter and charge the battery completely. The battery is charged when the light on the power cable changes from orange to green.
2. Leave the computer connected to the power adapter and in the fully charged state for at least two hours.
3. Disconnect the power adapter and run the laptop on battery power. Continue using the computer until it goes to sleep. (Be sure to save all of your work before it goes to sleep.)
4. Shut down the computer (or put it to sleep) for at least five hours.
5. Connect the power adapter and leave it connected until the battery is fully charged again.

What's happening behind the scenes? When your computer goes to sleep, the battery still has a little power left to store the RAM's state in the hard drive. (This is called *safe sleep mode*.) Over the next five hours, all of the remaining power drains out of the battery—the battery itself essentially "shuts down." At that point, the battery's microprocessor will be "retrained" to know what an empty charge is.

If you have a hard time remembering to do stuff like this, download Apple's Calendar event (*http://www.apple.com/batteries/images/notebook_icalreminder .ics*, free) to remind yourself to calibrate the battery every month.

Battery Calibration Assistance

Manually calibrating your battery is effective, as long as you remember to do it—and how to do it. Those who could use some assistance should check out a third-party application called Watts (*http://binarytricks.com/*, $). It not only displays notifications when it's time to calibrate your battery but also guides you through the process, telling you what to do at every step. The Watts application interface is shown in Figure 37-5.

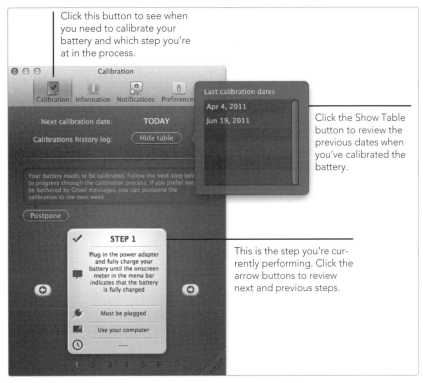

FIGURE 37-5: *Watts tracks past calibrations and guides you through the calibration process.*

If you like Watts, you can use its menu instead of the battery status menu. (The battery status menu can be disabled in the Energy Saver preferences.) The Watts menu provides access to additional information about your battery, including the capacity and charge cycles. You can also review the calibration steps and see historical capacity and calibration information.

Additional Ideas for Maintaining a MacBook's Battery

When it comes to the battery in your MacBook, an old axiom rings true: Everything in moderation. Be gentle, but not too gentle. The battery doesn't like extreme temperatures, being fully discharged every day, or being connected to the power adapter for extended periods of time.

With a little luck, and by following the tips in this chapter, you can get your MacBook's battery to stand the test of time and make it to the 1,000-cycle/5-year mark. Of course, you can always have it replaced if it doesn't make it that far. Apple can replace batteries whether or not they are covered under AppleCare. Depending on your model, the price ranges from $100 to $250.

Or better yet, replace the battery yourself by purchasing a new one from a third-party vendor like FastMac (*http://fastmac.com/laptop.php*). You can use the excellent tutorials on the iFixIt website (*http://www.ifixit.com/*) to learn how to replace the battery in your particular MacBook model.

38 Creating an Emergency USB Drive

It's a good idea to have a bootable emergency drive on hand, just in case disaster strikes your Mac. An emergency drive can help you repair the hard disk, reinstall the operating system, and restore from a Time Machine backup to get your computer back fast.

With previous versions of OS X, you could have used the installation DVD to fix problems. But Lion was Apple's first operating system sold in the App Store as a digital download—no physical disk is provided. What's a maintenance-minded Mac user to do?

Create your own bootable OS X USB drive, of course! It's easy, and if you've already purchased OS X and have a USB drive that's 1GB or larger, it's completely free. Carry it in your pocket or put it on your keychain so it's available if the worst-case scenario occurs. You'll thank yourself for taking the time to complete this project.

Project goal: Create an emergency USB drive capable of repairing the hard disk, reinstalling the operating system, and restoring from a Time Machine backup.

What You'll Be Using

To be able to get your Mac working if disaster befalls it, you'll use the following:

 Recovery Disk Assistant (*http://support.apple.com/kb/DL1433*, free)

Evaluating Your Emergency Drive Options

It can happen to any of us, even those who own brand-new Macs. First your computer starts freezing infrequently, then crashing more often, and then it won't start at all. For situations like this, you need an emergency drive on hand to start up your computer and troubleshoot the problem.

Emergency USB Drive

Creating a bootable USB drive is your safest bet. This device is self-contained and kept entirely separate from your computer—and any potential problems associated with it. But if you don't want to create a USB drive, you may have access to two other types of emergency drives, depending on when you purchased your Mac.

Recovery HD

Every Mac running OS X Lion and later has a hidden *Recovery HD* partition that can be used to boot the computer and repair the hard disk. (To use the Recovery HD partition as your startup disk, hold down ⌘-R at startup or, if that doesn't work, OPTION.) But the Recovery HD probably won't work if the internal hard drive is damaged. When you can't boot from the regular startup disk, chances are you won't be able to boot from the Recovery HD either.

Internet Recovery

Macs purchased after OS X Lion was released have an additional feature called *Internet Recovery*, which works even if your internal hard drive is damaged. If there's a problem with your computer, it can network-boot from Apple's servers. First, your computer's memory and hard drive are checked for major issues. If none are found, your Mac downloads and boots from a Recovery HD image. But even if your Mac has this feature, you'll still benefit from having an emergency drive, as it can take a while to download the Recovery HD partition.

Making Your Own Emergency USB Drive

The best option is a Recovery HD partition on a bootable USB drive. This drive provides you with all the tools you need to troubleshoot problems, repair the hard drive, reinstall OS X, and restore from a Time Machine backup. In short, it's the perfect safety net for those rare times when your internal hard drive is hosed.

✳ **WARNING:** **You cannot create a recovery disk while FileVault is enabled on your computer. Disable FileVault before proceeding with these instructions— you can enable it again after you have created the recovery disk.**

Here's how to create an emergency USB drive:

1. Connect a hard drive or USB drive to your computer. If the drive is larger than 1GB, consider partitioning it to make a 1GB partition for the recovery disk. (If you don't create a partition, this process will use all of the available space on the drive, no matter how large it is.)
2. Open the Recovery Disk Assistant application. It's available for free from Apple's website (*http://support.apple.com/kb/DL1433*).
3. Accept the license agreement. The Recovery Disk Assistant window appears, as shown in Figure 38-1.

FIGURE 38-1: *Select a disk or partition from the Recovery Disk Assistant window.*

4. Select the disk and then click **Continue**.
5. Authenticate with your administrator username and password. The Recovery Disk Assistant creates the recovery disk, as shown in Figure 38-2. The process takes approximately five minutes.

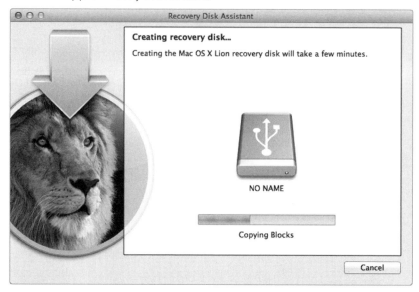

FIGURE 38-2: *Creating the recovery disk takes about five minutes.*

6. When the recovery disk has been created, click **Quit**.

Like the Recovery HD partition on your startup drive, the emergency drive is invisible when it's connected to your computer. The Finder won't provide any indication that it exists, but don't worry—it's there, waiting for your signal to help with a disaster.

Using Your Emergency USB Drive

Having an emergency drive doesn't do you much good if you don't know how to use it. Familiarize yourself now with the features available in recovery mode.

Here's how to use your emergency drive:

1. Connect the recovery drive to your computer.
2. Restart your computer and hold down the OPTION key.

✳ **NOTE: If firmware password protection is enabled, you will need to enter your firmware password to proceed.**

3. A list of startup drives appears. Select a network, if one is available. (This is required to reinstall OS X, as the necessary operating system files will be downloaded from Apple's servers.)

4. Select the emergency drive and then click the arrow directly below the drive. Your Mac starts in recovery mode.

Now you have four options for troubleshooting and recovery:

▶ **Restore From Time Machine Backup:** If you have a current Time Machine backup for your computer, you can use this option to restore from that backup. You'll be prompted to select a Time Machine backup drive, a backup snapshot, and a destination drive, which will be overwritten by your backup. See Chapter 36 for instructions on restoring from a Time Machine backup.

▶ **Reinstall OS X:** If the computer is crashing frequently, it might be a good idea to reinstall OS X on your internal hard disk. (Note that OS X is not actually stored on the emergency drive—the installer application is downloaded from Apple's servers.) Verify that you have backups before you do this.

▶ **Get Help Online:** If you have an Internet connection, this is a great way to do research on Apple's support website. The Safari web browser launches and allows you to visit any website, not just Apple's support website.

▶ **Disk Utility:** The old standby. Use Chapters 34 and 35 as a starting point for any problems with your computer.

There are also a few other applications available from the Utilities menu. You can find the Firmware Password Utility, Network Utility, and Terminal applications there.

Peeking Inside the Emergency USB Drive

Remember that the emergency drive is invisible? Here's a quick and dirty way to see it in the Finder. This is a cool way to take a peek inside the emergency drive and examine its files and folders. It's just for fun! Be careful not to change anything—you could really mess up your emergency drive by adding or removing files.

1. Open the Terminal application and type the following command:

```
defaults write com.apple.DiskUtility DUDebugMenuEnabled 1
```

2. Open the Disk Utility application.
3. Select **Debug ▶ Show Every Partition**.
4. From the sidebar, select **Recovery HD**.
5. Select **File ▶ Mount "Recovery HD"**.

Now you'll be able to see the Recovery HD in the Finder.

INDEX

Numbers

1Password, 154, 276, 282–285
  browser extension, 282–284
  integrating with Dropbox,
      284–285

A

abbreviations, in LaunchBar,
      training in, 70–71
actions. *See also* files, actions;
      folders, actions
  AppleScripts as, 153–154
  based on Bluetooth proximity
      monitor, 133–135
  configuring for Sidekick, 150–152
  location-based, 147–154
active application
  Divvy to resize, 36
  hiding, 5
  quitting, 4
active window, closing or
      minimizing, 5
Activity Monitor, 342, 344–345
adapter, for display port, 89
address bars, for site-specific
      browsers, 221
Adium, 135, 154
Adobe Flash Player (preference
      pane), 45
advanced alert, from script, 129
AirPort, disabling on laptop, 381
AirPort Express Base Station,
      255, 256
AirPort Extreme Base Station, 255
  connecting hard drive to,
      257–258
  connecting printer's USB
      cable to, 256
  connecting USB hub to, 262
  passwords, 261
alarms, for laptop, 136
Alarms application, 183, 185–187
album cover artwork, 197
alerts
  Alarms application for
      advanced, 185–187
  creating basic, 184–185
  in Pester, 183, 184–185
  from script, 128, 129

Alfred (application launcher), 58,
      60–67
  for computer control, 66
  Dictionary application and,
      63–64
  for math, 62
  Preferences window, 65
  setting up, 60–63
  system commands in, 66
Alfred Powerpack, 60, 66
Amazon, 202
  EC2 cloud computing
      platform, 306
  for Tor relay, 327
AND operator, in Spotlight, 23
anonymity on Internet, 297, 319–327
Apache web server, 246–247
AppCleaner
  removing applications with,
      43–45
  SmartDelete in, 44
appfirewall.log file, viewing, 311
Apple
  cloud music service, 190. *See
      also* iTunes Match
  Developer website, 130
  FileVault recovery key
      storage by, 333
Apple ID, 190
  linking to iCloud, 230
AppleJack, 359
AppleScript, 121–130
  as action, 153–154
  capabilities, 122
  changing into folder action, 140
  dictionary, 126–127
  executing, 66
  for file and folder actions,
      137–146
  flow-control structures, 127–128
  In Range script, 133, 134
  launching, 130
  learning by example, 125–126
  Out of Range script, 133, 134
  use with applications, 126–127
  user interface for scripts,
      128–130
  variables, 127
  voice commands, creating
      with, 105
  writing and running first, 123–124

AppleScript 1-2-3 (Soghoian and
      Cheeseman), 130
AppleScript Editor, 123–126
application firewall, 308
application launchers. *See also*
      Alfred
  configuring Spotlight as, 59–60
  LaunchBar, 67–76
application switcher, opening files
      with, 31
application-level keyboard
      shortcuts, 4
  changing and adding, 8–10
applications
  AppleScript use with, 126–127
  automatically starting at login,
      13–18
  converting websites to, 219–227
  crash, and hard disk repair
      needs, 356
  hiding all except active, 5
  iCloud use with, 231–232
  quitting active, 4
  quitting for power
      conservation, 382
  receipt for installed, 350
  removing, 41–46
      with AppCleaner, 43–45
      with Launchpad, 42–43
  resuming at login, 16–17
  routing data through Tor,
      323–324
  saving script as, 130
  switching between, 30–31
      with Mission Control, 34–35
Applications folder, 57
Apptivate, 12
AppZapper, 46
archive file (disk image), 110
archiving
  email with MailSteward, 165–169
      finding messages in
      MailSteward archive,
      168–169
  folders, 145
Areo Snap (Windows 7), 37
audio alerts, from Pester, 185
Aurora, 53
authentication, after enabling
      FileVault, 332

X